Holy Redeemer Catholic Church

1 2 2 7   E a s t   B r i s t o l   R o a d   •   B u r t o n ,   M i c h i g a n   4 8 5 2 9

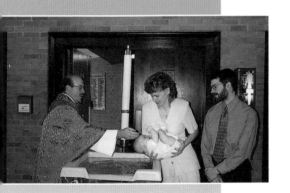

Dear Parishioners,

It is always a privilege to learn more about our faith and its history. Thus, I am pleased that we have this beautiful history of our diocese for our enjoyment. Not only does this carefully crafted book take us briefly, yet decisively, through the history of the Catholic Church in the United States, it focuses in on the unique heritage of our region and diocese.

As we move toward the 75th anniversary of our diocese in the next decade, this pictorial history should help us appreciate all the more the great work God has accomplished in our midst. You will find out more about our bishops, how various diocesan offices and councils came into being and work, as well as how various ethnic groups offered their unique gifts to the whole Church in our diocese.

Each parish has a page dedicated to it, including ours. You will perhaps see many priests, deacons, lay ministers, and fellow Catholics with whom you are familiar in these pages. In sum, you will learn just how profoundly the Holy Spirit has been at work in the diocese since the renewal started at the Second Vatican Council. As we continue the bring this Council to its yet unfulfilled realization, may we be inspired, guided, and be more learned as a result of this fine History of the Diocese of Lansing.

Let us go boldly forth in Christ,

Fr. Bill Wegher

Rev. William F. Wegher, STL
Pastor

D1498085

Living In Joyful Hope

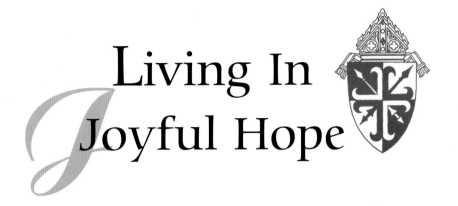

A History of the Diocese of Lansing

George C. Michalek

Foreward

Sixteen years ago during our Golden Jubilee in 1987, our first history *'Diocese of Lansing Parish Historical Sketches'* was published. This cherished and useful book was a labor of faith and love for its author Father George Michalek, Vice Chancellor. In the Preface, Bishop Povish wrote: "Our principal aim of the 50th Jubilee was expressed in the phrase, "Festival of Faith". A secondary, but by no means unimportant aim, was to make our members more aware of their history as People of God."

When asked to author a second updated and extensive history, Father Michalek expressed enthusiasm and agreed to undertake this massive project. I wrote: "Your literary disposition and love of history are well established and recognized through your previous work." I am very grateful to Father Michalek who devoted countless hours to researching, compiling and writing this inspiring and practical book.

This book is timely in view of our Holy Father's recent concern: 'the loss of Christian memory.' Knowing and cherishing our roots and realizing and admiring the faith and courage of our Catholic forebears is essential for our identity. Our history teaches, guides and inspires us. Knowing the faith, hope and love of countless Catholics is a reservoir of spiritual energy that impels us to continue generously the mission of Christ and his Church.

This book is a testimony to the faith, fidelity and fortitude of our people. We have been richly blessed with the unity and strengh of dedicated and remarkable Catholics.

I echo Bishop Povish: "This book makes our members more aware of their history in an interesting and most readable way." Enjoy!

In Christ, The Lord of History

† Carl F. Mengeling
Bishop of Lansing

HE MUST INCREASE

Dedication

This sixty-fifth anniversary history of the Catholic Diocese of Lansing is dedicated to those seven pioneer priests who first ministered the sacraments to devoted immigrant faithful longing to deepen their relationship with Jesus Christ.

- Rev. Gabriel Richard,
  1801-1832,
  Pastor at St. Anne, Detroit

- Rev. Patrick O'Kelly,
  1831-1839,
  Washtenaw, Livingston
  and Jackson Counties

- Rev. Bernard O'Cavanaugh,
  1834-1839,
  Livingston County

- Rev. Thomas Morrissey,
  1835-1839,
  Washtenaw, Livingston
  and Jackson Counties

- Rev. Anton Kopp,
  1836-1843,
  Clinton County

- Rev. Martin Kundig,
  1839-1842,
  Genesee County

- Rev. Thomas Cullen,
  1839-1862,
  Washtenaw, Livingston
  and Jackson Counties

These men of faith labored between 1831 and 1841, which was the first decade of parish establishments in what is now the Diocese of Lansing.

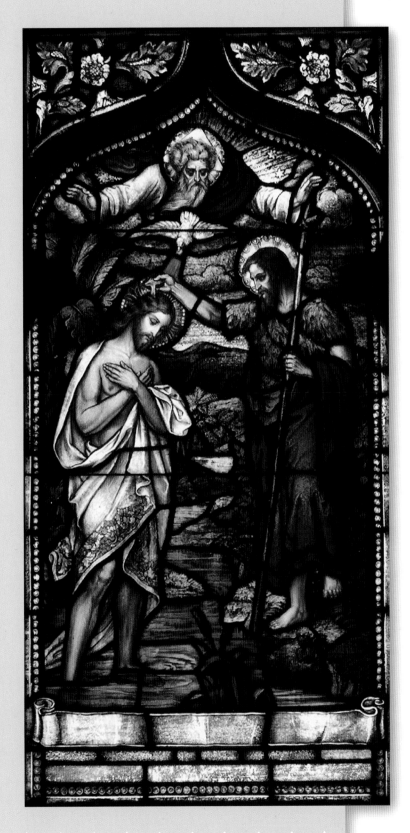

Acknowledgements

Ever since my appointment as archivist on October 1, 1979, I have hoped that a diocesan history might be compiled. Gathering, sorting and filing material over the last twenty-four years has been rewarding and frustrating at the same time. There is always the desire that other documentation be located and that there be more time. On October 1, 2002, Bishop Carl F. Mengeling met with Mr. Christian Riehl of Éditions du Signe and agreed to the publication of a history of the Diocese of Lansing. I then began working one day a week, most of my days off and most of my weekends on this book. This continued until the text and photographs were submitted.

The book would have never come about without Bishop Mengeling and the generous support and help of many others. I especially thank Loni Hackney and Jule Stafford who were the typists for parts one and two. Barbara DeGrand and Marilyn Elworth were very generous in taking the time to proofread. I am grateful to Barbara DeGrand for also serving as a research assistant and helping with the captions for the photographs. Kudos also go to the archive volunteers, Frances Michalek and Ila Parker, for their continued assistance. I am most grateful to the priests at St. Mary Cathedral for allowing me to use the living room as an office for writing the text. The carpet disappeared for months under my folders of information. Mark Lynch of E and S Graphics is to be commended for the maps. Patrick O'Brien and the staff of Faith magazine and Mary Jo Gilliland and the staff at Liturgical Commission Publishings are also to be acknowledged for the tremendous help they provided with the photographs.

Two congregational archives: the Adrian Dominican Sisters and the Sisters, Servants of the Immaculate Heart of Mary were very generous and provided information on the involvement of their communities in teaching public school children. I am grateful to Sr. Marilyn Francoeur, O.P., at the Dominican Archive and Ms. Donna Wesley and Sr. Mary Ann Untener at the I.H.M. Archive for their assistance.

Lastly I thank my parents, George and Frances Michalek, for always encouraging me to forge ahead. This project has been all consuming, but I rejoice in seeing it through to completion.

Rev. George C. Michalek

Table of Contents

Shepherds Who Cared for Our Area

The following Bishops ministered to Catholics in this area prior to the establishment of the Diocese of Lansing:

Quebec

The Most Rev.
Edward D. Fenwick

The Most Rev.
Frederic Rese

François de Montmorency Laval (vicar apostolic)	1658 – 1674
(bishop)	1674 – 1688
Jean-Baptiste de la Croix Chevrière de St. Vallier	1688 – 1727
Louis-François Duplessis de Mornay	1727 – 1733
Pierre-Herman Dosquet	1733 – 1739
François-Louis Pourroy de L'Auberivière	1739 – 1740
Henri-Marie de Pontbriand	1741 – 1760
Jean-Olivier Briand (administrator)	1760 – 1766
(bishop)	1766 – 1784
Louis-Phillippe Mariauchau D'Esglis	1784 – 1788
Jean-François Hubert	1788 – 1797

Baltimore

John Carroll	1796 – 1810

Bardstown

Benedict Joseph Flaget	1810 – 1822

Cincinnati

Edward Dominic Fenwick	1822 – 1832

The Most Rev.
John S. Foley

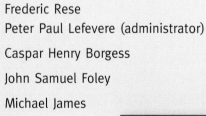

The Most Rev.
Caspar H. Borgess

Detroit

Frederic Rese	October 6, 1833 – December 30, 1871
Peter Paul Lefevere (administrator)	November 22, 1841 – March 4, 1869
Caspar Henry Borgess	April 24, 1870 – April 16, 1887
John Samuel Foley	November 4, 1888 – January 5, 1918
Michael James	November 18, 1918 – January 20, 1937

The Most Rev.
Michael J. Gallagher

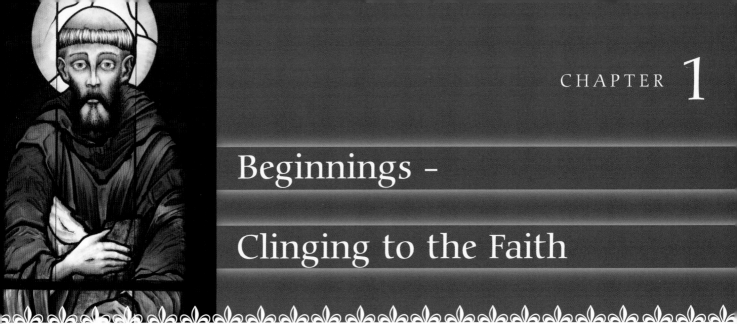

CHAPTER 1

Beginnings –
Clinging to the Faith

Planting the Cross in New France

Catholicism was brought to North America by devout soldiers, settlers and clergy from Spain, England, and France, who clung to their faith as they adapted to life in the New World. First, the Spanish Empire established colonies in the south and the west. Along the Atlantic seaboard the Maryland colony was founded by English Catholics who wanted to practice their faith freely. Lastly there were the evangelistic efforts within the territories of New France. It was the French efforts to bring the faith to the New World that most directly affected the origins of Christianity in Michigan.

Jacques Cartier reached the New World and on July 24, 1534, planted a cross on the Gaspé Peninsula off the Gulf of St. Lawrence claiming the area for Francis I of France. The missionaries with Cartier first preached to the Indians the following year at the areas later settled as Quebec and Montreal. French involvement in a series of wars prevented serious efforts at colonization for another sixty years. The Franciscans, known in New France as "Recollets", came to the settlement of Quebec shortly after its founding in 1608. Explorers went out from Quebec in 1622, and the first Frenchman, Etienne Brulé, reached the upper peninsula of Michigan. The Recollets returned to France in 1629, but evangelization continued under the Jesuits who had arrived in 1625. They were dependent directly on the Holy See.

Two Jesuits, Charles Raymbault and St. Isaac Jogues, were the first priests to visit the state of Michigan. They visited the Sault in 1641. The majority of the immigrants to New France came from the province of Normandy. The capital and archepiscopal see of Normandy is Rouen. In 1647 the archbishop of Rouen began to appoint the Jesuit superior as a vicar general of the archdiocese. This arrangement continued until François de Montmorency Laval was appointed Vicar Apostolic (head of a vicariate apostolic, an administrative unit which may precede the formation of a diocese) of New France in 1658. He was consecrated a bishop on the 8th of December in Paris. Sixteen years later, in 1674, Quebec became a diocese dependent directly upon the Holy See. The diocese encompassed all of North America exclusive of the English colonies on the Atlantic seaboard and the Spanish colonies in the Southwest.

The famed missionary and explorer, Rev. Jacques Marquette, came to New France in 1666 and two years later he founded the first permanent settlement in Michigan at the Sault. In May 1673, Louis Joliet and Fr. Marquette set out from St. Ignace to explore the Mississippi. Fr. Marquette died in 1675 near Ludington, Michigan. This was also the year that the first Mass was celebrated in the interior of the lower peninsula. Rev. Henri Nouvel offered the Holy Sacrifice of the Mass on December 3, 1675, somewhere between what is now the city of Saginaw and the junction of the Flint and Shiawassee rivers. It was not only Frenchmen who were at that first Eucharist but also Native Americans who had been converted to

Catholicism. Fr. Nouvel spent the winter of 1675-1676 in the interior of the lower peninsula reaching as far as Mecosta and Isabella counties. He then returned to the St. Ignace mission.

The founding of Detroit and of St. Anne Parish in 1701 was a significant event in the history of Michigan Catholics. The mission of St. Ignace cared for Catholics in the Northern half of the lower peninsula. The care for Catholics in the lower half of the peninsula was entrusted to St. Anne Parish in Detroit and to St. Joseph Mission in Niles, which had been founded a score of years earlier.

Baltimore Becomes a Diocese

Even though the United States achieved independence after the Revolutionary War, it did not gain control of the upper midwest for several years. In 1784, Baltimore was created as a vicariate apostolic. Five years later the vicariate apostolic was elevated to diocesan status. The boundaries of the Diocese were contiguous with those of the United States. However, the British troops did not leave Michigan until 1796, so Michigan remained under the political control of the British and the spiritual jurisdiction of the Diocese of Quebec. That year the Bishop of Quebec, Jean François Hubert, recalled his priests who were stationed in Michigan to Quebec and the Bishop of Baltimore, John Carroll, sent Sulpicians to St. Anne Parish. Rev. Michael Levadoux was the pastor of St. Anne Parish from 1796-1801. Rev. Gabriel Richard came to Detroit in June 1798 to serve as Fr. Levadoux's assistant. Ties to Quebec remained strong. When Fr. Richard succeeded Fr. Levadoux as pastor, he prepared over 520 persons for the Sacrament of Confirmation, which was administered by the Bishop of Quebec, Pierre Denaut, in 1801. Bishop Denaut came at Bishop Carroll's invitation. In 1816 it was again the Bishop of Quebec (then Joseph Plessis) who came to Detroit to preside at Confirmation.

Fr. Gabriel Richard

Fr. Richard was an energetic man who did much for Michigan. In 1809, he published the first newspaper in Michigan. He co-founded the University of Michigan in 1817. He was elected as the representative to Congress from the Territory of Michigan in 1823. Four years later the Holy See issued a Papal Bull (decree) establishing Detroit as a diocese and naming Fr. Richard its first bishop. When knowledge reached Rome of the scandal caused when a civil lawsuit was brought against Fr. Richard (who on the Bishop's orders had excommunicated someone married outside the church) the decree was suppressed. Fr. Richard died in September 1832, one of the last victims of a cholera epidemic. Worn out from ministering to the sick, he contracted the disease himself.

During Fr. Richard's tenure at St. Anne Parish, Michigan was transferred twice to new dioceses. In 1808, the Baltimore diocese was divided; Boston, New York, Philadelphia and Bardstown were created as suffragan sees to the metropolitan see in Baltimore. (A suffragan see is a diocese grouped with an archdiocese to make a province. The archdiocese is also known as the metropolitan see.) Benedict Joseph Flaget was appointed the first bishop of the new diocese in Kentucky, which covered the U.S. territory west of the Alleghenies and from Tennessee north, an area that included the state of Michigan. Overwhelmed by the task of administering such a large diocese, he initially resisted his appointment. He reconsidered and after accepting the position he went to France to recruit help. He was consecrated in 1810 and arrived in Bardstown the following year. Despite the difficulty of travel in the early 1800's, Bishop Flaget visited parishes in Michigan, but he still believed that his diocese was too large to administer adequately. In response to this problem, Pope Pius VII decreed the establishment of a new diocese in Cincinnati on June 19, 1821. The Michigan Territory was part of this new diocese. The Dominican missionary Edward Dominic Fenwick was appointed the first bishop. Bishop Flaget consecrated Bishop Fenwick in January 1822.

Bishop Fenwick first visited Detroit in 1822, but he did not reach the missions of northern Michigan until 1829. In 1831, Bishop Fenwick made a tour of the northernmost Indian missions. He was accompanied on the tour by a native of Slovenia, Rev. Frederic Baraga. Bishop Fenwick was returning from this visit to the Michigan Indian missions when he died of cholera in September 1832 (thirteen days after the death of Fr. Richard).

Fr. Patrick O'Kelly

Fenwick was Bishop of Cincinnati and Richard was pastor of St. Anne Parish in Detroit when the decision was made by Richard to send Rev. Patrick O'Kelly to visit Irish Catholics in Washtenaw County. Fr. O'Kelly was born in County Kilkenny, Ireland. He was ordained about 1820. By 1822, he was working in the Rochester area of New York State. By 1829, he was working with Irish immigrants in Detroit. He became one of the six assistants of Fr. Richard at St. Anne. Fr. O'Kelly is considered the apostle to Washtenaw, Livingston and Oakland counties. During Lent in 1831, Fr. O'Kelly developed plans for parishes in Northfield Township and Ann Arbor. In June 1831, Fr. O'Kelly signed his last entries in the St. Anne's baptismal register. Shortly thereafter he took up residence in Washtenaw County and later that year he began the first church in Green Oak Township in Livingston County.

Diocesan Development in Michigan

The Holy See created the Diocese of Detroit for the Michigan Territory on March 8, 1833. The former vicar general of the Diocese of Cincinnati, Rev. Frederic Rese, was appointed the first bishop. He was consecrated a bishop in Cincinnati in October. He entered Detroit the following January. The diocese included Michigan, Wisconsin, Minnesota, the eastern portions of North and South Dakota and the northern half of Iowa. The borders of the diocese were limited to Michigan when the Diocese of Milwaukee was created in 1843. The growth of the Catholic faith led to the establishment of a vicariate apostolic in the upper peninsula in 1853. The diocese of Sault Ste. Marie was formally created in 1857. The next diocese to be created was Grand Rapids in 1882. The new diocese did not include western and central southern Michigan because of the influence of Bishop Caspar H. Borgess to keep the city he loved, Kalamazoo, in the Detroit diocese. He loved the city to such a degree he retired, died and was buried there.

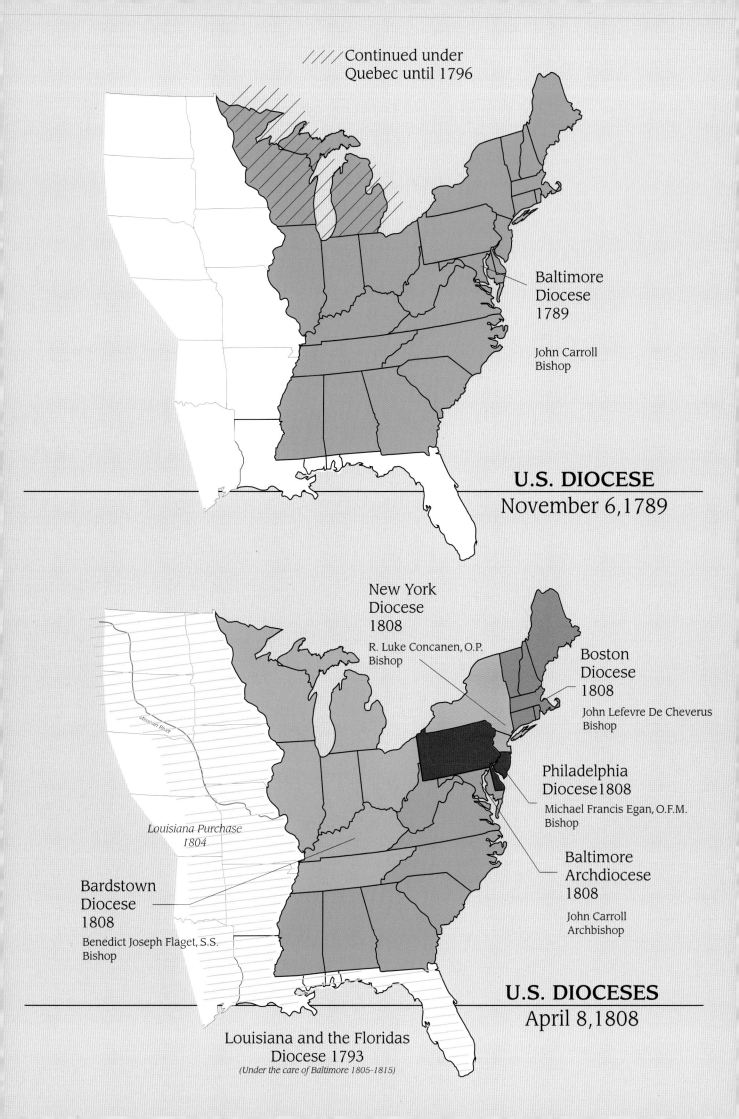

Continued under
Quebec until 1796

Baltimore
Diocese
1789

John Carroll
Bishop

U.S. DIOCESE
November 6, 1789

New York
Diocese
1808

R. Luke Concanen, O.P.
Bishop

Boston
Diocese
1808

John Lefevre De Cheverus
Bishop

Philadelphia
Diocese 1808

Michael Francis Egan, O.F.M.
Bishop

Baltimore
Archdiocese
1808

John Carroll
Archbishop

Missouri River

Louisiana Purchase
1804

Bardstown
Diocese
1808

Benedict Joseph Flaget, S.S.
Bishop

U.S. DIOCESES
April 8, 1808

Louisiana and the Floridas
Diocese 1793
(Under the care of Baltimore 1805-1815)

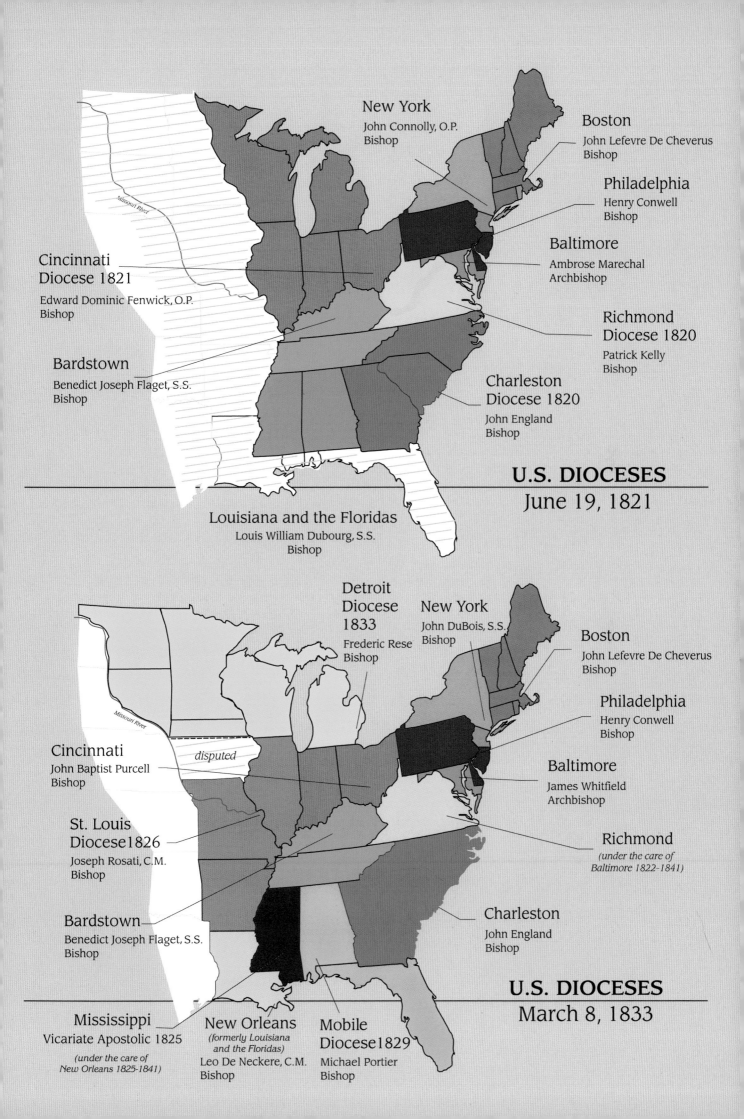

New York
John Connolly, O.P.
Bishop

Boston
John Lefevre De Cheverus
Bishop

Philadelphia
Henry Conwell
Bishop

Cincinnati
Diocese 1821
Edward Dominic Fenwick, O.P.
Bishop

Baltimore
Ambrose Marechal
Archbishop

Richmond
Diocese 1820
Patrick Kelly
Bishop

Bardstown
Benedict Joseph Flaget, S.S.
Bishop

Charleston
Diocese 1820
John England
Bishop

Missouri River

U.S. DIOCESES
June 19, 1821

Louisiana and the Floridas
Louis William Dubourg, S.S.
Bishop

Detroit
Diocese
1833
Frederic Rese
Bishop

New York
John DuBois, S.S.
Bishop

Boston
John Lefevre De Cheverus
Bishop

Philadelphia
Henry Conwell
Bishop

Cincinnati
John Baptist Purcell
Bishop

disputed

Baltimore
James Whitfield
Archbishop

St. Louis
Diocese 1826
Joseph Rosati, C.M.
Bishop

Missouri River

Richmond
*(under the care of
Baltimore 1822-1841)*

Bardstown
Benedict Joseph Flaget, S.S.
Bishop

Charleston
John England
Bishop

Mississippi
Vicariate Apostolic 1825
*(under the care of
New Orleans 1825-1841)*

New Orleans
*(formerly Louisiana
and the Floridas)*
Leo De Neckere, C.M.
Bishop

Mobile
Diocese 1829
Michael Portier
Bishop

U.S. DIOCESES
March 8, 1833

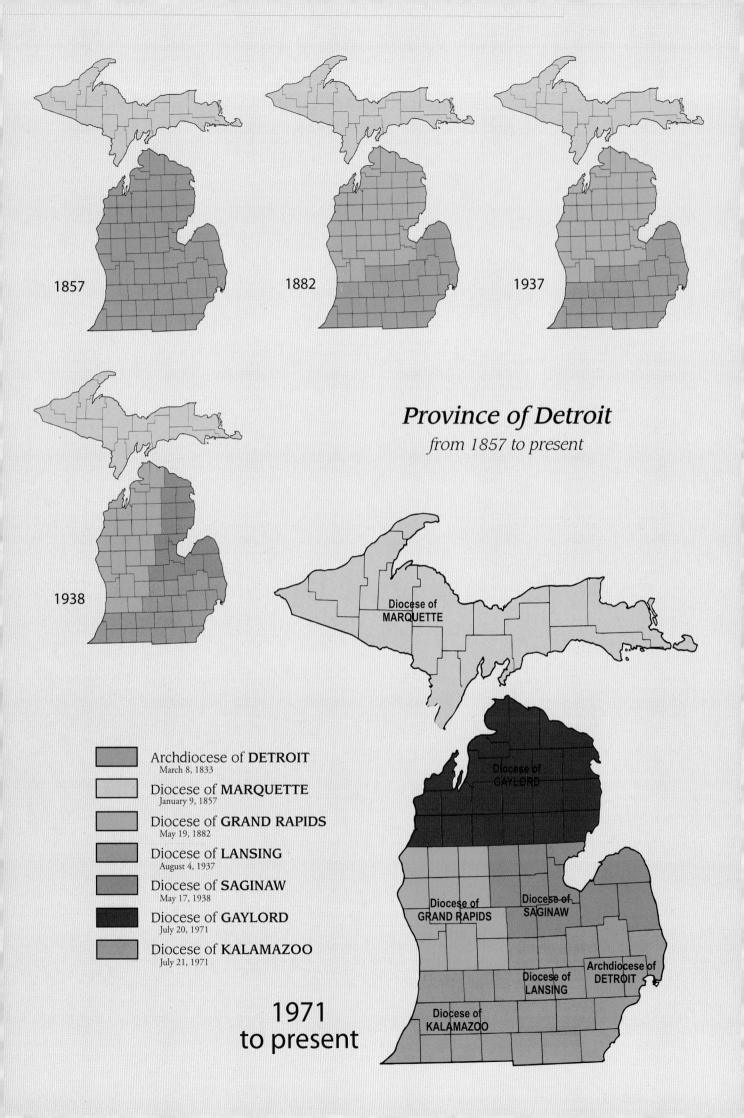

1857

1882

1937

1938

Province of Detroit
from 1857 to present

Diocese of
MARQUETTE

Archdiocese of **DETROIT**
March 8, 1833

Diocese of **MARQUETTE**
January 9, 1857

Diocese of **GRAND RAPIDS**
May 19, 1882

Diocese of **LANSING**
August 4, 1937

Diocese of **SAGINAW**
May 17, 1938

Diocese of **GAYLORD**
July 20, 1971

Diocese of **KALAMAZOO**
July 21, 1971

Diocese of
GAYLORD

Diocese of
GRAND RAPIDS

Diocese of
SAGINAW

Archdiocese of
DETROIT

Diocese of
LANSING

Diocese of
KALAMAZOO

1971
to present

Earliest Eucharistic Celebrations

Fr. Patrick O'Kelly's efforts led to the organization of the first Catholic communities in Washtenaw and Livingston counties in 1831. Rev. Thomas Morrissey served in the Washtenaw and Livingston mission field from 1835–1839. Rev. Bernard O'Cavanaugh was active in Livingston County in the late 1830's. Either Fr. O'Kelly or Rev. Thomas Cullen presided at the first Mass in Jackson County in 1836. The St. John the Evangelist community in Jackson became a parish in 1856. The same year the first Mass was celebrated in Jackson County, the German Catholics led by Rev. Anton Kopp came to Westphalia in Clinton County. Rev. Martin Kundig said the first Mass in Flint in 1841 while on his way to Saginaw and Bay City. After Rev. George Godez replaced Fr. Kopp in Westphalia in 1843 he began visiting outlying Catholics. He presided at the first Mass in Shiawassee County where a log chapel dedicated to St. Patrick was erected in 1847. The first Mass in Ingham County was celebrated by Fr. O'Kelly for Irish settlers at Bunkerhill in 1845. Lansing, the "see city", would not have Mass celebrated until the fall of 1854 when German immigrants offered their home for the service. It was from Monroe that priests first went to Lenawee and Hillsdale counties. Rev. Simon Saenderl, C.SS.R., part of the Redemptorist Community in Monroe, visited both Adrian and Hillsdale in 1846. He took a census of Catholic families in the area. The number of Catholics counted in the census prompted the decision to establish St. Mary, Adrian, in 1853 and St. Anthony, Hillsdale, in 1858. The first celebration of the Eucharist in Eaton County was a nuptial Mass celebrated in 1855 in the log cabin of the newlyweds two miles west of Bellevue.

Ethnic Parishes

The immigration of the Irish Catholics to south central Michigan was the chief impetus for organization of parishes. They began arriving in significant numbers in the late 1820s. A steady stream continued for over fifty years. Over twenty-five of the earliest parishes were predominately Irish in their origins. The next wave of Catholic immigrants came from Germany. In 1836 the settlers of Westphalia brought their priest, Fr. Anton Kopp, with them from Germany. St. Joseph, Adrian, would be founded nearly thirty years later as another German speaking parish. The last exclusively German parish was Most Holy Trinity in Fowler which was organized as a mission in 1872. German immigrants were also active members of many other parishes as the minority ethnic group to the Irish majority.

First Communicants 1911

Eastern Europeans were the next significant wave of immigrants to form parishes. The Poles were statistically the largest group within this category and they formed four parishes beginning with St. Joseph Parish in Jackson in 1902. All Saints Church in Flint opened in 1910. The last two to organize were St. Casimir in Lansing and St. Stanislaus in Jackson, which were established as missions in 1916 and 1919 respectively.

The Slovaks and Bohemians organized three parishes in the present Diocese of Lansing. St. Mary Queen of Angels in Swartz Creek began in 1912 as a mission of All Saints in Flint. Two years later it achieved parochial status. St. Joseph, Owosso, and Sacred Heart, Flint, opened in the 1920's. Since Czech and Slovak immigrants came in smaller numbers they often just became active in the predominately Irish parishes already in existence. They generally were the poorest and held the balcony seats for which the least amount of pew rent was paid. (Pew rent was the major source of income for parishes before the envelope system was instituted to collect donations. Parishioners paid rent to sit in a particular pew for a particular Mass.) The Hungarians were the last Eastern European group to form an ethnic parish, founding St. Joseph in Flint in 1921.

The ethnic parishes were distinguished in ecclesiastical terms as national parishes. National parishes did not have defined boundaries but were for all who generally spoke the language of a particular group. National parishes were usually based on language and ethnic heritage. They could also be based on race. In 1929 Christ the King Parish in Flint was founded for Black Catholics. Two ethnic groups, the Italians and the Belgians, formed large minorities in Resurrection Parish, Lansing, and St. Thérèse of Lisieux Parish in Lansing respectively.

After World War II, migrant workers from the Southwest and Mexico began to settle year round in the diocese. The summer migrant programs were no longer adequate to care for the needs of Hispanic Catholics. In 1957, Our Lady of Guadalupe in Flint and Cristo Rey in Lansing were established. More recently, in 1980, Sacred Heart Chapel and the Hispanic Cultural Center in Jackson was established.

The most recent Catholic immigrants to the area have been the Vietnamese. A mission for the Vietnamese was founded at St. Mary Cathedral in early 1982. The parish of St. Andrew Dung-Lac in Lansing was created on the feast of their patron saint in November, 1998.

Anti-Catholic Prejudice

After World War I there was a great rise in anti-Catholism. This was evidenced at the state level by the drives in 1920 and 1924 to outlaw parochial schools in Michigan. Bishop Michael J. Gallagher of Detroit joined in a coalition with Lutherans and Christian Reformed to fight off the attacks. One priest recalled that when his parents moved to Lansing in 1920, they were the third Catholic family in the neighborhood. A cross was burned by Klansmen within a week of their arrival as a warning to the increasing number of "papists". In the 1920's in Morrice the Klan burned a cross in the front yard of the Protestant superintendent because he had imprudently hired a Catholic teacher.

Clinging to the Faith

Almost three centuries had passed from the time the first Jesuit missionary visited Michigan until the diocese of Lansing was created in May 1937. Over a century had passed since the first parish communities had been established. Successive waves of immigrants - Irish, German and Eastern European - had come to Michigan seeking a better life for themselves and their children. The worst of the Great Depression was past. When the State of Michigan celebrated its centennial in January 1937, it was a celebration of growth and progress. Before the decade was out there would be much more change, more tragedy in another world war, more opportunities to pray and more reasons for clinging to the faith.

Joseph Henry Albers
J.C.D.

Born: March 18, 1891, Cincinnati, Ohio

Parents: Henry Albers and the former Anna Alf

Ordained a Priest St. Peter in Chains Cathedral Cincinnati, Ohio
June 16, 1916

By Henry K. Moeller, Archbishop of Cincinnati, Ohio

Consecrated a Bishop St. Peter in Chains Cathedral
December 27, 1929

Consecrator: John T. McNicholas, O.P., Archbishop of Cincinnati, Ohio

Co-Consecrators: Francis W. Howard, Bishop of Covington, Kentucky

Francis J.L. Beckman, Bishop of Lincoln, Nebraska

Motto: As Auxiliary Bishop of Cincinnati, Ohio:

Divinum auxilium nobiscum (Divine Assistance Be with Us)

As Bishop of Lansing:

Fides vincet mundum (Faith Conquers the World)
1 John 5:4

Bishop (Titular) of Lunda and Auxiliary of Cincinnati, Ohio

December 16, 1929 - August 4, 1937

Bishop of Lansing August 4, 1937 - December 1, 1965

Died: December 1, 1965, Lansing, Michigan

Buried: December 6, 1965, St. Joseph Cemetery, Lansing, Michigan

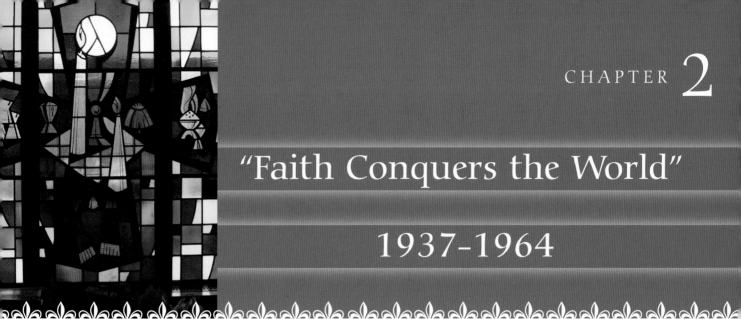

CHAPTER 2

"Faith Conquers the World"

1937-1964

The Formation of the Diocese

In 1937 four new chanceries were established in the United States when His Holiness Pope Pius XI established dioceses in Patterson, New Jersey; Camden, New Jersey; Owensboro, Kentucky and Lansing, Michigan. The Diocese of Lansing was established May 22nd of that year. Three dioceses (Newark, New Jersey; Louisville, Kentucky; and Detroit, Michigan) were raised to the rank of archdiocese. The public announcement of the creation of the new diocese of Lansing was on June 1st. That month also marked the 300th anniversary of the birth of Fr. Jacques Marquette. The new bishop of Lansing made reference to that fact in his installation sermon.

The Most Reverend Edward (later Cardinal) Mooney was installed as the first archbishop of Detroit in Blessed Sacrament Church in Detroit on August 3, 1937. After the impressive service, his first act as metropolitan (the chief bishop of an ecclesiastical province) was to install the first

The honor of your presence is requested
at
The Formal Establishment of the
Diocese of Lansing
and the
Installation of its First Bishop
The Most Reverend Joseph H. Albers, D.D., J.C.D.
St. Mary's Cathedral
Wednesday morning, August fourth,
Nineteen hundred and thirty-seven,
at ten thirty o'clock.
His Excellency, The Most Reverend Edward Mooney, D.D.,
Archbishop of Detroit,
Presiding.
Sermon by
His Excellency, The Most Reverend John T. McNicholas, O.P., S.T.M.
Archbishop of Cincinnati.

Invitation to the Establishment of the Diocese, August 4, 1937

Bishop of Lansing, Joseph H. Albers. Archbishop Mooney and Bishop-elect Joseph H. Albers, who had been Auxiliary Bishop of Cincinnati since 1929, boarded the train in Detroit and traveled to Lansing. They were greeted by a crowd of about 5,000 at Union Station, which is known today as Clara's Restaurant. The welcoming committee was led by the patriarch of Lansing Catholics, the Rev. John O'Rafferty. A procession formed and proceeded to St. Mary Cathedral. There was still much anti-Catholic sentiment in Lansing. St. Mary parishioners recall that the Klu Klux Klan arranged for a number of young boys to throw eggs at the procession just as it approached the Cathedral. The police were tipped off and the eggs were confiscated before any were thrown.

The following day, Archbishop Mooney presided over the formal establishment of the Diocese of Lansing and the installation of Joseph Albers as its first bishop. His Excellency, The Most Reverend John T. McNicholas, O.P., preached the sermon. Fr. O'Rafferty, dean of the Lansing clergy and rector of the Cathedral, led the sixty-six priests of the Diocese in professing their obedience to the newly-installed Bishop by kissing his ring. Five archbishops, forty-four bishops, hundreds of priests, sisters and laity witnessed the installation. The Governor of Michigan, Frank Murphy, and the Mayor of Lansing, Max Templeton, were among the civic officials in attendance. The clergy of the Diocese hosted a luncheon at the Hotel Olds for the nearly 600 visiting priests and hierarchy. That evening the laity came out in great numbers for a civic celebration held at Prudden Auditorium at 8:00 P.M. to welcome Bishop Albers to Lansing. The governor and mayor both spoke. Mr. William Hermes spoke on behalf of the laity of the new diocese and Rev. John A. Gabriels spoke on behalf of the clergy. The Boys Vocational School Band provided two musical selections.

When he was consecrated a Bishop, Albers chose as the motto of his episcopate *"Divinum auxilium nobiscum"* (Divine Help Be With Us). This motto was chosen shortly after the stock market crash of 1929. Bishop Albers chose a new motto when he came to Lansing. He had sent invitations to his installation as Bishop of Lansing to his World War I chaplain buddies who had served with him in France. This reunion of chaplains and the escalating military armament influenced his choice of a new motto. Bishop Albers chose *"Fides vincet mundum"* (Faith Conquers the World).

Getting Started

Fr. O'Rafferty offered Bishop Albers half of the rectory at 223 Seymour to serve as the temporary episcopal residence and chancery. The bishop had much work to do to organize the new diocese. His first correspondence with his clergy was a thank you letter for the good wishes they had extended on his installation. Compiling statistical information about priests and parishes was the subject of correspondence later in the month. This letter also outlined chancery procedures. The chancery office hours were from 10:00 A.M. to 12 noon daily except Sunday.

The Marian Pact for priests was soon organized. The condition for membership was to celebrate three masses as soon as convenient after the death of a member of the pact. The last item addressed by Bishop Albers in his first month as bishop was an instruction to the clergy on their duty to remind parents of the serious obligation to send their children to a Catholic elementary, high school, or college whenever possible. On August 30th, the first diocesan official, Rev. Joseph R. Byrne, was appointed chancellor and secretary to the bishop. He soon found out, as did all the diocesan clergy, that Bishop Albers' model for all decisions was to follow the way things were done in Cincinnati. Many copies of letters issued by the Cincinnati chancery served as prototypes of letters sent from the Bishop's office.

Vocations

Although a director of vocations was not appointed for almost 20 years, vocations were a concern of Bishop Albers from the start. Beginning in September 1937 an annual collection was established to raise funds for the education of those studying for the priesthood. A fundraising goal was set for each parish. The annual seminary collection was discontinued in 1955. The following year support of seminarians became a part of the Diocesan Development Fund. The day after three new counties were added to the Diocese in May 1938, a letter was sent to the priests regarding diocesan practices. Bishop Albers wrote that he should be informed of any young man who desired to study for the priesthood. On the feast of the Conversion of St. Paul in 1939, Bishop Albers directed that a campaign of prayer be started by priests, sisters and school children for more vocations to the priesthood and sisterhood. Thus the traditional practice in many parishes began of praying the Our Father, Hail Mary and Glory Be after Mass for vocations.

By 1947, March was designated as Vocation Month. This was tied in with the Feast of St. Joseph, Patron of the Universal Church. The intercession of St. Joseph was sought for vocations to the priesthood and religious life. In his annual vocation letters Bishop Albers often stressed that the need for more religious women was even more critical than the need for more priests.

Indulgences

The first letter regarding indulgences was sent to the priests in late October 1937. Bishop Albers requested that the priests announce to their parishioners at Sunday Masses October 31st and at All Saints Day Masses that indulgences for the Poor Souls in Purgatory could be gained in two ways. First by visiting any church or public oratory from noon November 1st to midnight November 2nd. Confession, reception of Communion, and praying the Our Father, Hail Mary and Glory Be to the Father six times were also required. The second way to gain the indulgence was to pray for the dead while visiting a cemetery between All Souls Day and the conclusion of its novena on November 9th.

The other indulgence which Bishop Albers often wrote about was the Portiuncula Indulgence, one of the oldest in the Church. The Portiuncula Indulgence was first given in the fourteenth century at the Portiuncula Chapel near Assisi. In 1939, this indulgence was limited to eleven designated churches in the Diocese (generally one per county). There were so many requests to make the indulgences more widely available that the Holy See allowed for its extension to 47 parishes in the Diocese in 1946. The Portiuncula Indulgence was categorized as a *toties quoties* indulgence meaning that it could be gained more than once on the same day.

Spiritual Concern for the Laity

The spiritual life of the laity was also a concern of the new bishop. The schedule of Forty Hours Devotions was sent out early in November 1937. The devotions were always scheduled to begin at the Cathedral parish during the first week of Advent. Each week at least one parish in the Diocese was scheduled to

hold this devotion of Adoration of the Most Blessed Sacrament. Traditionally adoration began after the last Mass on Sunday and concluded with a eucharistic procession and Benediction on Tuesday evening. Tuesday evening became a clergy gathering night because all the neighboring clergy were invited to the closing of Forty Hours.

In mid-December 1937, a letter was sent out instructing that the Holy Name Society be organized or reorganized in each parish on Holy Name Sunday, January 9, 1938. All members of the parish, young and old, were encouraged to join the organization.

The founding of the Lansing Particular Council of the St. Vincent De Paul Society in July 1941 brought the positive contributions of this organization to the attention of Bishop Albers. Two other particular councils had been formed: in Battle Creek in 1935 and in Flint in 1939. Rev. Earl V. Sheridan, head of Catholic Charities, prepared a report on the work of the society. The report was mailed to every pastor. The accompanying letter encouraged conferences to be established in every parish, rural as well as urban. By 1943, there were eleven parish conferences in the Flint Particular Council, seven in the Lansing Council, and two in the Battle Creek Council.

Clergy Conferences

Fr. Byrne, the bishop's secretary, sent out a notice that the first diocesan conference of pastors of the new diocese was to be held at Nazareth Academy in Kalamazoo at 1:30 P.M. on December 6, 1937. The first of a series of "Instructions to the Clergy" followed the meeting. Priests were also given notice that parish expenses exceeding $250.00 must have prior written approval from the chancery. (It wasn't until 1958 that this spending ceiling was elevated to $500.00.) After the first conference, a pattern of spring and fall conferences emerged. Sometimes there were general conferences considering policies and practices. The theological conferences usually focused on some issue in Moral Theology, Liturgy or Canon Law. The conferences were generally held by deaneries and organized by the dean once the topics and dates were established by the chancery.

At the fall general conference of 1941 it was announced that hospital insurance would be made available to each priest at a cost of $9.00 a year. At the same conference the development of adult study clubs in conjunction with the Confraternity of Christian Doctrine (CCD) program was encouraged. The September 1946 general conference discussed the following goals set by the Bishop for parish life:

a) Intensify and reorganize all parish societies.

b) Organize active high school Alumni Associations.

c) Organize Catholic Youth Organization (C.Y.O.) for youth 18 to 25, on parochial and inter-parochial basis.

d) Organize Boy Scout troops in all parishes, especially larger parishes.

e) Organize a St. Vincent de Paul Conference in each parish.

f) Institute the Federal School Lunch Program in all parishes with elementary and high schools.

Serious Fire

Early in January 1938, fire swept through the chancery side of St. Mary rectory. Fortunately there was a firewall between the two sides of the double residence. The only entry from one side to the other was on the first floor. Bishop Albers was overcome by smoke and collapsed. He was found on the floor near a rear window and was carried down a ladder by firemen. He was then taken to the rectory dining room and there the firemen used an inhaler to revive him. The Sisters of Charity, who staffed St. Mary Cathedral School, brought blankets and hot water bottles to keep him warm. Bishop Albers had weakened lungs as a result of being gassed in the trenches during his service as an army chaplain in World War I. The firemen and doctors worked for nearly 30 minutes before Bishop Albers was revived. An article in the Lansing State Journal of January 10th stated that physicians had to administer powerful stimulants to revive his heart. Nearly $10,000 of damage was caused by the fire and water damage, but most importantly the life of the bishop had been spared.

At the time of the fire in 1938, the middle building was the rectory and chancery.

Lent

Lenten regulations were issued on February 21, 1938. Wednesdays and Fridays of Lent were days of abstinence as well as Ember Saturday and Holy Saturday until noon. Fasting was required every day of Lent except Sundays. On these days only one full meal and two light meals were allowed for those between age 21 and 59. In accordance with the indult granted by the Holy See, Bishop Albers dispensed the working classes and those of their households from abstinence so that they could eat meat once a day during Lent except on Fridays, Ash Wednesday and before noon on Holy Saturday. The priests were asked to remind the faithful that those who were impoverished, under-nourished, ill, or convalescing, and women bearing or nursing children were not obligated to the fast and abstinence laws. For each of the twenty-six Lents that Bishop Albers shepherded the Diocese, a letter addressed to "Reverend dear Father and Beloved Faithful" was read at all masses the Sunday before Lent began. The faithful were reminded to fulfill their Easter duty to receive confession and communion between the First Sunday of Lent and Trinity Sunday. The Lenten practices of prayer, fasting and almsgiving were highly recommended for the penitential season. Weekly Lenten devotions in each parish included the Way of the Cross and Benediction of the Blessed Sacrament. These were usually held on Friday evenings and often repeated on Sunday afternoon or evening. Another night of the week devotions were to include a Lenten sermon and Benediction. Only great devotion to St. Joseph or St. Patrick could ever be a cause to set aside the ban on socials, amusements, theater and dances during this penitential season. Lenten sermon outlines were distributed to the priests. In 1947 the Bishops of Michigan issued their first joint regulations for fast and abstinence for the season of Lent. In 1956, an evening Mass was allowed once a week during Lent in order to encourage more people to attend Mass and receive Holy Communion. The last Lenten sermon outlines were distributed in 1961. The topic that year was the need for personal responsibility.

Chrism Mass

In recent decades the Chrism Mass on Holy Thursday has become the premier gathering of the faithful from across the Diocese. In 1938 the situation was different. The Pontifical High Mass was held at 10:00 A.M. in the Cathedral. The pastors and assistants in the vicinity of Lansing were asked to attend after their services were completed. (It was not till the reform of Holy Week in the mid fifties that services were moved from mornings and returned to afternoon and evenings.) The Holy Oils were then (as now) placed in small bottles and boxed together. The oils were distributed from: St. Mary Cathedral, Lansing; St. Philip, Battle Creek; St. Mary Star of the Sea, Jackson; St. Augustine, Kalamazoo; and St. John, Benton Harbor. The pastors of the other named churches were instructed to send their assistants to the Cathedral to pick up the oils between noon and 2:00 P.M. It was also noted that to defray the cost, an offering of at least $1.00 was expected from each parish. This was changed in 1942 to read that a substantial offering was expected.

Beginning with the 1956 letter, Lansing area priests were asked to urge their parishioners to attend the Chrism liturgy. It was noted in the letter that Holy Communion could not be distributed either to the clergy or to the laity at this Mass. The next year, by virtue of special permission from the Holy See, Holy Communion would be distributed to the laity. This privilege did not extend to the clergy who were expected to receive at the *Missa Coena Domini* in the evening. Again the instructions were given to invite the laity throughout the Diocese to attend the Chrism Mass. The schools in the Lansing deanery sent delegations of students. A booklet was prepared to be distributed to all attending. The booklet contained a translation of the Mass and of the liturgy of consecration of the oils.

Devotions and Novenas

A devotion is an exterior expression of an interior desire to imitate Christ. Devotions played an important part in Bishop Albers' vision of "faith conquering the world". In promoting the devotional life of the laity and clergy he saw faith being strengthened.

Since the Cathedral in Lansing is dedicated to the Blessed Mother, it is not surprising that a letter was sent out in late April 1938 directing that May devotions be arranged in all parishes. The devotions consisted of the Rosary and the appropriate Marian prayers in conjunction with Benediction. There were letters sent by Bishop Albers to encourage the Rosary Devotions in October as well. Rosary devotions consisted of the recitation of at least five decades of the Rosary, the Litany of the Blessed Virgin Mary and the Memorare.

Bishop Albers felt that a strong devotional life nourished the flock entrusted to his care. On May 10, 1938, he issued a letter to be read at all the Masses calling for a novena in every parish to be celebrated between the Ascension and Pentecost. On the seventh Sunday of Easter the Blessed Sacrament was to be exposed after the last Mass until Holy Hour and Benediction in the evening. This was to be done in union with the International Eucharistic Congress being held that year in Budapest, Hungary. Bishop Albers began the novena at the Cathedral by celebrating the first ordination to the priesthood in the Diocese. In addition to the Marian devotions and the Pentecost Novena, there was also the Blessed Sacrament Novena held each Lent. Bishop Albers continued to encourage all of these devotions and novenas throughout his episcopate.

Chancery Staff

By the summer of 1938 the Bishop had his staff in place. Very Reverend John R. Hackett was the Vicar General; Fr. Bryne continued as Chancellor but was also given responsibilities as the *officialis* (head) of the tribunal. He continued in this capacity until July 1950. Because of these added responsibilities, Fr. Byrne's position as priest secretary to the bishop was given to Rev. Adolph A. Oser. In August, Rev. Henry M. Mayotte was appointed director of the Catholic Student Mission Crusade (a forerunner to the Missions Office) efforts in the Diocese. Fr. Mayotte did not have an office at the chancery and neither did Fr. Hackett. The chancery staff consisted of Bishop Albers, Fr. Byrne, Fr. Oser and lay staff. Mr. Leo Walsh set up the fiscal books for the Diocese. He continued in the post of bookkeeper until the end of February, 1939. While he was bookkeeper there was a pay entry "St. Mary Cathedral steno". Miss Josephine Perry was the cathedral stenographer and she served the Diocese as secretary as long as her future husband (Mr. Walsh) was the bookkeeper. Mr. Walsh was succeeded by the long serving Miss Frances C. Monroe.

Diocesan Boundaries

Besides Marian Devotions, the Pentecost Novena and the first diocesan priesthood ordination, May 1938 also brought changes in the diocesan boundaries. On May 16th, the counties of Allegan, Barry and Ionia were transferred from the Lansing diocese to the Grand Rapids Diocese. A week later the counties of Genesee, Livingston and Shiawassee were transferred from the jurisdiction of the Archdiocese of Detroit to the Diocese of Lansing. The Diocese was stabilized (until 1971) as being composed of 15 counties: Berrien, Branch, Calhoun, Cass, Clinton, Eaton, Genesee, Hillsdale, Ingham, Jackson, Kalamazoo, Livingston, St. Joseph, Shiawassee and Van Buren.

Deaneries Established

At the end of June 1938 the Diocese was divided into five deaneries. The deans were the Very Reverends John O'Rafferty for Lansing, Maurice Chawke for Flint, John R. Hackett for

Kalamazoo, Joseph Coyle for Jackson and Eugene Cullinane for St. Joseph. Later that year the deans met with the local clergy to clarify parish boundaries. In February 1939, the deans organized the theological conference which focused among other things on the obligation to attend Sunday Mass and the indulgence attached to the Way of the Cross. Beginning with the 1939 Chrism Mass the deans oversaw the distribution of the Holy Oils in the outlying regions.

Clergy Retreats

Yet another tradition established in June 1938 was the annual priest retreat at St. Anthony's in Comstock outside of Kalamazoo. The facility belonged to the Sisters of St. Joseph of Nazareth, Michigan. Rev. Charles P. Bruehl of St. Charles Seminary in Overbrook, in suburban Philadelphia, Pennsylvania, preached the first retreat. The retreat went from Monday evening at 8:00 P.M. till Friday morning after morning Mass. The lists of priests who were assigned to each of the two June retreats were mailed from the Chancery. Pastors were expected to make an offering of at least $20.00 and assistants were expected to give at least $10.00. Participants were expected to rise at 5:50 A.M. and be ready for meditations and Prime at 6:15. The day ended with Benediction and a conference at 8:00 P.M. Retreatants were expected to retire at 9:45 P.M. These retreats at St. Anthony's continued until the opening of the Portiuncula in the Pines Retreat House at DeWitt. The DeWitt retreat house opened in the fall of 1955 and the next year the annual retreats were held there. Because of the limited space at DeWitt, five retreats rather than two (as previously scheduled) were held. As facilities at the retreat house expanded, the number of retreats decreased.

Education Office Begins

In 1938 the groundwork was laid for the opening of an office of education, when Bishop Albers sent Rev. Jerome V. MacEachin, (Fr. Mac) to Catholic University of America. Fr. Mac completed his masters degree in education and returned to the Diocese in 1940. Upon his return, he was given a full time parish assignment and responsibility for the Catholic schools in the Diocese. Until Fr. Mac returned, Bishop Albers ran the school system. The first school calendar was issued for the year 1938-39. In April 1939 the Bishop requested that the practice of a three day retreat be introduced in every parish high school.

Teachers' Institute, 1961, (left to right: Sr. Anne Celeste, O.P., from St. Joseph in St. Joseph; Sr. Philomena, S.S.J., from St. Augustine in Kalamazoo; Rev. Xavier Harris, O.F.M., keynote speaker; Sr. Marguerite, S.C., from St. Mary Cathedral in Lansing; Sr. Mary Frederic, I.H.M., from St. John in Jackson)

Fr. MacEachin organized the first Institute for Teachers in the Diocese in October 1944. These conferences continue in a modified form to this day. Another innovation during Fr. Mac's tenure was the organization of home-school councils across the Diocese. The councils fostered better communication between the parents and school staff. The support they gave the school through fund raising and organizing sports programs was tremendous.

Regional Divisions of the Diocese of Lansing

Five Deaneries
June 30, 1938 - July 21, 1971

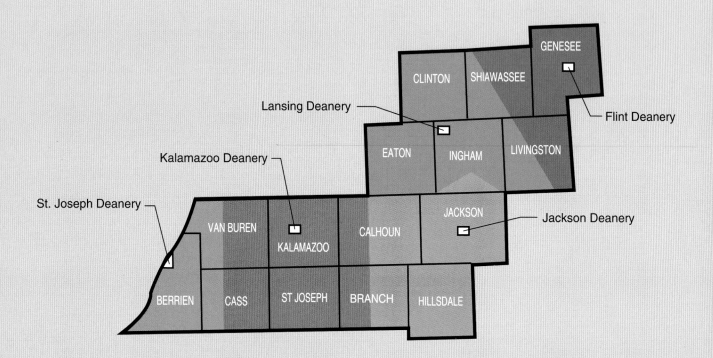

Lansing Deanery

Kalamazoo Deanery

St. Joseph Deanery

Flint Deanery

Jackson Deanery

GENESEE

CLINTON   SHIAWASSEE

EATON   INGHAM   LIVINGSTON

VAN BUREN

KALAMAZOO   CALHOUN   JACKSON

BERRIEN   CASS   ST JOSEPH   BRANCH   HILLSDALE

Six Regions of the Diocese of Lansing
October 9, 1972 - May 27, 1977

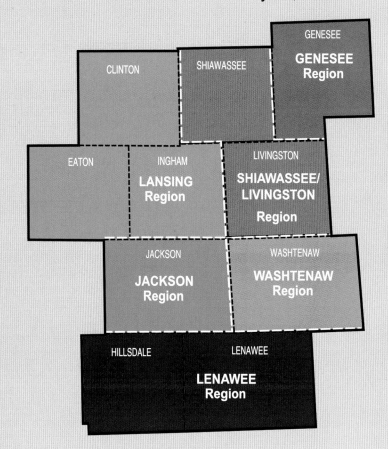

GENESEE

CLINTON   SHIAWASSEE   **GENESEE Region**

EATON   INGHAM   LIVINGSTON

LANSING Region   **SHIAWASSEE/ LIVINGSTON Region**

JACKSON   WASHTENAW

JACKSON Region   **WASHTENAW Region**

HILLSDALE   LENAWEE

LENAWEE Region

Five Regions of the Diocese of Lansing
May 27, 1977 - June 1, 1990

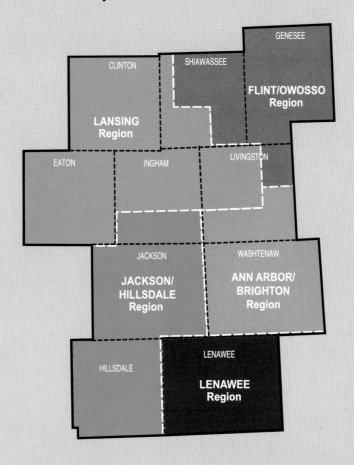

Six Regions of the Diocese of Lansing
June 1, 1990 -

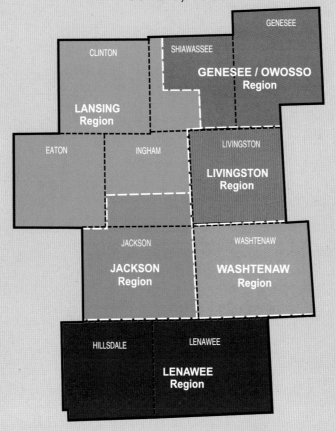

Catholic Charities

Accompanying Fr. Mac to Catholic University in 1938 were Revs. Maurice Olk and Earl V. Sheridan. They were sent to receive the background necessary to organize the Catholic Charities Office. In 1940 Fr. Sheridan founded the first Catholic social service agency of the Diocese in Flint. Eight years later Rev. John D. Slowey organized the Catholic Charities Office in Lansing. A decade later in 1958, Rev. Francis J. Murray opened the Catholic Charities Office in Kalamazoo.

The opening in 1940 of Holy Angels Convent at St. Michael Parish in Flint for the Franciscan Sisters of the Poor was another effort of Bishop Albers to foster social services in the Diocese. The Sisters worked in conjunction with the Catholic Charities office in Flint. They soon established the Holy Angels Sandwich Program for the poor.

Eucharistic Congresses

Bishop Albers had a firm belief in the spiritual value of eucharistic devotions. He repeatedly seized opportunities to make the priests and faithful aware of the National Eucharistic Congress in New Orleans in 1938 and the International Eucharistic Congress in Budapest that same year. In conjunction with the eighth National Eucharistic Congress held in October 1938 in New Orleans, Bishop Albers directed that the Confraternity of the Blessed Sacrament be formed in each church and mission in the Diocese. A pamphlet explaining the purpose, organization, privileges and indulgences of the confraternity was sent out by the diocesan director, Rev. Herman D. Fedewa, the pastor of St. Joseph Parish in Howell. The priests were asked to preach about the Blessed Sacrament and the Eucharistic Congress, to hold eucharistic devotions on the

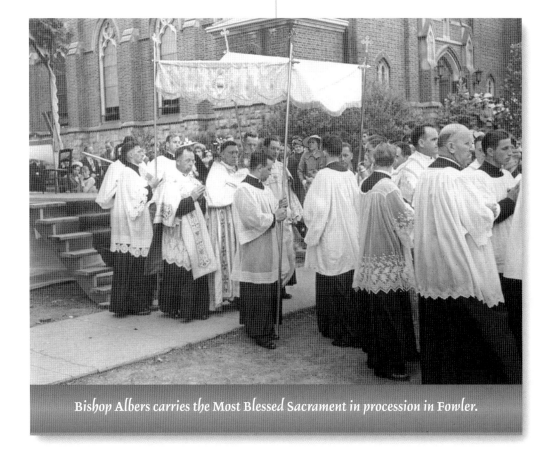

Bishop Albers carries the Most Blessed Sacrament in procession in Fowler.

Sunday of the Congress, and to encourage all the faithful to receive Holy Communion that day. Eucharistic devotions culminated in the Diocesan Eucharistic Day held at Most Holy Trinity Parish in Fowler on June 11, 1939. In preparation for the Eucharistic Day a Holy Hour was conducted in every parish in the Diocese. Again all Catholics were encouraged to receive Communion on the day of the celebration, even if they could not actually attend the devotions in Fowler. A second Diocesan Eucharistic Day was held the following year at Nazareth. Gas rationing during World War II affected the ability to travel and brought an end to the annual event.

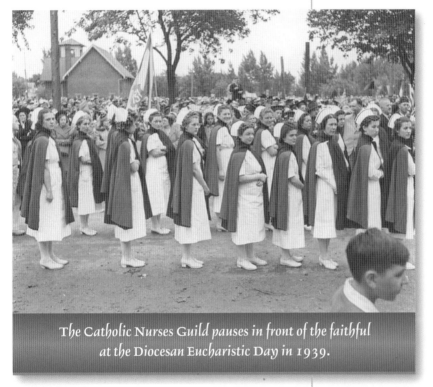

The Catholic Nurses Guild pauses in front of the faithful at the Diocesan Eucharistic Day in 1939.

Legion of Decency

Prompted by concern for the moral fiber of the faithful, Pope Pius XI called for an annual renewal of a pledge to stay away from motion pictures offending "the truth and Christian morality". At their annual meeting in Washington in 1935 the U.S. Bishops directed that the Legion of Decency pledge be renewed each year during the octave of the feast of the Immaculate Conception. Each year of the Albers episcopate beginning in 1938, a letter was sent from the chancery reminding pastors to renew the pledge with their parishioners at Sunday Mass. The pledge was repeated after the priest gave a sermon condemning indecent and immoral films. The pledge also condemned motion pictures which glorified crime or criminals. The Legion of Decency was established in the U.S. in 1934 and it rated all movies. Members promised to avoid movies which were classified as B (morally objectionable in part or all) or C (condemned). The classification lists were to be posted in church vestibules and on school bulletin boards.

Confraternity of Christian Doctrine

In 1905 Pope Pius X directed that the Confraternity of Christian Doctrine be established in every parish. When the Diocese came into existence the Confraternity was already officially established in some parishes but was lacking in many others. The organization of branches of Confraternity of Christian Doctrine (C.C.D.) received a boost in early September 1940 when a regional conference was held at Sacred Heart Seminary in Detroit. Bishop Albers sent out a letter to all the priests urging them to attend the conference. Sisters were also encouraged to attend. They shouldered the responsibility for formal religious education outside the home. Besides teaching in schools all week they went out (usually on Saturday mornings) to teach in parishes having no schools. (See the pages entitled Adrian Dominicans and Sisters, Servants of the Immaculate Heart of Mary for further information.)

The first recorded Catechetical Sunday observed in the Diocese was held October 9,

Adrian Dominicans

The sisters were assigned to the parishes listed in bold type where they taught school. In the same parishes they also taught CCD for the years given. In addition, they traveled to the parishes listed in regular type to teach CCD during the years indicated.

Residence	Parish/Mission	Years taught CCD
Adrian	**St Joseph**	1951-1968
Adrian	**St. Mary**	1945-1968
Albion	**St. John**	1959-1970
Brighton	**St. Patrick**	1942-1980
Chelsea	**St. Mary**	1948-1968
	Manchester, St. Mary	1956
Deerfield	**St. Alphonsus**	1936-1969
	Blissfield, St. Peter	1941-
East Lansing	**St. Thomas Aquinas**	1949-1968
	Laingsburg, St. Isidore	1953-1963
Jackson	**Queen of the Miraculous Medal**	1939-1967
	Concord, St. Catherine	1953-1967
Lansing	**Resurrection**	1944-1971
	Laingsburg, St. Isidore	1938-1953
	Charlotte, St. Mary	1943-1960
	East Lansing, St. Thomas	1943-1949
	Grand Ledge, St. Michael	1943-1961
	Fowlerville, St. Agnes	1947-1959
	Williamston, St. Mary	1947-1959
	Lansing, St. Therese	1949-1950
	Lansing, Immaculate Heart of Mary	1949-1955
	Lansing, Cristo Rey	1963-1968

Residence	Parish/Mission	Years taught CCD
Owosso	**St. Paul**	1945-1969
Morrice	St. Mary	1930-1961
Durand	St. Mary	1946-1961
Paw Paw	**St. Mary**	1952-1971
	Mattawan, St. John Bosco	1953-1955
	Decatur, Holy Family	1954-1972
Pinckney	**St. Mary**	1956-1969
St. Joseph	**St. Joseph**	1950-1966
	Hartford, Immaculate Conception	1946-
	South Haven, St. Basil	1946-
	Watervliet, St. Joseph	1946-
	Coloma	1950-1951
	Bridgman	1952-1963
	Three Oaks, St. Mary	1952-1966
Sturgis	**Holy Angels**	1949-1971
	Mendon, St. Edward	1953-1963
Tecumseh	**St. Elizabeth**	1962-1970
Ypsilanti	**St. John**	1941-1976
	Whittaker, St. Joseph	1942-1943
	Willow Run, St. Alexis	1950-1957
	Ypsilanti, St. Ursula	1962-1963

Adrian Dominican sisters are shown with their Saturday morning CCD classes at St. Mary, Morrice, in June 1948.

Sisters, Servants of the
Immaculate Heart of Mary (IHM)

**The sisters were assigned to the parishes listed in bold type where they taught school.
In the same parishes they also taught CCD for the years given. In addition, they traveled to
the parishes listed in regular type to teach CCD during the years indicated.**

Residence	Parish/Mission	Years taught CCD
Ann Arbor	**St. Thomas the Apostle**	1941-1976
	Ypsilanti, St. John	1922-1923
	Milan, Immaculate Conception	1940-1949
	Ann Arbor, St. Patrick	1940-1941
		1949-1950
	Ann Arbor, St. Francis	1950-1952
Battle Creek	**St. Philip**	1933-1971
	Bellevue, St. Anne	1943-1969
	Battle Creek, St. Joseph	1947-1949
	Nashville, St. Cyril	1952-1969
	Dowling	1962-1967
	Lacey, Our Lady of Great Oak	1967-1969
Benton Harbor	**St. John**	1937-1978
	Buchanan, St. Anthony	1947-1965
	New Buffalo, St. Mary	1958-1964
	Benton Harbor, St. Bernard	1967-1968
Coldwater	**St. Charles**	1922-1976
	Hillsdale, St. Anthony	1924-1956
	Coldwater State School	1947-1971
	Union City, Our Lady of Fatima	1949-1968
Dexter	**St. Joseph**	1921-1982
	Pinckney	1954-1956

Residence	Parish/Mission	Years taught CCD
Fenton	**St. John**	1950-
	Howell, St. Augustine	1954-
Flint	**St. Matthew**	1928-1970
	Flint, Christ the King	1936-1938
	Durand, St. Mary	1936-1938
	Flint, Michigan School for the Deaf	1939-1968
	Flint, Holy Redeemer	1940-1946
	Gaines, St. Joseph	1946-1954
	Howell, St. Augustine	1946-1954
Flint	**St. Michael**	1922-1970
	Swartz Creek, St. Mary	1922-1951
	Davison, St. John	1929-1930
	Fenton, St. John	1933-1950
	Flushing, St. Robert	1930-1951
	Flint, St. Joseph	1955-1966
	Flint, St. Michael Byzantine	1955-1966
	Flint, St. Pius	1957-1961
Jackson	**St. John**	1933-1975
	Jackson,	
	Queen of the Miraculous Medal	1937-1938
Mount Morris	**St. Mary**	1937-1995
	Birch Run	1938-1948

Sisters of St. Joseph Nazareth, MI

Residence	Parish/Mission	Years taught CCD
Battle Creek	**St. Joseph**	1949-1990
Bangor	**Sacred Heart**	1957-1967
Charlotte	**St. Mary**	1961-1983
Comstock	**St. Anthony**	1942-1956
Davison	**St. John**	1946-1971
	Otisville, St. Francis Xavier	1949-1971
Dowagiac	**Holy Maternity of Mary**	1952-1967
	Cassopolis, St. Ann	1952-1967
	Silver Creek, Sacred Heart of Mary	1952-1955
	Marcellus, St. Margaret Mary	1952-1957
Flint	**St. Agnes**	1942-1977
Flint	**St. John Vianney**	1948-1971
Flint	**St. Mary**	1925-1987
	Deerfield, St. Augustine	1942-1946
	Gaines, St. Joseph	1942-1946
Grand Blanc	**Holy Family**	1956-1985
Hillsdale	**St. Anthony**	1956-1977
Kalamazoo	**St. Augustine**	1937-1971
Kalamazoo	**St. Monica**	1958-1975
Kalamazoo	**St. Joseph**	1924-1989

Residence	Parish/Mission	Years taught CCD
Lansing	**St. Therese**	1951-1987
Lansing	**St. Gerard**	1961-1985
Lansing	**Immaculate Heart of Mary**	1958-1977
Leslie-Bunker Hill	**St. Cornelius and Cyprian**	1937-1964
Mattawan	**St. John Bosco**	1957-1969
Michigan Center	**Our Lady of Fatima**	1960-1967
Niles	**St. Mary**	1926-1974
	Dowagiac, Holy Maternity of Mary	1945-1952
	Cassopolis, St. Ann	1952
	Silver Creek, Sacred Heart of Mary	1955-1975
Parchment	**St. Ambrose**	1959-1969
St. Johns	**St. Joseph**	1924-1989
Three Rivers	**Immaculate Conception**	1949-1967
		1979-1989
	White Pigeon, St. Joseph	1948-1967
Watervliet	**St. Joseph**	1952-1975
	Hartford, Immaculate Conception	1952-1975
Williamston	**St. Mary**	1959-1986
	Fowlerville, St. Agnes	1959-1986

1949. Bishop Albers directed the priests to preach on "The Catechism". They were to emphasize its dignity and the honored place it should have in the life of every Catholic. This celebration was first held at the request of the Sacred Congregation of the Council in Rome and the Confraternity of Christian Doctrine.

Another (the fourth) regional C.C.D. congress was held in September 1952 in Lansing. The congress was held in conjunction with the 15th anniversary of the establishment of the Diocese. As a prelude to the congress two institutes for priests concerning the work of the C.C.D. were held during July at Benton Harbor and Flint. As a result of the institutes, two goals were established: 1) to foster adult discussion clubs, and 2) to pursue a common course for teaching religion to high school students. The members of the institutes recommended that each priest director should set up a parish C.C.D. executive board and enlist the help of the laity as teachers. These boards were to implement the discussion clubs and high school programs. The Creed was chosen as the subject of study for the school year 1952-53 for both discussion clubs and public high school students. In November 1952, Bishop Albers appointed Rev. Anthony P. Majchrowski, assistant at All Saints in Flint, to serve as diocesan director of the C.C.D. He retained that position for nearly a decade. In the same letter approving Fr. Majchrowski's appointment Bishop Albers stressed the importance of enlisting the aid of "devoted laymen and women" in the Confraternity work. The following year in September, another meeting of the clergy covering the Confraternity work was held in St. Mary Cathedral Hall. Two days later on Catechetical Sunday, a Diocesan Confraternity Conference was held. Each parish was asked to send two or more delegates, preferably from the parish boards of the Confraternity. The first session focused on religious education for children, while the second session featured a demonstration of a discussion club by an active club from St. Michael Parish in Flint. Nearly 250 people attended the conference. The subject for high school and discussion clubs for 1953-54, was "the Sacraments, the Mass and the Liturgical Year" from the "St. Paul Series". Efforts to establish C.C.D. branches in every parish continued.

Honoring the Bishop

After seeking the advice of the consulters (advisors required by Canon Law) of the Diocese Bishop Albers announced in April 1940 that the time had come to build a suitable bishop's residence. To finance this venture the first diocesan appeal for funds was launched. The seventy-four parishes and missions contributed $31,623.34. The funds were used toward the purchase of the Reuter Mansion in Eaton Rapids. The residence is now known as The English Inn. The following year on June 17th, a Solemn Pontifical Mass was celebrated by Bishop Albers at the Cathedral to observe the twenty-fifth anniversary of his ordination to the priesthood. Representatives from every parish were invited. The priests and people were asked to express their congratulations by sending spiritual bouquets (a promise to recite certain prayers for the intention of the recipient) to the Bishop.

World War II

World War II began with Nazi Germany's invasion of Poland on September 1, 1939. Britain and France declared war on Germany two days later. On September 7th, Bishop Albers issued a letter to the clergy instructing that in every parish public prayers for peace be instituted. The *oratio imperata* (the requested prayer designated by the Bishop as the second oration at the beginning of Mass) *pro pace* was to be recited at all Masses until further notice. The school children were especially asked to join in Pope Pius XII's Crusade of Prayer for Peace.

A letter from Bishop Albers dated January 2, 1940 asked that parishes provide Catholic young men going into military service with a small crucifix, rosary, medals and a prayer book. The first war relief collection was taken up during Lent 1940.

After the bombing of Pearl Harbor, Bishop Albers wrote a letter dated December 11, 1941, which was addressed to the clergy and beloved faithful. He told them:

Rev. John R. Day

Bishop Albers in his chaplain's uniform with family, circa 1918.

Rev. Gilbert H. Gruss

World War II Chaplains

Rev. Joseph E. Whelan

Rev. John R. Day	Army	1940-1943
Rev. Gilbert H. Gruss	Navy-Marines	1943-1946
Rev. George A. Higgins	Army (Field Artillery)	1941-1945
Rev. John E. Madden	Army Air Forces	1942-1943
Rev. James Leo McCann	Army	1943-1946
Rev. Alphonsus J. Olk	Navy	1943-1945
Rev. Francis E. Timmons	Army Air Forces	1944-1946
Rev. Norbert B. Wheeler	Army Air Forces	1944-1947
Rev. Joseph E. Whelan	Army (Infantry)	1940-1945
Rev. Joseph E. Wieber	Navy-18th Marines (Engr)	1942-1947
Rev. George B. Zabelka	Army Air Corps	1944-1946

Rev. George A. Higgins

Rev. Joseph E. Wieber

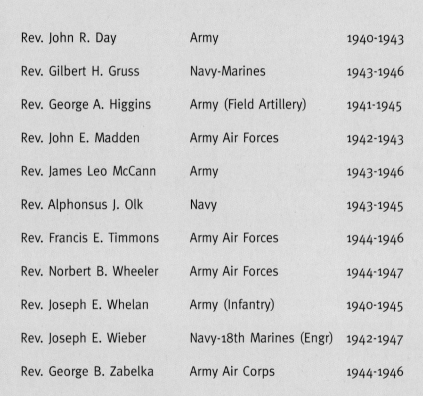

Rev. Norbert B. Wheeler

Major General Geoffrey Keyes congratulates Capt. George A. Higgins awarding him the Legion of Merit for performance of outstanding services during the Italian campaign.

Rev. George B. Zabelka

Rev. Francis E. Timmons

"Sad as the hour is we must not lose heart but rather take courage, strength and consolation that God in His Divine Providence watches over the world and has His reasons, which He has not made known to us, in permitting this war to come upon us."

Later that month pastors were encouraged to establish in their church vestibule a "Roll of Honor" with the names of the men serving with the armed forces.

Having served as an Army Chaplain in World War I, Bishop Albers knew first hand the tragedy of war. He was very supportive of the eleven priests of the Diocese who entered the armed forces as chaplains. Two other priests served as auxiliary chaplains at military facilities in Battle Creek. Rev. John R. Day had served in World War I as a Protestant chaplain. In World War II he served as a Catholic chaplain. Rev. George B. Zabelka's experience as a chaplain with the Army Air Corps that dropped the bomb on Hiroshima led to his decision to become a peace activist.

As the priests and laity of this diocese went off to war, Bishop Albers urged more fervent and more frequent prayers for peace. He asked the clergy to pray unceasingly that those dying in combat might receive the grace to receive the Sacraments or at least to make an Act of Contrition. In a letter dated May 23, 1942 he stated:

"As soon as possible after official word has been received by relatives announcing the death of a son or brother, pastors are directed to forward to us in the Chancery the name and address of the bereaved parents or relatives as we wish to send a personal letter of condolence to those who have sacrificed so much for God and country."

In the spring of 1944 all awaited the invasion of Europe by the Allied Forces. Bishop Albers wrote his priests on May 25th:

"Whenever the invasion begins I trust that you will immediately urge your parishioners to attend daily Mass, receive Holy Communion and redouble their prayers."

In the fall the faithful were urged to turn to God in gratitude and thanksgiving. When victory came church bells were to be rung for fifteen minutes after the news was broadcast. Each parish was to offer a special High Mass of Thanksgiving followed by Adoration of the Blessed Sacrament and closing with Benediction.

War Relief

Even before the United States entered the war, war relief efforts began. The first war relief collection was held in March 1940. It continued each Lent on Laetare Sunday for many years after the war. A clothing drive began as a war relief effort in the fall of 1944. The drive slogan was "One usable garment from every parishioner." The diocesan quota of 53,000 pounds of clothing was surpassed by 30,806 pounds. Catholics were asked to participate in a United Nations Clothing Collection in April 1945. Another clothing appeal for the children of Europe, the Philippines and China was launched in August through the auspices of the National Council of Catholic Women. The clergy were asked to respond to a special appeal for the needy priests in war torn areas. The U.S. Bishops sponsored a campaign in Advent 1945 to collect canned foodstuffs for Europe. In the Diocese 170,827 pounds of foodstuffs was collected. This averaged out to one ton of canned goods from each of the sixty-six parishes and eighteen missions. In May of 1946 a food drive for the children of Europe and the Far East was held. The total diocesan contribution was 313,928 cans of food which had an estimated cash value of $28,399.17. The diocesan quota had been 100,000 cans. A clothing drive was held in November 1946 and a Thanksgiving Food Collection was held in 1947. In 1949 the Thanksgiving Week Collection was for clothing, shoes and bar soap. This was the first of a long series of Thanksgiving Clothing Drives which continued throughout the Albers episcopate. Rev. William J. Flanagan, pastor of the Cathedral, chaired most of these drives. Rev.

Earl V. Sheridan, head of Catholic Social Services, coordinated the settlement of displaced persons in the Diocese.

With the December 1950 outbreak of the Korean War, portions of the annual Lenten appeal were sent to Asia. In 1950 the appeal was renamed the Bishop's Fund for the Victims of War. By 1956 the appeal was known as the Bishop's Relief Fund.

Third War Loan

A combination of patriotism and financial acumen was behind the War Bond Drive which the Diocese sponsored in 1943. As in the previous World War, Catholic participation in bond drives was stressed as their patriotic duty. Since anti-Catholic sentiment labeled Catholics as subjects of a foreign power (the Pope), Catholic pastors stressed the need to support the nation. It was necessary to demonstrate that there was no conflict between being a Catholic and being an American. With the 1943 drive, support for the country and the Church were combined. This was the first drive addressing a broad spectrum of needs. The first diocesan appeal three years

before had been focused on raising funds for the bishop's residence. The slogan of the new drive was "A Bond From Every Family". Parish organizations as well as each school classroom were encouraged to purchase a war bond which would be redeemed by the Diocese at its maturity for "the needs of religion." These needs were specified as the following: adequate diocesan offices; the care of orphans; and the education of poor boys to the priesthood.

St. Vincent Home

When the war bond drive was held, the building of an orphanage was a prominent goal. The diocesan consulters advised Bishop Albers to use a fourth of the war bonds for the purpose of building an orphanage. They also recommended a special assessment of 10% of the previous year's ordinary income of the parishes in 1945 to supplement the building fund. The next step in making the orphanage a reality was the five

Bishop Albers with four residents of St. Vincent Home.

deanery meetings held in April and May, 1950. At the meetings the need for the orphanage and the building plans were explained to the priests. The 1950 Diocesan Development Fund (D.D.F.) drive raised nearly half a million dollars and the 1951 D.D.F. collected another $120,000. All contributors were invited to the cornerstone laying of the new home on July 22, 1951. The 1952 D.D.F. collection was also specified for St. Vincent Home.

Diocesan Development Fund

The organization of the D.D.F. (as noted above) was closely intertwined with the founding of a Catholic orphanage in Lansing. From 1950 to 1952 the fund was used solely for St. Vincent Home. In 1953 the following goals were listed for the campaign: the needs of mission churches; work among the Spanish Speaking; and development of diocesan offices. Wage earners were asked to give $5 or more according to their income. The establishment of the Student Center at Michigan Agricultural College (M.A.C.) became a major goal in 1954. Bishop Albers celebrated the twenty-fifth anniversary of his consecration as a bishop in 1954. He informed the priests that any monetary donations he received could be given to the Student Center at M.A.C. Msgr. Herman P. Fedewa was appointed first general chairman for the D.D.F. in 1956. He remained chair throughout the Albers years. This was also the first year parish lay chairmen were chosen. The lay chair was to divide the parish into districts for fundraising solicitation. Each solicitor was not to have more than ten households upon which to call. The Bishop attended dinner meetings in each deanery at which the pastors and lay chairmen were present. Each wage earner was asked to give one day's wage or a minimum of ten dollars. Larger donations could be paid as a pledge over a period of six months. Individual parishes were not assigned goals but the diocesan goal was $300,000. Special issues of the *Catholic Weekly* were prepared and distributed free of charge to help parishes understand the work

of the D.D.F. Bishop Albers was pleased to announce in August that the campaign had met its goal.

The designated projects for 1957 included the Mexican (also commonly called the Spanish Speaking) Apostolate, the student centers in East Lansing and Kalamazoo, education of the thirty-four seminarians and St. Vincent Home. A pulpit exchange was arranged for pastors to preach in neighboring parishes on the D.D.F. The John McCarthy Associates were the consultants behind the 1957 drive. The designated needs for the 1961 campaign were the Spanish Speaking Apostolate, education of seminarians, St. Vincent Home, the new Catholic Charities office in Kalamazoo and the acquisition of new parish sites. The funding for the 1963 drive went to St. Vincent Home, the Mexican Apostolate, seminarian education, the retreat house in DeWitt, regional high schools and the C.C.D. program.

Rural Concerns

In 1945 the Sisters of St. Joseph in Kalamazoo hosted the national meeting of the Catholic Rural Life Conference. Bishop Albers invited the faithful from rural areas of the Diocese to take part in the two day conference. Members of 4H clubs were especially encouraged to attend. When the national conference was held in Saginaw in 1952, participants from farm areas of the Diocese were again encouraged to participate. Regional meetings of the conference were held in October 1957 in Westphalia for the eastern part of the Diocese and in Sturgis for the western portion of the Diocese. The theme of the conference was "Christian Solutions for Farm and County Problems." Among the topics addressed were: migrant agricultural labor, religious instruction for farm and county youth, vocations to the sisterhood from small communities and vocational guidance for rural youths.

Provincial Activities

Two institutions with long term effects in Michigan had their beginnings in 1948. Boysville near Clinton was opened in September for high school boys who were troubled. The project was sponsored by the five dioceses in the Province of Detroit in collaboration with the Knights of Columbus. Priests were notified that applications would be cleared through Rev. Earl V. Sheridan of Catholic Charities in Flint. The following month the cornerstone of St. John Provincial Seminary in Plymouth was laid. When the seminary opened in the fall of 1949 seminarians from the Lansing diocese were a part of the original student body.

Holy Year 1950

The twenty-fifth Holy Year in the history of the Church was inaugurated on Christmas Eve 1949 when His Holiness Pius XII opened the Holy Door of St. Peter Basilica in Rome. The Holy Year was rung in across the Diocese of Lansing when parishes rang bells after the noon Angelus on Saturday, December 24. Many parishes also celebrated the special Midnight Mass on New Years Eve. This privilege was also allowed on New Years Eve 1950. During the year a diocesan pilgrimage was organized to visit Rome. On Christmas Day 1950, Pope Pius XII announced that he was extending the Holy Year to the universal church for the year 1951. The conditions for gaining the Jubilee Plenary Indulgence for a total remission of the temporal punishment due to sin were mailed to the parishes in January 1951.

The Newman Club at Michigan State College sponsored a Holy Year pilgrimage to Rome in 1950. Newman chaplain, Rev. Jerome V. MacEachin, stands just to the right of the Holy Father, Pius XII.

The most important event of the 1950 Jubilee Year occurred on the vigil of All Saints Day when His Holiness, exercising his infallibility, defined the Dogma of the Assumption of the Blessed Virgin Mary into Heaven. An Assumption Triduum was held in the Diocese on October 29-31. Bishop Albers was in Rome for the historic occasion.

Marian Celebrations

Pope Pius XII called for a Marian Year in 1954 to commemorate the centenary of the definition of the Dogma of the Immaculate Conception. The feast of the Annunciation, March 25th, was observed as the Priests Marian Day throughout the world. Each deanery held an outdoor liturgy to observe the Marian Year. "Madonna Week" was celebrated from May 1 to May 7, Mother's Day. At the close of the Novena each parish was consecrated to the Immaculate Heart of Mary. The Marian Year ended on December 8th and the parishes were encouraged to conclude the year with a novena in honor of the Immaculate Conception. The following year the first observance of the new Feast of the Queenship of Mary was inaugurated in the Diocese with an outdoor liturgy at Memorial (Sexton) Stadium in Lansing on May 31st at 7:30 P.M.

Vocations Office

In order to foster more vocations to the diocesan priesthood as well as to provide a more thorough method of examining the applicants, a director of vocations was appointed. Rev. William G. Hankerd received the assignment late in 1957. A system was put in place whereby all the applicants to the seminary were visited by Fr. Hankerd in their homes. Applications were to be made in January or February each year. The visitations occurred in March and April. No boys with scores less than 110 in standard IQ tests were to be accepted. Due to the shortage of seminary space, new students were only accepted for ninth grade or first year college. During the Hankerd years (1957-1966), it was customary for diocesan priests to give vocation talks in parish schools in nearby parishes. These talks were usually given in November. Representatives of religious communities gave talks in March.

Council of Catholic Women

Early in his episcopate, Bishop Albers put his stamp of approval on the Holy Name Society and St. Vincent De Paul Society for men. No organizations for women received such diocesan-wide approval until 1952. In 1940 Bishop Albers promoted the League of Catholic Women but only in the Flint deanery. The organization meeting of the Council of Catholic Women was held on May 26, 1952 at St. Mary Cathedral. Mrs. Agnes Fedewa of

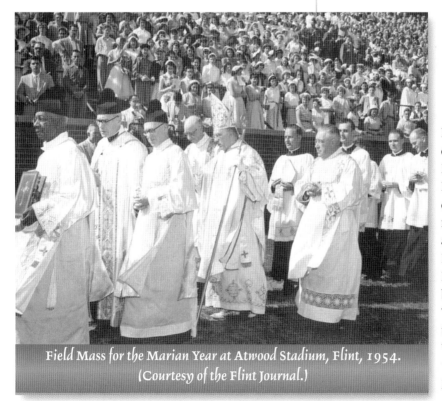
Field Mass for the Marian Year at Atwood Stadium, Flint, 1954. (Courtesy of the Flint Journal.)

St. Casimir Parish in Lansing was appointed by Bishop Albers as the first diocesan president for a term of one year. The first diocesan meeting had been preceded by the first deanery meetings at which officers were elected.

Bishop Albers is pictured with some 1960 Council of Catholic Women officers (left to right) Thelma Rann from St. Mary, Morrice; Marguerite Huhn from St. Michael, Grand Ledge; Joan Klotz from St. Thomas Aquinas, East Lansing; and Eugenia Hurlbert from St. Mary, Kalamazoo.

Catholic Weekly

Early in 1954 the priests were asked if it would be worthwhile to publish a Lansing edition of the *Catholic Weekly* which had been published in the Saginaw Diocese for over a decade. The weekly would focus on the life of the Diocese. Their response was enthusiastic and plans were made to print about 15,000 copies for distribution to parishes. Bishop Albers met with Fr. Neil O'Connor of the Saginaw edition of the *Catholic Weekly* to discuss details. In his April 13, 1954, letter to the clergy, Bishop Albers described his hope for the paper "to be a means of uniting the people, of intensifying their faith, and of

Rev. Neil O'Connor and Bishop Albers with the inaugural issue of The Catholic Weekly

helping in the work of spreading the gospel." In July it was announced that Mrs. Rosemary Howley of Lansing had been hired by Fr. O'Connor as his news representative. All information to be printed in the Lansing edition was to be sent to her. The first edition of the paper came out on Sunday, August 1, 1954. Among the weekly features Bishop Albers felt should be highlighted when presenting the new paper to the faithful were "Catholic News of the Week in Review" and the "Question Box." A bright young priest of the Saginaw diocese, Rev. Kenneth J. Povish, took over writing the "Question Box" column in 1954.

DeWitt Retreat House

Aerial view of the retreat house property

A local Catholic paper was one of Bishop Albers' dreams realized. The following year another hope was realized. The Hungarian Franciscans laid the cornerstone for their retreat house known as Portiuncula in the Pines on June 26, 1955. The retreat house was located on a farm they purchased on the edge of the village of DeWitt. Bishop Albers, desiring to create broad interest in the lay retreat movement, asked priests to attend the cornerstone laying ceremony with two to four parishioners who would be potential parish leaders in the movement. Bishop Albers stressed the extraordinary amount of good the retreat movement achieved in bringing men and women closer to God. The retreat house was dedicated on October 9th.

Third Orders

The first Secular Franciscan Fraternity for the Lansing Diocese is thought to be the chapter founded at Holy Cross Parish in Lansing in 1927. Conventual Franciscans had founded the parish in 1924 and laid the foundation for a "third order Franciscan" fraternity as it was then known. The Fraternity moved to St. Mary Cathedral Parish in the 1930's and reached a membership of about 100 before returning to its roots at Holy Cross. In 1955, the St. Basil Fraternity in South Haven organized and was canonically established in 1958. It was the influence of the Hungarian Franciscans that led to the formation of fraternities of Secular Franciscans in the Flint and Lansing deaneries. The Hungarian Franciscans staffed St. Joseph Parish in Flint and in January 1956 the St. Joseph Fraternity began to meet. This group was canonically established in 1959. The Portiuncula in the Pines Retreat House in DeWitt was then within St. Thérèse, Lansing, parish boundaries. On September 23, 1962, twenty-one St. Thérèse parishioners were invested in the Third Order of St. Francis Secular. With the profession of twenty of these individuals the following year, the Our Lady of the Angels Fraternity was formally established. In 1964, the North American Federation of the Third Order of St. Francis established the Thomas E. Murray Training Center for Tertiaries at a property on Lake Noah near Three Rivers. The following year the center was moved to a larger facility near Mansfield, Ohio. A Franciscan fraternity has also been established in Jackson.

The Adrian Dominican Sisters were the motivation behind the formation of Third Order of St. Dominic groups at St. Paul Parish in Owosso and St. Thomas Aquinas Parish in East Lansing. In both of these parishes Adrian Dominican Sisters staffed the schools. The St. Paul Chapter was organized in January 1950 with six members and grew to nearly fifty members. The St. Thomas Aquinas Chapter was organized about the same time and both chapters continued until the late 1960's.

Spanish Speaking Apostolate

Member of the Spanish Speaking Apostolate plan their annual "Holiday in Mexico" held in November 1959; standing: David Pizana, Erasmo Hernandez, Reynuldo Trevino, and Benito Zamora; seated: Margaret Orvis, Dolores Delgado, Rev. William McKeon, Ruben Alfaro, and Julia Gonzales

In March 1949, a survey was sent to pastors from the bishop's office asking for statistical information on migrant workers. A question about how many priests would be able to hear confessions in Spanish was included on the form. Suggestions for how to care for the spiritual needs of migrants were also requested. Three years later Bishop Albers wrote to the clergy again requesting statistical information on the number of Spanish-speaking persons who were permanent residents or migrant workers. He indicated that three or four clusters of Spanish speakers had been identified in the larger cities of the Diocese. Each of these groups had between 200 to 400 souls. In 1957 Our Lady of Guadalupe, Flint, and Cristo Rey, Lansing, were established for the Spanish-speaking. Lansing activities for the Spanish-speaking were featured at the eleventh conference of the National Council for the Spanish Speaking held in May 1962 in Milwaukee, Wisconsin. Rev. William J. McKeon, the first Lansing diocesan priest assigned to the Spanish Speaking Apostolate, was the national council president at the time. Priests, seminarians, religious and laity all participated in the diocesan migrant program. Fiestas like the one held August 16, 1964, at Keeler were extremely popular. Nearly a thousand people participated in the field Mass at which fourteen children made their First Holy Communion. The front porch of a home served as a canopy for the altar upon which Rev. Gilbert O. Rahrig offered the Mass. Religious instruction, confessions, music and a meal rounded out the festivities.

Migrant workers 1966.

Liturgical Changes

There is a misconception that liturgical changes all followed the Second Vatican Council. This is far from the truth. The Sacraments and the celebration of Holy Week all underwent changes in the decades preceding the Council. On June 29, 1941, the Sacred Congregation of the Sacraments in Rome issued an instruction about the preliminary

investigation of all parties entering marriage. The Marriage "A" form (M-A) and the Marriage "B" form (M-B) came into existence and their use was required for all marriages beginning July 1, 1942. Changes in the Sacrament of Confirmation occurred in 1947 when pastors were given the authority to administer the sacrament to those in their parishes who were in danger of death.

The changes in the Holy Week liturgies began in 1951. This was the first year that the Easter Vigil could be celebrated in the evening. The Mass proper could not begin until midnight but the preliminary service was recommended to start at 11:00 P.M. The following year permission to use the experimental rite was renewed for three years. In November 1955 a new order of service for Holy Week was mandated for every parish to take effect the following year. The clergy were advised of this in mid-February. A week later a ten-page outline was sent to them. In February 1957 the new order of service was modified again, resulting in basically the same order as we have today. Clergy conferences were soon held to explain the changes.

The Sacred Congregation of Rites issued an Instruction concerning the Sacred Liturgy in September, 1958. The following year three changes were implemented. The active participation of the faithful in the Eucharist was the motivation for the changes. First, the practice of praying the Rosary during Mass was officially discouraged. Second, commentators were introduced to lead the congregation in the Latin responses to be said with the priest. Third, the faithful were to recite the *Sed Libera nos a Malo* (Deliver us from evil) at the end of the Lord's Prayer, making the sentiments of the whole prayer their own. An eight week series of instructions during the homily at Mass began on October 18, 1959. Articles in the *Catholic Weekly* paralleled the Sunday sermon topics. By the end of the eight weeks the congregation had been introduced to reciting together the parts of the Mass which were generally sung by the choir at High Mass; i.e., Kyrie, Gloria, Credo Sanctus, Benedictus and Agnus Dei. More new liturgical rulings were received on December 3, 1960.

Ecumenical Council

On the feast of the Conversion of St. Paul in January 1959, Pope John XXIII announced the coming Ecumenical Council. A council had not occurred for nearly ninety years. Prayers invoking the guidance of the Holy Spirit were offered for years before the initial session was opened on October 11, 1962. Four Lansing bishops were present that day. Bishop Albers was accompanied by his auxiliary bishop, M. Joseph Green, who had been consecrated two months prior. Bishop Albers' successor, Alexander M. Zaleski, was in attendance as an auxiliary bishop of Detroit. The Fourth Bishop of Lansing, Carl F. Mengeling, was present as well. He was a student priest in Rome and acted as a page during the council sessions.

The first document to be issued by the Second Vatican Council was the *Constitution on the Sacred Liturgy*. The constitution, entitled *Sacrosanctum concilium*, was promulgated just days before the second session of the Council concluded on December 8, 1963. When the bishops returned home the implementation of the changes began. In January 1964, eight priests were assigned to form the Diocesan Liturgical Commission. Officers of the new commission were chairman, Rev. Paul V. Donovan, and secretary, Rev. William J. Fitzgerald. Five lengthy communiqués from this commission during the year and the priests' liturgy day in November helped the clergy and faithful understand and embrace the changes.

Cursillo Movement

The Cursillo de Cristiandad (a Short Course in Christian Living) Movement came to Michigan in August 1961. Holy Cross Parish in Lansing hosted the first Spanish-speaking Cursillo in the state from August 10th through 13th. Thirty-eight men attended. Rev. Donald McDonnell of San Jose, California, had worked among the Spanish-speaking migrant workers in the Diocese that summer. While at the home of Mrs. Joan Klotz, the Spanish-speaking chair of the Diocesan Council of Catholic Women, Fr. McDonnell first proposed that a Spanish-speaking Cursillo be held in Lansing. Two weeks after receiving Bishop Albers' blessing on the proposal, the Cursillo was conducted by a team from Lorraine, Ohio. (The first English Cursillo in Michigan was held in St. Joseph Parish in Saginaw in 1962.)

Women's Cursillo at Cristo Rey Church, c. 1963

The Ohio team was headed by Rev. Antonio Hernandez. He also directed the second Cursillo held in the Diocese in November at Cristo Rey Church in Lansing. When the third diocesan Cursillo was held in March 1962, the assistant pastor of St. Mary, Jackson, Rev. Kenneth L. Faiver, served as the spiritual director. He was assisted by Rev. Richard A. Simons of Our Lady of Guadalupe in Flint. Bishop Albers' support of the movement was evidenced by his attendance at the closing of the March Cursillo. Cristo Rey became the headquarters of the Cursillo movement with Fr. Faiver's enthusiastic support after he became pastor there in June 1962.

Nearly 1,000 delegates attended the sixth National Cursillo Movement in America convention at Michigan State University in August 1964. The general chairmen were Chief Justice Thomas M. Kavanagh of the Michigan Supreme Court and State Senator John P. Smeekens, President Pro Tem of the Michigan Senate. The men represented different political parties but both had been active as rectors of Cursillos in the Diocese. Mrs. Joan M. Klotz of St. Thomas Aquinas Parish in East Lansing served as executive secretary for the meeting. The delegates passed a resolution requesting an episcopal moderator. Auxiliary Bishop Green promised to present the request at the national bishops' meeting. He was later appointed the national episcopal moderator.

Training Lay Teachers of Religion

A new era in religious education began in the fall of 1961 when training schools for lay men and women were established in each deanery. The number of Catholic children in public schools was estimated at 21,453, while the number in Catholic schools was thought to be 33,756. Official C.C.D. textbooks were chosen beginning in the fall of 1961. The Sadlier Company series "On Our Way" was mandated for the religious education of elementary school children. The designated high school texts were published by the Chicago C.C.D. office.

Diocese of Lansing
Confraternity of Christian Doctrine
School of Religion

REPORT CARD

Name ....
Parish ....
Teacher ....
Grade .... Year 19...... to 19......

RECORD OF PROGRESS

	I	II	III	IV	Av.
Knowledge of Religion					
Cooperation Makes effort to improve					
Does Required Home Assignments					
Attendance — Classes held					
Classes attended					

PROGRESS CODE

VG — Very Good   F — Fair
G — Good   U — Unsatisfactory

CCD School of Religion report card

The following year Fr. Majchrowski was succeeded by Rev. John M. Grathwohl as diocesan director of C.C.D. The first diocesan training course for teachers was concluded in May 1963. Close to 500 adults were awarded certificates as confraternity teachers. In the fall of 1963, a second two-year training course was initiated at centers across the Diocese. For those who had already completed the basic C.C.D. training course, a curriculum of intermediate and later advanced courses was prepared in the fields of scripture, liturgy, Church history and moral theology. A special methods class for teaching religion to the mentally retarded was offered in Jackson by Rev. Raymond Ellis of Detroit. In the fall of 1964, two Sisters of St. Joseph from Nazareth, Michigan, began working at the newly opened C.C.D. office in Lansing. Sisters Angela LaBranche and Thomas Marie Carley were to assist in the development of parish programs and to be a part of the faculty for the teacher training programs.

Diocesan Milestones-1962

The twenty-fifth anniversary of the Diocese was held on May 22, 1962. Bishop Albers was the celebrant of the Pontifical High Mass and

Archbishop Dearden and Bishop Albers at the Silver Jubilee of the Diocese

Archbishop John Dearden of Detroit preached the sermon. All the servers were priests of the Diocese. Representatives from every parish were issued tickets to the liturgy. In July, it was announced that the first auxiliary bishop of Lansing had been appointed. Former bishop's secretary and vice-chancellor, Michael Joseph Green was elevated to the episcopate on August 28th. The consecration was broadcast live on Channel Six in Lansing. Bishop Green served the Diocese until his appointment as Bishop of Reno, Nevada, on March 10, 1967.

Michigan Catholic Conference

The bishops of Michigan founded the Michigan Catholic Conference (M.C.C.) in 1963 to serve as the lobbying and services branch of the Church in Michigan. Among the first ways the M.C.C. impacted the Diocese was its opening of a job training center for the economically disadvantaged in the former Cathedral Grade School and the issuance of the non-discrimination contract clause for church employees, both in 1964.

Parish High Schools Begin To Consolidate

The transition from parish high schools to regional high schools began during the latter part of Rev. Francis T. Martin's term as superintendent of schools. Regional high schools began in Lansing in the fall of 1963 when Msgr. John Gabriels and Msgr. John O'Rafferty High Schools opened. Msgr. Gabriels High School replaced Resurrection High School and was built for the parishes on the east side of Lansing. Msgr. O'Rafferty High School replaced St. Mary Cathedral High School and was built for parishes on the west side of Lansing. The following year Msgr. John Hackett and Msgr. Francis O'Brien High Schools opened in Kalamazoo. The former St. Augustine Parish High School closed and the two regional

schools replaced it. The newly built Msgr. Hackett High School was for boys and the former St. Augustine site became Msgr. O'Brien High School which was for girls.

The Health of Bishop Albers

The experiences of being gassed in World War I and almost dying of smoke inhalation in 1938 contributed adversely to the Bishop's health. Other ailments arose over time and he was often hospitalized with pneumonia and bronchitis. St. Lawrence Hospital even had a bishop's suite for his care. During the years of 1948, 1949 and 1957 he had lengthy stays in the hospital. The duties of the growing diocese were taking their toll on his physical condition. The twenty-fifth anniversary of the Diocese was his last moment of glory. The appointment of Fr. Joseph Green as his auxiliary bishop later that year was an indication of the bishop's need for assistance. The Bishop attended the first two sessions of the Ecumenical Council but not the third. He requested a co-adjutor bishop in 1964. Bishop Zaleski was appointed in October, 1964. Bishop Albers' health steadily declined and he entered eternal life December 1, 1965. He was buried in St. Joseph Cemetery in Lansing, a cemetery he had founded.

Faith Conquers the World

When Bishop Albers became bishop of Lansing in 1937, he chose as his motto a paraphrase of a passage of scripture from the First Letter of John, Chapter 5 verse 4, *Fides vincet mundum*, "Faith Conquers the World." "Faith" represented life with God and the "world" represented secularization and life apart from God. Repeatedly throughout his episcopate his articulated motivation for his decisions was to increase the faith of the laity and the clergy. He instituted diocesan retreats for priests and invited the Franciscans to build a retreat house for the laity. He worked to institute the Confraternity of Christian Doctrine program in every parish so that the faith might be passed on to public school children, and to increase the discussion clubs in which adults participated. He promoted organizations for the laity, like the Council of Catholic Women, League of Catholic Women, St. Vincent de Paul Society and the Holy Name Society, all of which would nurture faith. He promoted lay renewal movements like the Catholic Action and Cursillo. His concern for the poor was evidenced in the establishment of Catholic Charities offices in Flint, Lansing and Kalamazoo. He truly tried to live the scripture "For whatever is begotten by God conquers the world. And the victory that conquers the world is our faith." (1 John 5:4) Faith conquering the world was his hope-filled vision.

Growth in the Albers Years

	1937	1964
Parishes	59	97
Missions	23	19
Elementary Schools	29	71
Pupils in Catholic Grade Schools	7,379	30,177
Public School Pupils in Religious Instruction	4,354	18,536
High Schools	18	20
Pupils in Catholic High Schools	2,236	6,987
Public School Pupils in Religious Instruction	1,510	8,658
Catholic Hospitals	6	6
Diocesan Priests	84	189
Religious Order Priests	17	33
Brothers	1 (1945)	28
Sisters	616 (1945)	797
Seminarians	30	152
Catholic Population	67,270	212,533
Baptisms	2,611	9,332
Converts	525	1,553
Marriages	1,045	2,074

The Most Rev. Joseph H. Albers, First Bishop of Lansing

Alexander Mieczyslaw Zaleski
S.S.L.

Born:	June 24, 1906, Laurel, New York
Parents:	Antoni Zaleski and the former Bronislaza Jarnulewicz
Ordained a Priest	The American College, Louvain, Belgium July 12, 1931
	By John Murray, Archbishop of St. Paul
Consecrated a Bishop	Cathedral of the Most Blessed Sacrament, Detroit, Michigan May 23, 1950
	Consecrator: Edward Cardinal Mooney, Archbishop of Detroit
	Co-Consecrators: Stephen S. Woznicki, Bishop Elect of Saginaw
	Allen J. Babcock, Auxiliary Bishop of Detroit
Motto:	*Manus tua ducet me* (Your Hand Shall Lead Me) Psalm 139:10

Bishop (Titular) of Lyrbe and Auxiliary of Detroit

March 28, 1950 – October 7, 1964

Apostolic Administrator of the Archdiocese of Detroit

October 25, 1958 - January 28-1959

Coadjutor Bishop and Apostolic Administrator of the Diocese of Lansing

December 15, 1964 – December 1, 1965

Bishop of Lansing	December 1, 1965 – May 16, 1975
Died:	May 16, 1975, Miami, Florida
Buried:	May 21, 1975, St. Joseph Cemetery, Lansing, Michigan

CHAPTER 3

"Your Hand Shall Lead Me"

1965-1975

New Bishop Installed

Although the announcement of the auxiliary bishop of Detroit, Alexander M. Zaleski, as the Co-adjutor Bishop and Apostolic Administrator at the Diocese of Lansing had been made public on October 14, 1964, the installation was delayed until the bishops of the state could return from the third session of the Second Vatican Council which concluded November 21st. Archbishop John Dearden of Detroit presented his trusted adviser to the priests and laity of the Diocese on December 15, 1964. An 11:00 A.M. Mass at the Cathedral was followed by a luncheon at the Civic Center. An informal reception followed the luncheon. Because of the limited number who could attend the installation ceremonies, a special reception for the laity to meet Bishop Zaleski was arranged two days later at Gabriels High School (presently Lansing Catholic Central) auditorium.

The New York native had come to Michigan to attend the Polish seminary at Orchard Lake. He remained in Michigan and was ordained for the Diocese of Detroit in 1931. When Bishop Zaleski was ordained as auxiliary bishop for the Detroit Archdiocese in 1950 he chose for his episcopal motto a line from Psalm 139:10 *"manus tua ducet me"* (Your Hand Shall Lead Me).

Diocesan Liturgical Commission

Implementation of the changes to the liturgy called for by the *Constitution on the Sacred Liturgy: Sacrosanctum Consilium*, had begun in the diocese with the creation of the Liturgical Commission in 1964. To keep the

Diocesan Liturgical Commission, January 1969

priests abreast of the changes, demonstrations of the Mass facing the people were held at three regional locations in February 1965. In May of that year the Liturgical Commission began sending all the priests a subscription to *Living Worship*, a monthly bulletin published by the National Liturgical Conference in Washington, D.C. In the cover letter sent with the May issue, Rev. Paul V. Donovan, the chair of the Liturgical Commission, explained that the purpose of the bulletin was to keep priests in touch with the best liturgical practice available. The Commission also sponsored a "Liturgy and Architecture" study day that architects within the diocese were invited to attend. Mr. Robert E. Rambusch, secretary of the National Liturgical Conference and a respected New York architect, gave the keynote address. Mr. Rambusch was later chosen by Bishop Zaleski to direct the renovation of St. Mary Cathedral. The other featured speaker was Rev. William J. Sherzer who chaired the Provincial and the Detroit Liturgical Commissions. In 1966 Bishop Zaleski continued to implement liturgical changes by granting permission for the reception of Holy Communion under both species on special occasions.

Rev. James S. Sullivan took charge of the Liturgical Commission in 1966 and it entered a period of intense activity. It was reorganized in November to include more laity. On May 1, 1967, the Commission began to publish commentaries on the readings and intercessions for weekday Mass. Fr. Sullivan had initially recruited the seminarians to write, edit and print the commentaries, but a staff person was soon hired to oversee editing and printing the commentaries. The Commission met monthly and initiated many projects. One of these was the "Survey of Liturgical Progress in the Diocese". The results were published in May 1968. The priests were asked how their parishioners reacted to the liturgical changes.

One hundred and nine priests reported the changes were enthusiastically received. Two priests felt there was negative response and twenty-eight priests felt the response was one of indifference. The commission tried to focus its efforts in accord with the survey results.

The weekday commentary service was so successful that a weekday homily service was published beginning in January 1969. The cost of an annual subscription to either service was $5.00. In January 1970 the Commission began to commercially publish both the commentary and homily services and sponsored the first diocesan study day for members of parish liturgical commissions. Bishop Zaleski gave the welcome and Rev. Gerald Broccolo, secretary of the Liturgical Commission of the Archdiocese of Chicago, gave the keynote "How to Live the Liturgy". Five workshops were offered: for lectors, readers and commentators; for musicians; for sacristans; on liturgical art; and for parish liturgies, including school and neighborhood. In February workshops were held for the priests to prepare them for the new liturgical rites that went into effect on Palm Sunday 1970. The highlights of the sessions held in East Lansing, Flint and Kalamazoo were the videos of Rev. Joseph Champlin, the executive director of the National Liturgical Commission, discussing the pending changes. Bishop Zaleski also requested that the workshops include a discussion from the pastoral viewpoint regarding the best age for First Confession and First Holy Communion. Out of this came the experimental practice of receiving First Holy Communion without first receiving the Sacrament of Penance.

By July 1970 the Liturgical Commission had a two page list of their publications. *Guidelines for Parish Liturgical Committees* and *Love Heals: A Spiritual Program for the Sick* had been published the previous month. A second edition of the fifty-four page *Sacristan's Manual* was published in order to include the changes effective at

Liturgical Commission Publications

the beginning of Holy Week in 1970. The annual subscription for commentaries or homilies for daily and Sunday Masses was $12.00.

During the first week of March 1971 workshops were held for clergy in Flint, Jackson, Lansing and Paw Paw to explain the changes for Holy Week, the sacrament of baptism and the new funeral rite, which took effect November 1st. The same issues were addressed for parish liturgical committee members later that month.

In December 1971 permission was granted within the province of Michigan to use an interim rite for the Sacrament of the Sick. The Liturgical Commission hosted seminars at St. Joseph Hospital in Flint and at St. John School in Jackson for priests, religious, doctors, nurses and others having responsibility for caring for the ill or aged. The seminars were held in February 1972. That same month *Dialogue: Liturgy Newsletter of the Diocese of Lansing* made its appearance. It continued throughout the Zaleski years.

The diocesan Liturgical Commission continued to meet and make proposals to Bishop Zaleski about a variety of issues, including the time of Saturday weddings. Fr. Sullivan, the head of the Liturgical Commission and now auxiliary bishop of the Diocese, took on more responsibility as the Bishop's health deteriorated. The workshops and the issues of the *Dialogue* kept everyone informed of the latest interim rites - their changes, ramifications and effective dates. The rites of Penance and Confirmation were in transition at the time of Bishop Zaleski's death in 1975.

Education Office

The Schools Office was dramatically transformed during the Zaleski years. Rev. William F. Meyers was the key figure in the transformation. Fr. Meyers had completed a

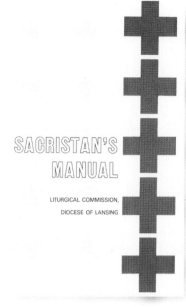

doctorate at Notre Dame in 1963. The title of his doctoral dissertation was *The Role of the Lay Teacher in Catholic Education.* Upon completion of his doctorate at Notre Dame, while administrator of St. Ann Parish in Cassopolis, Fr. Meyers was appointed a part time Assistant Superintendent of Schools. The following year Fr. Meyers was assigned to work full time in the Schools Office in Lansing. On May 20, 1965, Bishop Zaleski appointed Fr. Meyers as Superintendent of Schools and Mr. William Blackburn as Assistant Superintendent. Rev. Francis T. Martin (former superintendent) was appointed to the new diocesan school board. The ten member board (six lay men and women, one religious order priest, two diocesan priests and one religious sister) convened May 27th and elected Mr. Robert Mooney of St. Thérèse Parish in Lansing as president of the board. Fr. Martin was elected vice president and Fr. Meyers served as executive secretary.

Rev. William F. Meyers

When Fr. Meyers began his term as Superintendent, the *Catholic Weekly* reported 37,000 students in seventy parish elementary schools, sixteen parish and four regional Catholic high schools. In his six-year tenure as superintendent, the Catholic school system underwent drastic change. When he left there were nine high schools and fifty-nine elementary schools with a combined enrollment of some 26,000 students. In addition to the decrease in enrollment, the schools began to experience significant changes in personnel, from a predominance of women religious to primarily lay teachers. The salaries paid women religious were significantly less than the salaries required to employ lay teachers. Increased salaries necessitated increased tuition, which in turn contributed to a decrease in the numbers of parents who could afford the increased costs. There was also a shift in accountability. The schools were now required to follow diocesan policies set by the Diocesan Board of Education with the approval of the Bishop, instead of the guidelines and policies of the religious orders.

As a precondition to receiving state aid for auxiliary services, a system of accountable school boards was established. Although efforts at receiving parochi-aid failed, parish, regional and diocesan school boards emerged. In early September 1965, area boards of education were established 1) to coordinate local school procedures, 2) to provide further liaisons with local public school authorities, and 3) to implement diocesan policies. Bishop Zaleski presided at a meeting of all the newly appointed regional board members at Gabriels High School in Lansing. The establishment of parish school boards soon followed.

The scope of the education office broadened in May 1966 when new full time staff were added to the office. Rev. William J. Fitzgerald became director of the new department of Religious Education. For the first time, direction of religious instruction for parochial and public school children was united. Two laymen, Mr.

Rev. Matthew J. Fedewa presented a gift by David Neering

George Martin and Mr. James Rauner were added as full time staff under Fr. Fitzgerald. Rev. John M. Grathwohl, who had been director of the C.C.D. office, assumed the position of coordinator of religious programs for state institutions and summer bible schools. The two Sisters of St. Joseph who had assisted Fr. Grathwohl continued in their positions. Two other religious women joined the staff: Sr. Leslie Hartway, O.P., became director of curriculum services and Sr. Christine Davidson, S.S.J., became director of reading and language arts programs. Rev. Matthew J. Fedewa became director of spiritual activities for youth in the new Religious Education Department. Fr. Fedewa had developed the TEC (Teens Encounter Christ) program, which was a retreat movement for high school seniors. In his new position he was to direct TEC, days of recollection and organize apostolic activity in schools and high school C.C.D. programs.

Fr. Meyers' efforts expanded the mission of the Schools Office so that it became an Office of Education, caring for public and parochial school children as well as continuing education for adults.

The change at the diocesan level was clearly reflected at the parish level. The scope of the parish school boards, which had been limited to the parish schools, was now expanded to include parish religion education programs for public school children and adult education. The term "school board" was abandoned in favor of "parish education commission".

TEC

English language Cursillos began with great regularity in 1963. A number of men from St. Philip Parish in Battle Creek were enthusiastic about how the Cursillo movement had invigorated their faith. They wanted to share this experience with their sons and approached Rev. Matthew J. Fedewa, who was the assistant

Diocesan of Lansing Youth Apostolate T.E.C. Lodge # 81, May 1968

at St. Philip. These lay men worked with Fr. Fedewa to put on a program for senior class boys of St. Philip High School. The program was held at the Fatima Retreat House at Notre Dame, Indiana. In 1965, while attending summer school at Loyola University in Chicago, Fr. Fedewa revised the program developed for the Notre Dame retreat and named the new program Teens Encounter Christ (TEC). He tried to make the three day experience reflect the annual liturgical experience of Lent, Easter and Pentecost. The former nurses' dormitory at Leila Post Hospital in Battle Creek became available for use as a teen retreat center. It was christened the "TEC Lodge" and the first TEC retreat was offered there in October 1965. Each parish high school was asked to send two or three male seniors for the first TEC. They returned to their parishes excited about their faith. The other young assistants teaching in parish high schools across the diocese became involved in assembling teams to direct the weekend retreats. The Cursillo movement provided a large contingent of volunteers. The weekends alternated between retreats for boys and retreats for girls. News of this dynamic youth retreat reached Chicago through Fr. Fedewa when he returned to summer school there. Several priests and sisters from Chicago brought young people from their high schools. The TEC movement spread from Chicago and Cincinnati to the other dioceses in Illinois and Ohio. TEC eventually became a nation-wide program.

Diocesan Census

In an effort to determine the needs of the flock entrusted to his care, Bishop Zaleski appointed Rev. Francis J. Murray to spearhead a diocesan census in the spring of 1966. The Bishop recalled that a census conducted when he served in the Detroit archdiocese yielded helpful pastoral information. In each parish Fr. Murray set up the following census offices: priest moderator, chairman and secretary (other than the parish secretary). The chair would assist in the direction and selection of section leaders (one per every 400 households). In September, deanery meetings were held at St. Mary (Jackson), St. Augustine (Kalamazoo), St. Joseph (St. Joseph), St. Michael (Flint) and St. Mary Cathedral (Lansing). A census manual was distributed. It dealt with the aims of the census, its benefits, census boundaries, census committees and parish committee responsibilities. The issue of parish boundaries had to be addressed because the responsibility for visiting every house fell to the parish in which it was located.

During early October, training sessions were held for all section leaders and parish committees. Then the help of enumerators was enlisted. Census Sunday was held on October 23rd. In a letter read to the faithful the week before Census Sunday, Bishop Zaleski stressed the importance of acquiring general information about the religious practices of baptized Catholics. The form developed for the census is still used in many parishes today. Another survey questionnaire was left at every Catholic home to seek information on Catholic practices and on the opinions of the laity concerning issues related to the Church. The statistical information (except identity) from the census questionnaires was then keypunched onto IBM punch cards. A preliminary parish summary report was sent out in April 1967. The diocese-wide tabulation of the survey was distributed in December 1967. Among other results, the survey indicated that forty-nine percent of the people who responded had read some of the documents of Vatican Council II. Forty-one percent approved the abolishment of Friday abstinence while forty-five percent opposed it. The remaining fourteen percent had no opinion.

Ecumenical Commission

The *Decree on Ecumenism* of the Vatican Council II directed each diocese to form its own Ecumenical Commission. Early in 1966 the Auxiliary Bishop of the Diocese, M. Joseph Green was named chairman of the new commission. Diocesan Directives for Ecumenical Practice were soon issued. In May Clergy conferences were held in Lansing and Kalamazoo to set the directives in their theological context. The presenters at the conferences were Revs. Francis Zipple, James A. Murray and John Hardon, S.J. After Bishop Green's appointment to Reno in March 1967, Fr. Murray led the commission. In March 1968, the commission surveyed ecumenical practice across the diocese.

Renewal through Vatican II

It was not enough to implement the directives of the Council. Bishop Zaleski, a well trained theologian, wanted the faithful to understand the basis of renewal. The creation of the Office of Renewal through Vatican II was first announced in June 1966. Rev. William J. Rademacher took up his duties as director of the new office on July 1st. During September, three day training sessions were held at the TEC Lodge in Battle Creek and the Portiuncula in the Pines Retreat House in DeWitt. Priests, religious and laity all shared in these sessions. Teachers in the Catholic school systems were given the first opportunities to attend the training sessions.

A completely different approach was developed for use at the parish level. The first document to be studied was the *Dogmatic Constitution on the Church: Lumen Gentium.* Six laymen, one from each deanery, were chosen to serve on a diocesan executive board. The

Renewal through Vatican II Workshop # 1, September 1966

executive committee for implementation was later expanded to twenty-three members. Each pastor chose a lay chairperson for his parish. Pastors were given a sermon outline from which to preach about the Renewal through Vatican II program. All parish chairs attended an orientation meeting the third week of September and the parish group leaders received leadership training the last week of September. The executive board developed two formats: the adult education format (a lecture/seminar series) and the home discussion group format. The adult education component began with a thirty-minute lecture followed by a forty-five minute seminar. From each seminar, proposals for the practical implementation of the conciliar decree at the parish and diocesan level were developed. Discussion groups in homes followed the seminar portion of the adult education segment.

Parish assemblies were held during the second full week of December. Recommendations for renewal were gathered from those participating in the adult education and the home discussion groups. Deanery assembly delegates were elected at the parish assemblies. A synthesis of the parish suggestions was prepared in topical order and forwarded to the deanery chairperson. Bishop Zaleski attended the deanery assemblies held in late December 1966 and early 1967 at which he concelebrated (a very new practice) the Mass with twelve of the senior clergy of the deanery. The same process used in the parish setting was used at the deanery level. The synthesis of the deanery recommendations was then presented to Bishop Zaleski for his consideration.

A thirty minute program about the Renewal through Vatican II project was prepared and shown over three television stations across the diocese. WILX in Jackson, WKZO in Kalamazoo and WJRT in Flint all aired the program on January 8th as a public service. WJIM (Channel 6 in Lansing) was the only station approached that refused to use the program or arrange for free time.

The *Decree on the Ministry and Life of Priests*: *Presbyterorum Ordinis* was the Vatican II document studied by the clergy at study days arranged during Lent and Easter season 1967. Nearly 450 women religious attended a March meeting at which they studied the Vatican II *Decree on the Renewal of Religious Life: Perfectae Caritatis*. The initial suggestion of organizing a priests' senate and a sisters' senate arose at these meetings. The first publication of the Office of Renewal, *Renewal Through Vatican II Newsletter*, was issued on March 31, 1967. The headlines stated that Bishop Zaleski had appointed an *ad hoc* committee to study the possibility of developing parish pastoral councils in the diocese. The committee was chaired by Mr. Jerry Walke of Jackson and was composed of one religious sister, two laywomen, three laymen and six priests.

More television time was devoted to a second thirty-minute program featuring Bishop Zaleski entitled "Renewal: Here and Now", which was broadcast on Renewal Sunday, November 12, 1967. A second Flint television station and the Lansing station were added to the original list of stations broadcasting the program. The Diocesan Renewal Congress at the Lansing Civic Center on Sunday, February 18, 1968, was a tremendous success. An estimated 5,000 people attended. The Congress was held as the climax of the fall study

Renewal Congress at Lansing Civic Center, February 1968

program on the Vatican II *Decree on the Apostolate of the Laity: Apostolicam actuositatem*. The highlights of the Congress were made into a thirty-minute documentary entitled "Church Renewal Congress". It was shown on television stations in Flint, Jackson, Kalamazoo and Lansing on April 28th. At the Congress, Bishop Zaleski endorsed the formation of a parish pastoral council in each parish by June 1, 1968.

About 18,000 people had participated in the first two years of the renewal program. During the third year Bishop Zaleski encouraged participants to focus on the *Constitution on the Sacred Liturgy*. The Liturgical Commission and the Renewal Office made this a joint effort. The heart of the 1968-69 program was the "Liturgical Week" held in November. It was patterned after a parish mission and was conducted by a team of liturgy specialists. In the spring of 1969, Fr. Rademacher accepted the opportunity to pursue graduate studies and the Renewal Office closed.

Priest Resignations

In October and December 1966 the first priests of the diocese decided to resign from the active ministry in the wake of the changes of Vatican II. Many priests found it very difficult to contend with the conflicting visions and expectations of the priesthood which followed the Council. Some felt the changes did not go far enough; others felt the changes went too far. Each side claimed that their position was the original intent of Pope John XXIII. There was much unrest and talk of dissent, especially after Pope Paul VI's encyclical *Humanae Vitae*. Nearly thirty priests resigned during the Zaleski years. The most difficult year was in 1969 when six priests left. The resignation of five priests in 1972 made it the second highest number. Those closest to Bishop Zaleski knew what a heavy cross this was for him.

High School Consolidations

The closing of two parish parochial high schools in Lansing, St. Mary and Resurrection, resulted in the formation of two regional high schools, O'Rafferty and Gabriels. A much more difficult task was to close two or more parish high schools and create one regional school. Fr. Meyers spent much of his energy doing just that. The first city in the diocese where this occurred was Jackson. St. Mary and St. John High Schools were closed in the spring of 1968. That fall Lumen Christi High School opened. The next year St. John and St. Bernard Parish High Schools in Benton Harbor were combined forming Lake Michigan Catholic High School. In 1970 the two high schools (O'Rafferty and Gabriels) in Lansing were forced to combine for financial reasons. Lansing Catholic Central was opened at the Gabriels site. The Luke M. Powers Educational Center in Flint opened in the fall of 1970 after the closing of seven high schools: St. Agnes, Holy Redeemer, St. John Vianney, St. Mary, St. Matthew, and St. Michael all in Flint; and St. Mary in Mt. Morris.

Consultative Bodies

Most of the consultative bodies of the diocese began in the Zaleski years. A good number first appeared in the dynamic year of 1966.

A diocesan music commission was formed in May 1966. The commission consisted of Rev. Gerald Boyer, pastor at St. Agnes, Fowlerville, Brother Gregory Horning, O.F.M., music director at the Franciscan Retreat House in DeWitt and Mr. David Ferland, music director at St. Mary Cathedral in Lansing. Mr. Ferland chaired the commission, which was established to authorize use of suitable musical settings of the propers of the Mass for the vernacular liturgy and to correct any abuses. An eight-member board of consultants, all parish musicians, was appointed in the summer.

A four-member building commission was also created in May 1966 to review building plans for all proposed construction projects in the diocese. A construction contractor, Mr. Basil Kennedy of St. Joseph Parish in Howell, served on the building committee assisting Rev. Edward G. Donahoe of St. Luke Parish in Flint, Rev. William Koenigsknecht of St. Thérèse Parish in Lansing and Rev. Adolph W. Nadrach of St. Monica Parish in Kalamazoo.

As a result of the work of the Renewal Through Vatican II Office three new advisory bodies took shape. The Priests' Senate (now known as the Presbyteral Council) and the Sisters' Council were formed and the initial efforts for a diocesan pastoral council began. During Lent 1967 the priests studied the council document on priesthood, *Presbyterorum Ordinis*. In April the first balloting for election to the Priests' Senate took place and its organizational meeting convened on May 2nd. The first officers were Rev. John J. Shinners, president; Rev. John P. Foglio, vice-president; and Rev.

James A. Murray, secretary. From the beginning the Lansing Council has been affiliated with the National Federation of Priest Councils. In 1969 the priest personnel commission was established on the recommendation of the Senate. The personnel (or appointments) commission was well received by most of the priests.

The first Vicar for Religious, Rev. John M. Steffey, was appointed August 1, 1966. He met with a steering committee to organize a Sisters' Council in April 1968. The first meeting was held in June and in September Sister Adelma (Eileen) Fitzpatrick, I.H.M., was elected president. The Lansing Sisters' Council was affiliated with the Leadership Conference of Women Religious. During the 1970's it had its own newsletter, *Council Communique*. The council advised the bishop on issues relative to religious women until it disbanded in 1991.

First Priests' Senate, May 1967

Sisters' Council, February 1970

In December 1968 a twenty-two member steering committee was appointed by Bishop Zaleski to develop a diocesan pastoral council. The formation of the steering committee was a response to the recommendation made the previous February at the Diocesan Renewal Congress that a council be established. The first meeting was held in January at St. Mary Cathedral rectory. Mr. Louis A. Radelet of St. Thomas Aquinas in East Lansing was elected chair of the steering committee. The council lost one of its chief proponents when Fr. Rademacher left the Renewal Through Vatican II office for graduate studies in June 1969. When a number of other members resigned, a lack of common vision among the remaining members and the bishop's declining health led to the steering committee's demise.

The Michigan Catholic Conference instituted a program for lay employee retirement benefits in October 1966. The program for priest pensions was developed by the Priests' Senate in 1968 and approved by Bishop Zaleski to take effect on January 1, 1969. The first retirement board was composed of: an active priest, Rev. D. Philip Dupuis; a retired priest, Rev. Gerald A. Owens; the bishop's representative, Rev. James A. Murray; and a lay representative, Mr. Lawrence Van Zwoll. Twenty-four disabled and retired priests became immediate beneficiaries of the $325.00 a month pension.

The Diocesan Finance Committee held its first meeting in March 1969. The committee members were three priests, three laymen and three *ex officio*. Besides the chancellor and vice chancellor, the other *ex officio* member was Howard C. Walsh, the first diocesan business manager. Mr. Walsh commenced his duties as business manager on June 1, 1967, and introduced standard accounting procedures in the parishes.

Rev. Francis J. Murray

The Joseph H. Albers Trust Fund was established in March 1972 to assist young men in pursuit of a seminary education. A seven-member board of trustees consisting of three priests and four lay people was set up to supervise the investment of funds.

Catholic Charities

During the mid to late 1960's qualified lay directors replaced the priest directors at St. Vincent Home and the Catholic social service agencies in Flint, Kalamazoo and Lansing. In 1965 Rev. Francis J. Murray ended his service as regional director of the Kalamazoo office and became the diocesan director of Catholic Charities. This was the first time the diocesan directorship was separated from a regional office directorship. A fourth diocesan social agency was opened in Jackson in October 1966. Mr. Chris E. Johnstone was the first director. The new agency focused on family counseling and assistance for unmarried parents in Branch, Calhoun, Hillsdale and Jackson counties. The Diocesan Charities Office actively supported interfaith housing efforts in Kalamazoo and Jackson. In Lansing the Particular Council of the St. Vincent de Paul Society constructed a fifty-five-unit housing

Diocesan Finance Committee, 1974

project. In cooperation with the Michigan Catholic Conference the Charities staff worked at coordinating and developing a "Right to Life" effort that sought to oppose the liberalizing of Michigan's abortion laws. Fr. Murray left the Catholic Charities Office in 1973 and was succeeded by Rev. Richard J. Groshek who was active in the resettlement of Vietnamese refugees which came under the Charities umbrella in the early 1970's.

Vocation Developments

The Home Seminary Program was developed by Rev. James S. Sullivan as an initiative to foster vocations to the priesthood. The program was designed to encourage high school students to consider vocations to the priesthood and religious life. During its first year of operation, 1968-1969, there were eighty-five applicants. Some twenty-five priests of the diocese served as spiritual moderators for the members. A newsletter, *The Wayfarer*, was begun in December 1974

In September 1969 the Albers House of Studies for first and second year college men was opened with eighteen applicants under the direction of Rev. William J. Fitzgerald. The Albers House was located at the former convent of St. Joseph Parish in Kalamazoo. Coursework was taken at Nazareth College or Western Michigan University. The Albers House closed after the creation of the Diocese of Kalamazoo. Another seminary house opened later during the episcopate of Bishop Kenneth J. Povish. It was located on Oak Street in East Lansing. The program was similar to the one at Albers House with some modifications.

In 1969 an Admissions Committee was formed and was composed of six priests, one brother and six lay representatives. The role of the Admissions Committee was to interview seminary applicants. Each candidate was interviewed by three members of the committee, who in turn made a recommendation and presented their findings to the entire committee for a vote.

A Seminarian Burse Committee was formed of ten laymen and two priests. The objective was to invest funds already available and to develop a burse for the future education of seminarians. The Burse Committee was combined with the Albers Trust Fund when it was established in 1972.

Home Seminary Program retreat, St. Joseph Home, Jackson

and was mailed to all home seminarians. One or more college seminarians were employed full time each summer to promote the program by visiting home seminarians.

Permanent Diaconate

A program of preparation for the permanent diaconate was developed in the late 1960's. Three priests were appointed as directors of the program for the diocese. The directors were assisted by the Admissions Committee in interviewing applicants. By 1969 there were three men enrolled in the program. After the death of his wife Agnes, Robert Henry Boehmer entered the charter deacon training

Deacon Robert H. Boehmer ordained by Bishop Alexander M. Zaleski, May 1971

program at Orchard Lake. He was ordained the first permanent deacon in the diocese by Bishop Zaleski on May 25, 1971, at the Cathedral. He served at St. Michael Parish in Flint. When Deacon Boehmer died in 1974, he was reported to be the oldest permanent deacon in the world.

Catholic Pentecostal Movement

The origins of the Catholic Pentecostal (now Charismatic) movement can be traced to the fall of 1966 at Duquesne University in Pittsburgh. The experience of being baptized in the Holy Spirit was central to this movement and was shared at a series of meetings held at South Bend beginning in March 1967. Two

individuals, Ralph Martin and Stephen Clark, who were very active in the Cursillo Movement and served on the staff at St. John Student Parish in East Lansing, attended the South Bend meetings where they met James Cavnar and Jerry Rausch. The foursome intended to work together on the campus of Michigan State University. These four men and other individuals from local prayer groups across Michigan began holding a monthly day of renewal, first in Williamston in October 1967, then in Lansing. The expected positions at MSU

Bishop Sullivan with the February 1974 permanent diaconate ordination class and spouses.

fell through and the foursome went to work at St. Mary Student Chapel in Ann Arbor. In November they held the first prayer meetings in their apartments. By February 1968 the group had become so large that they began meeting at the Newman Center. The United States Bishops' Committee on Doctrine, which was chaired by Bishop Zaleski, issued a statement in November 1969 cautiously encouraging the movement. From 1969 to 1971 the prayer group was an organization within St. Mary Student Parish. In the summer of 1971 the foursome left work at the Student Parish to work full time with the growing charismatic community. The Thursday open prayer meetings were transferred to the St. Thomas the Apostle Parish Hall in Ann Arbor which could accommodate the nearly 500 participants.

Between September 1970 and September 1971 a "covenant" community began to take shape. The first public commitment to the community took place then and the community was divided into sub communities. Households were set up and eleven coordinators were put into place, including the four original founders. By September 1971 the community magazine, *New Covenant*, had a circulation of 4,500 in forty-five nations. Catechetical programs like the "Life in the Spirit" seminar and the "Foundation in Christian Living" course were developed for the membership. In the early 1970's households of men and women desiring "to live single for the Lord" began to develop.

East Lansing became another center of the charismatic movement. The "Work of Christ" community evolved from the Wednesday evening prayer meetings at MSU. This community was established in June 1974 with eighty-seven people making a covenant commitment with each other and the Lord to live fully for God. Both the Ann Arbor and East Lansing covenant communities remained ecumenical. Parish prayer groups were often developed and supported by individuals who had been in or associated with a covenant community.

State Referendums

In the fall of 1970 "parochi-aid" came to the forefront of the issues considered by the voters of Michigan when "Proposal C" (the proposed constitutional amendment to prohibit public aid to non-public schools and students) was placed on the ballot. Bishop Zaleski looked to the Council of Catholic Women, the Knights of Columbus and the parish priests to rally the faithful in opposition to the amendment. Unfortunately the initiative passed and the Catholic schools systems suffered as a result.

An issue on the 1972 fall ballot was "Proposal B", the proposed constitutional amendment to radically liberalize access to abortion in the state. Bishop Zaleski chaired the "Respect for Life" Committee for the Michigan Catholic Conference (M.C.C.) The committee worked closely with the M.C.C. acting executive director, Mr. Thomas M. Bergeson, in developing the "Love and Let Live" program which was presented across the state to deepen Catholic understanding of the dignity of each human life. Early polls showed that Proposal B would easily pass. Parish pro-life groups were in their infancy and were loosely connected through the Office of Social and Community Services, (a.k.a. Catholic Charities). The groups, along with the Council of Catholic Women, the Knights of Columbus and the parish priests, played a critical role in encouraging the faithful to vote "no" on this life issue. The issue was handily defeated in every county of the diocese expect Washtenaw. In Clinton and Shiawassee counties the "no" vote was over 70%. Even though Proposal B was defeated soundly at the state level in November, the United State Supreme Court issued its infamous *Roe vs. Wade* decision the following January, marking abortion legal in all states.

Diocesan Boundary Changes

Just as Catholics were adjusting to the changes of Vatican II, the Holy See decided to re-draw the boundaries of the dioceses in Michigan.

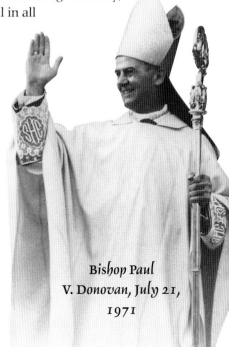

Bishop Paul V. Donovan, July 21, 1971

Pope Paul VI issued his apostolic letter *Qui Univerisae* on December 19, 1970. The letter, which was executed the following February, called for the creation of the Dioceses of Gaylord and Kalamazoo. The Diocese of Lansing lost seven counties (Berrien, Cass, St. Joseph, Branch, Van Buren, Kalamazoo and Calhoun) on its western side and gained two counties, (Washtenaw and Lenawee) on its eastern side. The fact that the Rev. Paul V. Donovan, a well-respected priest of the Diocese of Lansing, was chosen as the first Bishop of Kalamazoo made the transition easier for those involved in the western reorganization. Bishop Donovan was consecrated and installed as the first bishop at St. Augustine Cathedral in Kalamazoo on July 21, 1971, the day after Bishop Edmund C. Szoka was consecrated and installed at St. Mary Cathedral in Gaylord.

The incorporation of Washtenaw and Lenawee counties into the Diocese of Lansing was challenging. For some years people continued to write checks for the Diocesan Services Appeal to the "Archdiocese of Lansing", because they were accustomed to being part of the Archdiocese of Detroit.

The change in boundaries impacted many areas of diocesan life. The bucolic "Western Union" was gone and replaced by two more suburban counties that identified more closely with Detroit and Toledo than with Lansing. The academic profile of the diocese changed with the gain of the University of Michigan and Eastern Michigan University and the loss of Western Michigan University. Several other colleges were part of these changes as well. It was decided that the Lansing and Kalamazoo Council of Catholic Women would remain together for a period of time. Major outreach was needed to welcome those affiliates in Allegan, Barry, Lenawee and

Washtenaw counties. The Lenawee Council was not affiliated with the Lansing Council until 1974. In the area of Catholic Charities, the agency in Kalamazoo and St. Agnes Foundling Home were no longer a part of the Lansing diocese, while the diocese gained the agencies in Washtenaw and Lenawee counties. Boysville, outside of Clinton, was added under the umbrella of Catholic Charities. Two agencies dedicated to the Spanish Speaking Apostolate, the Community Action Center in Adrian and the Latin American Service Center in Blissfield, joined the migrant program already in place in the diocese. The only Catholic college (Nazareth) and religious Motherhouse in the old diocese (the Sisters of St. Joseph) became a part of the Diocese of Kalamazoo. The Dominican Sisters in Adrian and their college, Siena Heights, were welcomed into the new Diocese of Lansing.

Campus Ministers gather January 1975

Auxiliary Bishop

In late November 1971 Bishop Zaleski was hospitalized with an abdominal aneurysm. He was transferred to Henry Ford Hospital in Detroit for surgery. His strength and energy never returned and he requested an auxiliary bishop to assist him in leading the diocese. On

Bishops Donovan, Green and Zaleski with newly ordained auxiliary bishop James S. Sullivan September 21, 1972

Cardinal Dearden, was the principal celebrant and homilist at the funeral on May 21st, which was held two days before the twenty-fifth anniversary of Bishop Zaleski's episcopal ordination. Auxiliary Bishop Sullivan was appointed the Apostolic Administrator of the Diocese until the new bishop was named.

Your Hand Shall Lead Me

While Bishop Zaleski was earning his License in Sacred Scripture at the Biblicum in Rome, he grew to love the Psalms. It was very fitting that it was from the Psalms that he chose as his episcopal motto in 1950, from Psalm 139:10 *"manus tua ducet me"* which translates "your hand shall lead" or "guide me". Divine guidance was much needed by Bishop Zaleski. His episcopate spanned the problematic years following Vatican Council II. He had to contend with the conflicts arising from the expectations of some that more change was needed and the disappointment of others that too much change had occurred. The exodus of priests bore witness to the fact that the perceived expectations of the priesthood and the reality were in conflict. Bishop Zaleski's scholarly patience in facing these matters was a blessing for the Diocese of Lansing. During the turbulent decade 1965-1975 the whole diocese, under Bishop Zaleski's leadership, turned to the Psalms in hope and prayed that "Your hand shall lead us."

the Feast of St. Matthew, September 21, 1972, James S. Sullivan was consecrated as the second auxiliary bishop of Lansing. He had served Bishop Zaleski as secretary from 1966-1969 and as vice chancellor from 1968 until his elevation to the episcopate. Bishop Sullivan had been active in vocations work, developing the Home Seminary Program and serving as Vocations Director from 1969 to 1973. His work with the Liturgical Commission, which he chaired from 1966-1985, brought the diocese national recognition. Bishop Sullivan continued to serve the diocese until he was installed as Bishop of Fargo, North Dakota, in May 1985.

Bishop Zaleski's Final Illness

In February 1975 Bishop Zaleski suffered a stroke. He went to Florida to convalesce. While under doctor's care in Miami he was diagnosed with cancer. He died in Mercy Hospital in Miami on May 16, 1975. The Cathedral rectors, Revs. James A. Murray and Robert D. Lunsford, had gone to Florida to be with the Bishop and his family. They arranged to return to Lansing on the same airplane that carried the Bishop's body. The Metropolitan and close friend, John

The Most Rev. Alexander M. Zaleski, Second Bishop of Lansing

Kenneth Joseph Povish

Born:	April 19, 1924, Alpena, Michigan
Parents:	Joseph Povish and the former Elizabeth Yachaik
Ordained a Priest	St. Mary Cathedral, Saginaw, Michigan June 3, 1950
	By Stephen S. Woznicki, Bishop of Saginaw, Michigan
Consecrated a Bishop	Cathedral of the Immaculate Conception, Crookston, Minnesota September 29, 1970
	Consecrator: Archbishop Luigi Raimondi, Apostolic Delegate to the United States
	Co-Consecrators: Francis F. Reh, Bishop of Saginaw, Michigan
	James A. Hickey, Bishop of Cleveland, Ohio
Motto:	"To Accomplish His Work" John 4:34
Bishop of Crookston	July 28, 1970 - October 8, 1975
Bishop of Lansing	December 11, 1975 - November 7, 1995
Apostolic Administrator of the Diocese of Lansing	November 7, 1995 - January 24, 1996
Former Bishop of Lansing	November 7, 1995 - September 5, 2003
Died:	September 5, 2003, Lansing, Michigan
Buried:	September 11, 2003, St. Joseph Cemetery, Lansing, Michigan

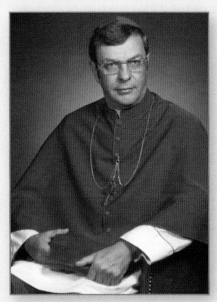

(Courtesy of Edwards Photographic Studio)

CHAPTER 4

"To Accomplish His Work"

1975–1995

Appointment to Lansing

On October 8, 1975, Pope Paul VI appointed Kenneth J. Povish (the fifth Bishop of Crookston, Minnesota) to fill the See of Lansing left vacant by the death of Bishop Alexander M. Zaleski. The appointment was made public on October 21st. In order to accommodate large numbers of the faithful, the installation of the new bishop was held in the Lansing Civic Center. A severe winter storm prevented many from being present. The Apostolic Delegate, Archbishop Jean Jadot, represented the pope at the installation. The Metropolitan, John Cardinal Dearden of Detroit, thirty-five bishops, one hundred and eighty priests and women religious from seventeen religious orders serving the

...to accomplish His work

The Bishop's Annual
DIOCESAN SERVICES APPEAL

Diocese joined the faithful in welcoming the new Bishop. When Bishop Povish was appointed Bishop of Crookston he chose as the motto of his episcopate a portion of John 4:34, "To Accomplish His Work". He retained this motto when he came to Lansing

Getting to Know Each Other

Two days later Bishop Povish ordained three transitional deacons at the Cathedral. The following week he met with the clergy of the Diocese at regional meetings held in Flint, Lansing and Saline. In January Bishop Povish's column, "Grace and Peace", made its first appearance in the *Catholic Weekly*. By reading this column many people of the Diocese became acquainted with their Bishop before he concluded his visitation of all the parishes. Trust and confidence in the new Bishop was demonstrated when the Diocesan Services Appeal achieved $700,000 in June 1976. This was the first time in four years that the DSA reached its goal.

Bishop Povish congratulates Monsignor MacEachin on the successful completion of the DSA campaign of 1976.

Catholic Women's Organizations

Every parish had a Rosary Altar Society or its equivalent. These groups were affiliated with the Council of Catholic Women. Bishop Povish's first appearance at a Council event was at the Lansing Region's annual Interfaith Day in February 1976. The following year at the national convention in San Antonio, Texas, Bishop Povish began his decade long service as National Episcopal Moderator of the Council of Catholic Women. The diocesan council presidents were very appreciative of his expertise and support. During Mrs. Frances Michalek's presidency, providing water tanks for Africa became a diocesan project. While Mrs. Michalek, from St. Mary, Morrice, was province director (1977-1979) the water tank project was encouraged at the regional and parish levels of the organization. The Diocese provided another province director to the state when Mrs. Jeanette Kirk from St. Mary, Manchester, served from 1991-1993. Bishop Povish had often expressed the desire to hold a provincial convention. In 1993 the Holiday Inn South in Lansing was the site of the first provincial convention. The keynote speaker was Susan Muto, Ph.D., who spoke on the "Power of Appreciation". Over 300 representatives from all seven Michigan dioceses declared the meeting a great success.

Two regions, Flint and Lansing, had other active Catholic women's groups in the Povish years. The Daughters of Isabella had very active chapters in Davison, Flint and Owosso. The Catholic Women's Club in Flint sought to promote the spiritual well being of its members and to serve as an auxiliary to the Franciscan Sisters of the Poor in their dedicated service to the less fortunate. In Lansing there was a Catholic Women's Club and a Catholic Business Women's Club. The special charitable focus of the Catholic Business Women's Club has been Catholic school libraries.

Marian Organizations

After the message of the Apparitions of Our Lady at Fatima in 1917 was approved by the Church, a world-wide organization was developed fostering devotion to Our Lady of Fatima. In the United States the World Apostolate of Fatima was commonly known as The Blue Army. Mrs. Edna Gilpin of Resurrection Parish in Lansing visited Fatima in 1958 and began a rosary prayer group when she returned. In 1975 two women, Karen LaFleche of St. Patrick Parish in Brighton and Martha Winslow of St. Mary Parish in Pinckney, arranged to have the National Pilgrim Virgin Statue brought to the diocese on tour. Bishop Sullivan, Apostolic Administrator of the Diocese, gave permission. A group coalesced to prepare for the arrival of the statue and to communicate with the national Blue Army headquarters in Washington, D.C. These events lead to the inaugural meeting of the Blue Army of the Diocese of Lansing at St. Agnes Parish in Fowlerville. The gathering occurred on September 8th, the Blessed Mother's birthday. Rev. E. Charles Jacobs, pastor of St. Agnes, recommended Rev. Andrew A. Czajkowski as spiritual director. This appointment was confirmed by Bishop Sullivan. Mr. John Walker of St. Gerard Parish in Lansing was elected the first president of the group after the constitution and by-laws were compiled by Mr. John DeRose. The group was chartered by the national office in 1976 and soon began sponsoring First Saturday vigil services across the Diocese and all night vigils to honor the feasts of the Sacred Heart of Jesus and the Immaculate Heart of Mary every year. Parish rosary prayer cells and the enthronement of the Sacred Heart in homes were actively encouraged. In the mid 1980's the group produced a series of programs for local cable public access television stations. Bishops Povish and Sullivan were frequent participants in the annual May and October Rosary Marches which were a means for spreading the message of Fatima across the Diocese. The Lansing chapter played an important role in the formation of the preamble of the national constitution in 1994.

The first meeting to organize the Marian Peace Center for greater Lansing was held at Thy Kingdom Come bookstore in Haslett. Mr. John W. Beutler chaired the gathering. The group was formally incorporated in December 1994 and Msgr. David M. Stotenbur served as the first spiritual director. The Center's apostolate is dedicated to focus individual lives on faith in God. They strive to accomplish this with the intercession of Our Lady Queen of Peace through conversion of hearts. The means used are: celebrating the sacraments, fasting, and prayer (especially eucharistic adoration and the rosary).

Office on Aging

Although the Office on Aging was opened in May 1973 by Bishop Zaleski, the most familiar programs that it sponsored were put in place during the Povish episcopate. J. Andre Tardif was the first director. He initiated regional councils on aging in Adrian, Ann Arbor, Flint, Lansing and Jackson. In September 1976 the first Senior Citizen Appreciation Week occurred. Bishops Povish, Green and Sullivan celebrated the Masses at six parishes representing the five regions and Shiawassee County. After Mass a meal was held and entertainment followed.

Mrs. Ellen McKay became coordinator of Aging Ministry on December 1, 1978. She continued the appreciation week and added an innovation. In 1981 prayer intention cards were introduced to the celebration. Seniors were asked to pray for specific intentions for the good of the Diocese. Mrs. McKay encouraged the founding of Councils on Aging in Livingston and Shiawassee counties and strengthened those already established. In response to a diocese-wide survey of the needs of senior parishioners the Senior Scripture Days were instituted in 1994. Sr. Donna Hart, I.H.M., was

the presenter on the theme "Scriptures: Promises Made, Promises Kept." Thirty-six people participated in the June session held at St. Francis Retreat Center in DeWitt. The program was repeated in August at Weber Center in Adrian.

Fortieth Anniversary of the Diocese

The fortieth anniversary celebration of the creation of the Diocese of Lansing occurred in May 1977. A statue of the Blessed Virgin Mary was carried in procession to the Cathedral. At the Cathedral Bishop Povish led the assembly in rededicating the Diocese to Our Blessed Mother. On the anniversary date the bishop announced the division of the Diocese into five regions; Adrian, Ann Arbor, Flint, Jackson and Lansing. This was done to facilitate overall pastoral planning.

Permanent Diaconate

Bishop Povish with the 1995 permanent diaconate class and their spouses.

Vatican Council II restored the permanent diaconate. In 1976 Rev. Douglas R. Osborn was assigned to the Cathedral and directed to lay the ground work for a permanent diaconate office. The permanent diaconate office began its training program in the Diocese with ten applicants in 1978. Deacon Samuel Bues and Mrs. Mary Tardif were other members of the diaconate office staff. During his episcopate Bishop Povish ordained sixty-seven men to the permanent diaconate in nine celebrations. In July 1986 Deacon Rogelio R. Alfaro of Cristo Rey parish in Lansing was elected to the board of the National Association of Hispanic Deacons. To honor the twenty-fifth anniversary of the restoration of the permanent diaconate, Bishop Povish presided at a diaconal convocation held at St. James Parish in Mason in June 1994.

Disabilities Office

Efforts were made in the 1960's to address the spiritual needs of those with physical and mental disabilities. In 1963 the Flint chapter of the International Catholic Deaf Association was

organized and in 1969 the Flint Area Chapter of Victorious Missionaries was established to advocate for and provide services to the mentally and physically handicapped. It was not until 1976 that Sr. Joan Feeney, O.P., was hired by the Diocese as the first full time consultant for special education for the disabled. The importance of this ministry was further recognized in September 1982 when the Office of Handicapper Ministry was established. Rev. George Kuryvial, O.M.I., who had already served as consultant for two years, was appointed the first director. Fr. Kuryvial initiated the *HELPS (Handicapper Educational Letter on Pastoral Services)* newsletter in January 1981. It continued to serve as a means of communication for over a decade. The office staff expanded in February 1984 when Sr. Marlene Taylor, A.D., began her work as the office outreach worker. After Richard G. Strife, Ph.D., assumed responsibility in 1987, the office took on a new name, Office of Ministry with Persons with Disabilities.

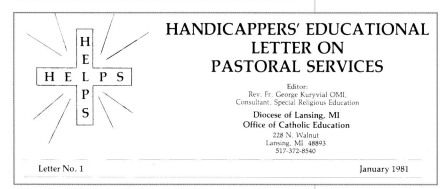

HANDICAPPERS' EDUCATIONAL LETTER ON PASTORAL SERVICES

Editor:
Rev. Fr. George Kuryvial OMI,
Consultant, Special Religious Education

Diocese of Lansing, MI
Office of Catholic Education
228 N. Walnut
Lansing, MI 48893
517-372-8540

Letter No. 1   January 1981

The Diocese of Lansing has a long tradition of ministry to the blind and deaf because the State School for the Blind was in Lansing and the State School for the Deaf was in Flint. In the early 1980's Catholic Inquiry for the Blind (an evangelical outreach to blind unchurched) was developed by a blind couple, Robert and Jennie Mahoney. Their efforts were soon incorporated under the Disabilities Office umbrella. In 1963 Rev. Earl W. Matte was appointed the first chaplain to the deaf community in Flint. Diocesan Services Appeal funds were set aside in 1981 to open a Catholic Deaf Office at St. Pius X in Flint. At that time Rev. Steven J. Raica was appointed director of the office. Annual retreats began the following year. In September 1983 Sr. Bernadette Mooney, O.P., was added to the staff as activity coordinator for programs which then existed in Flint, Jackson, Lansing and Ypsilanti. After Sr. Bernadette left the Diocese the care of the deaf community was assumed by the staff of the Disabilities Office.

Rev. George Kuryvial, O.M.I.,
and Louise Klein, special education teacher
at St. Mary, Westphalia

Regional Reconciliation Services

The present rite of penance became effective on the first Sunday of Lent in 1977. The following year during Lent an estimated 7,000 Catholics received absolution at regional penance services held at St. Mary Cathedral in Lansing, St. Francis of Assisi Parish in Ann Arbor, and at Luke M. Powers Educational Center in Flint. The theme was "Let's Prepare for Easter Together". On Palm Sunday in 1979, communal services were held in Lansing and Jackson. The services were extremely well received and brought many back to the practice of the faith. This third form of the rite of penance, commonly called general absolution, was a regular Advent and Lent experience until September 1988. At that time Bishop Povish banned the practice as a result of the decision reached at the summer meeting of the National Conference of Catholic Bishops.

![Bishop Povish preaches at reconciliation service at St. Mary Cathedral in April 1979.]

Bishop Povish preaches at reconciliation service at St. Mary Cathedral in April 1979.

Catholic Charities

One of the first areas that received Bishop Povish's attention after his arrival in Lansing was the reorganization of the Diocesan Office of Social and Community Service (a.k.a. Catholic Charities). A sixteen-member diocesan Christian Service Commission was announced as part of the reorganization which occurred in December 1976.

In April 1978 Bishop Povish endorsed the establishment of an eleven-member Justice and Peace Coalition. In response to the United States Bishops' pastoral letter, *The Challenge of Peace*, the Justice and Peace Office was opened on July 1, 1983. Mr. Myles McCabe served as the director for seven years. He instituted study sessions on the bishops' pastoral letters. Peace Sunday, the Sunday closest to the anniversary of the bombing of Hiroshima and Nagasaki, was a part of the diocesan life for over a decade. During Mrs. Christine Doby's tenure as director of the office a Justice Advocacy Network was established to ensure that the Catholic voice was heard in Peace and Justice issues at the state legislature.

The Bishop's Task Force on Alcoholism/ Chemical Dependency was organized in January 1981. The following November the first Alcoholism Awareness Week was observed in the Diocese. The task force goals of aware-

Chris Doby, Director of the Peace and Justice Office is flanked by diocesan secretary Arlene Woelfel and Director of Catechesis Peter Ries

ness, advocacy and evangelization were met by the annual awareness week, regional evenings of inquiry, retreats and workshops. Mary Morin in the Catholic Community Services (a.k.a. Catholic Charities) Office first served as coordinator for the Task Force.

In January 1985 Jeffrey Dongvillo joined Catholic Charities to head the Christian Service,

Parish Social Ministry and the Campaign for Human Development offices which were opened within the Charities department. The need for a full time position for Parish Social Ministry was quickly recognized and that position was created in the fall with Stephen Rall assuming the responsibilities. Four years later the Project Rachel Office was opened to assist women dealing with the trauma of an abortion.

County agencies experienced change in 1985. A new county-wide social service agency opened in February in Livingston County. The response was so great that within five months it was necessary to add another counselor to the staff. Later that year two independent agencies merged: Catholic Social Services of Lansing and St. Vincent Home. The new association provided a continuity of care for children unable to live with their family of

greater still. One of the Franciscan Sisters of the Poor, Sr. Claudia Burke, organized Catholic Outreach in January 1977 to provide emergency relief. In May 1981 the Catholic Committee of Concern (C.C.C.) was convened by Rev. James B. Bettendorf. With unemployment in the Flint area nearly 25% the C.C.C. announced in May 1982 that they would sponsor a soup kitchen. The North End Soup Kitchen opened All Hallow's Eve 1982 in Fr. Blasko Hall at the Sacred Heart Parish site. The need was so great that in 1987 a branch of Catholic Outreach opened in Davison and became known as Outreach East. In the late 1980's a temporary haven for battered women known as Shelter of Flint was opened under the auspices of Catholic Charities.

Charismatic Renewal

Sr. Claudia Burke, S.F.P., Founding Director of Catholic Outreach

Charismatic prayer groups gather at St. Mary Cathedral in November 1979.

origin through foster care, counseling, residential treatment and adoption services.

Meeting the needs of the poor has always been central to the Gospel message. In the Genesee region many programs had been provided by Catholic Charities, parish St. Vincent de Paul Societies and the Holy Angels Sandwich program operated by the Franciscan Sisters of the Poor. The need was

When Bishop Povish arrived in the Diocese he found two distinct expressions of the charismatic movement. There were covenant communities in Ann Arbor and Lansing and parish prayer groups. A third expression, the charismatic pastoral center, developed during his episcopate. Because of his broad experience, Bishop Povish served as chair of the National Bishops Conference Committee on the Charismatic Renewal.

The so-called Vatican of the Charismatic Renewal, located in Ann Arbor, was known as the "Word of God". The "Work of Christ" Community was based in Lansing. Both these covenant communities were ecumenical in nature. In 1976, concern for retaining a strong Catholic identity led the coordinators of the Ann Arbor group to open a dialogue with Bishop Povish about creating a Catholic Fellowship within the Word of God community. Rev. Robert D. Lunsford served as the bishop's liaison to the community. The dialogue resulted in a Catholic Fellowship being constituted into an association of the faithful in January 1979. On Pentecost Sunday 1981, the association received a new name, the "Christ the King Association". This group evolved into Christ the King Parish in Ann Arbor.

The second expression of the Charismatic Renewal was parish prayer groups. Their number merited Bishop Povish appointing Rev. David J. Hooper as liaison in July 1978. The following year a series of Pentecost charismatic Masses began in the Cathedral with Bishop Povish as celebrant. A fourteen-member Diocesan Service Committee for Charismatic Renewal was formed in the fall of 1980 to strengthen and develop parish prayer groups. In 1981 a diocesan charismatic newsletter entitled "Life in the Spirit" began. In the mid 1980's about thirty prayer groups were active in the Diocese. When the Diocese hosted the All Michigan Charismatic Conference in 1982, 1990 and 1991, Bishop Povish celebrated Mass for the participants.

A third expression of the Charismatic Renewal grew out of a parish prayer group and into a pastoral center within the Diocese. The Good Shepherd Montrose Charismatic Prayer group felt called to youth evangelization. Martha and Gordon Krupp spearheaded the first youth retreats at their home. The group separated from Good Shepherd Parish and became the Mt. Zion Prayer Community. The status of the community as a pastoral center was approved by Bishop Povish in 1988. The Youth to Youth Catholic Evangelization teams remain active and the Mt. Zion community has participated in several international outreaches including World Youth Day in Toronto.

Youth to Youth Catholic Evangelization 2001-2002

Vocations to Priesthood

Bishop Povish once wrote that the most important work he did as bishop of Lansing was ordaining priests. While Bishop of Lansing he ordained fifty-seven priests to serve the Diocese. In the year 1978, in five different celebrations, ten individuals were joined to the priesthood of Jesus Christ. That same year a vocations council was organized for the Diocese under the direction of Director of Seminarians, Rev. James R. Swiat. Its goal was to establish a vocations committee in every parish.

In the late summer of the following year the "Oak Street" residential facility in East Lansing opened. It served as a residence for young men contemplating priestly vocations while attending Lansing Community College and Michigan State University. Similar programs were established in Ann Arbor and Flint.

Bishop Povish with priests newly ordained June 12, 1993 and, at far right, Director of Seminarians, Rev. Mark Inglot

Education

Bishop Povish was an ardent supporter of Catholic education in all its forms – especially catechetical and formational programs for young people and adults. As bishop he regularly participated in the deliberations of the Diocesan Board of Education regarding the development of policies that would enhance those programs as well as provide professional development for the personnel engaged in those ministries.

Adequate financial resources were an ongoing concern to ensure the future of Catholic education. Bishop Povish encouraged the Department of Education and Catechesis to offer a series of in-services on development possibilities. Bishop Povish was actively involved in many fundraising efforts on behalf of Catholic schools. Among them was a successful two million dollar drive to pay off the debt of the Luke M. Powers High School in Flint. This drive was launched in October 1976. The Bishop also supported the annual Lansing Catholic Central High School Msgr. Jerome V. MacEachin Scholarship dinner, which was inaugurated in 1985. In 1990, he was involved in three campaigns: a multi-million dollar campaign for Lumen Christi High School in Jackson, the Catholic Education Campaign for Genesee County schools, and the Greater Lansing Catholic Education Foundation five million dollar campaign. In 1993 he was engaged in yet another fundraising campaign in the Jackson area. Many schools and parishes throughout the Diocese initiated their own educational trust funds during his episcopacy.

In 1981 St. Mary Cathedral hosted its first Catholic Schools Week liturgy. Monsignor Jerome V. MacEachin celebrated the Mass for students from the Ingham/Eaton/Clinton region of the Diocese. The liturgical celebration was well received and the following year Bishop Povish was the main celebrant at an event for students from schools all across the Diocese. The Mass is now traditionally held on the Monday of Catholic

Schools Week. The Cathedral is always filled with students, teachers, principals and parish priests who gather to pray for our Catholic schools and for those who work and study in them.

During Bishop Povish's tenure, regional boards of education were abolished. Subsequently, in 1985, the secondary schools were constituted as public juridic persons under Canons 113-116. Each school developed its own set of by-laws which complemented the Statutes for Interparochial schools. This system has served as a governance model for Catholic high schools across the country.

In 1986 Bishop Povish endorsed a diocesan chapter of the Federation of Catholic School Parents. Though it was short-lived, it was a witness to the importance Bishop Povish placed on parental involvement.

Prior to 1988 the Catholic elementary and secondary schools were not accredited by any private or national agency. Between 1985 and 1988, the Michigan Non-Public School Accrediting Association developed a set of rigorous religious and academic standards for accreditation. Bishop Povish endorsed the expectation that every elementary and secondary diocesan Catholic school would engage in the process and become fully accredited. Within a relatively short time all the diocesan schools achieved accreditation. In February 1991 Holy Family School in Grand Blanc was the first Catholic school in the state to be accredited. Such accreditation is reviewed and renewed annually; each school undertakes the full process every five years.

High standards were set for catechist formation during the Zaleski episcopate. An extensive resource handbook for parish leaders and catechist trainees was developed during the Povish tenure. During Bishop Povish's administration hundreds of catechists attained at least

Dr. Bruce Fech, Superintendent of Education, presents a candle representing the light of Christ in education programs to a representative of one of the forty-five elementary and five high schools during Catholic Education Week in January 1985.

one of the levels of diocesan certification. A certification program for Directors of Religious Education began in May 1989. Through the work of a committee comprised of religious education directors and school principals, the diocesan catechist formation program underwent a major revision that was completed in May 1991. Through these courses and other opportunities such as the biannual catechetical day, catechetical leaders continue to receive ongoing academic and spiritual formation.

In October 1990, responsibility for providing adult education in the Diocese was placed within the Office of Catechesis. In 1993 Bishop Povish appointed four regional adult education representatives who were paid a stipend to work with the diocesan director in providing assistance and resources to parish adult leaders. This arrangement remained in place until August 2002.

Marriage Preparation

After four years of planning, on October 13, 1980, John Cardinal Dearden, Archbishop of Detroit, held a news conference in Lansing announcing new marriage preparation guidelines for the Province. The desire to promote and protect the sacredness of marriage led to the institution of a six month preparation period. The effective date of the guidelines was January 1, 1981. One of the mandated components of marriage preparation was the pre-marriage inventory (P.M.I.). The Diocese sponsored a Marriage Preparation Convocation in April 1981 at Lansing Catholic Central. Workshops on parish-centered marriage preparation programs, communication, spirituality and sexuality were presented. Another workshop was held in the fall on pre-marriage inventories. Hundreds of married couples across the Diocese were asked to administer the P.M.I. to the engaged in their parish and to discuss the results in a series of meetings. Contact between the married and engaged couples served as a wonderful means of expressing the idea that marriage as a sacrament affects the whole parish. Couples shared their trials and triumphs with the engaged to help them realize the effort and beauty marriage entails. In 1983 the Liturgical Commission developed a pre-marriage resource manual entitled *To Love and to Honor*.

School Openings and Closings

After being closed for over ten years, St. Mary School in Pinckney reopened its doors to grades one through five in August 1983. Shortly thereafter it added a kindergarten program. Over the next three years St. Mary expanded its educational program by adding grades six, seven and eight.

A newly constituted parish, St. Martha in Okemos, began its educational program with a preschool in January 1993. The elementary school formally opened on August 13, 1993, and now provides a flourishing Catholic educational and formational program for children preschool through eighth grade.

Among the most painful experiences for Bishop Povish was the closing of four parish schools. St. Thomas the Apostle High School in Ann Arbor closed in June 1977. That fall Gabriel Richard High School opened on the St. Thomas site as a regional high school for the Ann Arbor-Ypsilanti area. The transition was eased by the leadership of Mrs. Diane B. Nowak, who served as the last principal of St. Thomas High School and the first principal

of Gabriel Richard High School. The last parish high school in the Diocese, Holy Rosary High School in Flint, closed in 1992. The closures of two elementary schools, St. Anthony School in Hillsdale, 1985, and St. Alexis School in Ypsilanti, 1995, brought much sadness to those parish communities and to the Bishop.

The Gabriel Richard State Class "D" Champion girls basketball team of 1993

Curriculum Development in Our Schools

From 1987-1994 curriculum guidelines with a distinctive Catholic identity were written for all subject areas K-8. The formation of a religion curriculum for grades K-8 began in 1989. There were very clear objectives for seven major themes: History of Salvation, Revelation, Jesus, Church, Sacrament, Prayer/Worship, and Christian Living/Morality. Bishop Povish assigned Rev. Robert D. Lunsford as the theological advisor for the committee. When the religion curriculum was completed, Bishop Povish gave his blessing for five years of in-services on the curriculum for all grade school teachers. In 1994 Bishop Povish approved the writing of a high school religion curriculum. He again assigned Fr. Lunsford as theological advisor. This curriculum, which was finalized in 1997, is in use in all the Catholic high schools and parish high school religious education programs in the Diocese.

Diocesan Pastoral Council

In September 1977 the first concrete steps were taken to organize a diocesan pastoral council during the Povish episcopate. A study committee was appointed and at their first meeting in October, Sr. Florence Powlicki, C.S.F.N., a pastoral associate at St. Casimir, Lansing, was appointed temporary secretary. The study committee became the steering committee and in January 1979 was elevated by Bishop Povish to the level of the interim council. Sr. Carol Jean McDonnell, O.P., was elected as the interim council's first chair. The following March over 900 Catholics participated in regional meetings to set temporary goals for the Diocese. That fall regional assemblies were held to prepare for the First Diocesan Pastoral Assembly held in November.

The meeting for the 380 delegates began with an open house at the Diocesan Center and Chancery. The grand opening of the first diocesan museum, located on the second floor of the Diocesan Center, coincided with the diocesan office open house. The museum was under the direction of Rev. Douglas R. Osborne. The diocesan goals adopted by the assembly were published and mailed to 60,000 households in the Diocese. The first members of the Diocesan Pastoral Council (D.P.C.) were elected at the assembly. In January 1981 Mr. Robert Grace, of St. Francis of Assisi Parish in Ann Arbor, was elected chair of the Diocesan Pastoral Council. Diocesan Assemblies were held

The Diocesan Pastoral Assembly at St. Michael, Flint, in 1984.

biannually in conjunction with the election of members to the D.P.C. The November 1990 assembly was held at the Kellogg Center at Michigan State University. Bishop Kenneth Untener of Saginaw was the keynote speaker on the conference theme "Good News for the Nineties: Prospective for the Decade". The three diocesan priorities approved by the assembly were the result of a three year parish-based consultation process to consider the future of the church. The following year regional meetings were held to gather practical suggestions for implementing priorities. At the 1990 assembly the new Diocesan Pastoral Council members were first selected by lot rather than by election.

The eighth and last diocesan assembly was held in 1994, and focused on the second diocesan priority adopted in 1990: to educate ourselves in the Catholic principles of social justice and expand awareness and action consistent with these principles. Mr. Ron Krietemeyer, director of the Social Justice Office of the Archdiocese of St. Paul/Minneapolis, was the keynote speaker. The month prior to the last diocesan assembly, the eleven-member Common Conference Steering Committee began to meet and plan for a new format.

Ethnic Ministry

When Bishop Povish came to the Diocese of Lansing, he built upon the foundation of the two Hispanic parishes in Flint and Lansing. During his episcopate Bishop Povish encouraged the Summer Migrant Program and was a regular visitor to the migrant camps where he celebrated Mass. The Spanish-speaking Cultural Center in Jackson was opened in March of 1980 to address the needs of that local Hispanic Community. Later that spring, a program of ministry to the Spanish-speaking was established as a pilot project at Cristo Rey Church in Lansing. The following year an *Encuentro Juvenile* (Youth Gathering) was held at the Luke M. Powers High School in Flint.

Two National Hispanic *Encuentros* in 1972 and 1977 led to the development of the Diocesan Spanish Speaking Commission which approved its by-laws in August of 1982. The Office for Hispanic Affairs was opened on July 2, 1984, in preparation for the upcoming *Tercer Encuentro* (Third Encounter) in 1985. As part of the preparation for this national *Encuentro*, a diocese-wide *Encuentro* was held in March 1985. Bishop Povish and a delegation of ten others took part in the national *Tercer Encuentro* held in Washington, D.C., in August 1985.

The result of the *Tercer Encuentro* was the development of a "Pastoral Plan for Hispanic Ministry" published by the National Conference of Catholic Bishops (NCCB) in 1987. In November of 1989 a second diocese-wide *Encuentro* was held to implement the guidelines set forth by the national plan.

Bishop Povish was also supportive of the Cristo Rey Community Center in Lansing, which provided much needed social services. He presided over the blessing of the new center on High Street on April 13, 1988.

The development of a specific "Black Theology" in the Catholic Church was an outgrowth of the national awareness of ethnic consciousness in the late 1960's and early 1970's. This took firm root in the Diocese of Lansing under the direction of Bishop Povish. In 1976 seven parishes (Christ the King, Sacred Heart, St. Agnes, St. Francis, St. Luke, St. Matthew, St. Michael) in Flint's inner city began meeting to address their common concern of ministry to dwindling numbers of parishioners in the midst of a rapidly growing Black non-

Catholic population. The group, whose membership fluctuated somewhat, became known as the Flint Catholic Urban Ministry. The Josephites, a religious order whose primary ministry is to the Black community, were invited to come to Flint to help assess the situation. After an extensive survey and on-site visit by a four member team, a proposal was submitted to the Bishop. The proposal recommended the establishment of an intercultural resource center. Bishop Povish endorsed the proposal and the DuKette Intercultural Center for Urban Ministry was dedicated on October 23, 1977, by Bishop Povish. Bishop Povish commissioned Sisters Nancy Trayler and Barbara Dakoske, both Home Visitors of Mary religious, to manage the center. The center was named after Rev. Norman DuKette, Lansing's first Black priest, ordained in 1926. The DuKette Center was designed to meet the needs of the Black Catholic community in the city of Flint. This was done through mission revivals, the formation of a gospel-oriented choir, vacation bible schools, and other unique programs.

Lansing's Fr. DuKette had achieved the status of dean of the Black clergy in the United States. Bishop Povish understood the unique historical role that the Diocese held. It became increasingly clear that ministry to the Black Catholic community needed to be expanded beyond the city of Flint. After extensive local, regional, and national consultation, a vision for diocesan-level ministry was formed. In September 1986, the first Black Catholic Diocesan Coordination Team was commissioned by Bishop Povish. In May 1987 he led the ten member delegation to the first National Black Catholic Congress of the 20th century in Washington, D.C. In April 1988 the Diocesan Coordination Team for Black Catholics presented a proposal to the Diocesan Pastoral Council for the establishment of an office for Black Catholic Ministry.

DIOCESE OF LANSING
BLACK CATHOLIC CONGRESS
SECOND DAY OF REFLECTION

Bishop Kenneth J. Povish, D.D.
Bishop Moses Anderson, S.S.E., D.D.—Keynote Speaker

SATURDAY, APRIL 30, 1988
9:00 A.M. - 6:00 P.M.
ST. MARY CATHEDRAL
219 SEYMOUR STREET
LANSING, MICHIGAN 48933

Black Catholic Congress Day of Reflection, held at the Cathedral April 30, 1988

The Black Catholic Ministry Office opened in March of 1990, with a part-time director, Mr. Willard C. Hooks, Jr. The office was established to address the unique experiences of persons of color within the Diocese. Bishop Povish was also a delegate to the Seventh National Black Catholic Congress in 1992, held in New Orleans.

The needs of the Native American population of the Diocese were acknowledged by Bishop Povish with a special day of reflection for Native American Catholics which was held at St. Thérèse Parish in Lansing in June 1989.

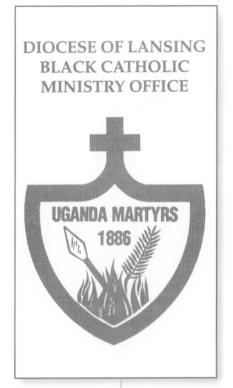

DIOCESE OF LANSING
BLACK CATHOLIC
MINISTRY OFFICE

UGANDA MARTYRS
1886

Professional Pastoral Ministers Association (PPMA) in December of 1986. (This was one of the first groups of its kind in the nation.) The following September, Mrs. Mary Tardif was appointed the first director of the Office of Lay Ministries. One of the duties assigned to the director was to serve as a liaison between the Diocese and the PPMA. A second duty was to establish and coordinate regular ministry training programs for parish volunteers. Many volunteers participated in programs such as Stephen Ministry and BeFriender Ministry. These ministries were designed to offer one on one support to people in crisis situations. The

Lay Ministry

To encourage the deepening of faith and to extend the opportunity for graduate studies among full time lay staff, Bishop Povish encouraged the institution of the Loyola Institute for Ministry Extension Programs in the Diocese in the fall of 1983. The program offers masters degrees in Religious Education or Pastoral Studies through Loyola University in New Orleans. Since its institution in the Diocese, over eighty-five people have earned their masters degrees through this extension program with concentrations in five areas of study.

The increase in lay members on parish staffs led to the formation of the

Bishop Povish with the seven newly commissioned lay ministers, September 9, 1995

first Stephen Ministers were commissioned in the Diocese on April 16, 1989, at St. Mary Parish in Flint for St. Mary and St. Leo the Great parishes. The first regional parish ministry institute was held in October 1989. BeFriender Ministry training sessions began in the Diocese in March 1994. At the time of the training program BeFriender Ministry had already been implemented at St. John, Fenton; Queen of the Miraculous Medal, Jackson; and St. John, Ypsilanti. In September the first BeFriender Ministers trained in the Diocese were commissioned at St. Joseph Parish in St. Johns. The inaugural meeting of the Listening Ministries Advisory Committee for the Lansing Diocese was held the following November. The committee's purpose was to be a support network for the Stephen Ministry and BeFriender Ministry programs at the parish level. Mary Tardif and Stephen Rall of Parish Social Ministry did much to see these programs take root in the Diocese.

The Church Ministries Institute was developed in the fall of 1989 to train lay ministers and permanent deacons. The Institute was an extension program of St. Mary College at Orchard Lake. A concern that 70 percent of the lay ministers in positions of leadership did not have proper training led Bishop Povish to convene a task force in August 1993 to study ways to prepare the next generation of "laborers for the harvest." Bishop Povish wanted lay ministry formation and education to be more affordable, more accessible and more attainable across the Diocese. He was very concerned that no one be refused training because of economic hardship. In response to these issues a new Ministry Formation Program was launched in March 1995 at St. James Parish in Mason with Bishop Robert Morneau speaking on "Called & Gifted/ Broken & Given." The Ministry Formation Program has agreements with Siena Heights University in Adrian and Loyola University in New Orleans. Educational and formational opportunities are offered at multiple times and locations with diocese and parish subsidized funding.

Desiring to give greater recognition to the service of lay people in parish and diocesan work, Bishop Povish began the commissioning of ecclesial lay ministers. The first class of twelve lay ministers completed their academic and spiritual formation through the Church Ministries Institute. Bishop Povish preached on the theme "Called, Gifted and Sent" at the commissioning liturgy at St. Mary Cathedral on October 10, 1992. Seven more ministers were commissioned in September 1995.

A medallion was given the lay ministers at their commissioning. It depicted an individual rising from the waters of Baptism, living in the shadow of the Cross and sustained by prayer.

New Faith Communities

In the twenty year episcopate of Bishop Povish six new parishes and missions were formed. Catholics in the Goodrich area held their first Mass on August 20, 1978. That community was first a mission of St. John the Evangelist Parish in Davison. Later the community took St. Mark the Evangelist as their patron. The Catholics at Montrose named their new community after the Good Shepherd and celebrated their first Mass on February 4, 1979. The Montrose mission was an outgrowth of St. Robert Parish in Flushing. Because of the shortage of priests, St. Mark and Good Shepherd have been headed by pastoral coordinators. In June 1979 Bishop Povish sent Rev. Charles E. Irvin to be the first pastor of the newly created parish of Holy Spirit in Hamburg. In June 1988 Rev. Jonathan W. Wehrle was asked to found the new parish of St. Martha in Okemos. The next parish opened was St. Mary Magdalen, founded on June 29, 1993, in Livingston county. Rev. David F. Howell was entrusted by Bishop Povish with the pastoral care of the new parish. The sixth faith community was formed from the merger of St. Alexis and St. Ursula parishes in Ypsilanti. The first liturgy for the new parish, dedicated to the Transfiguration of Our Lord, occurred on January 9, 1994. Rev. David M. Franco, O.S.F.S., was the first pastor of Transfiguration Parish.

Diocesan Services Reorganized

In the first fifteen years of the Povish episcopate, over twenty diocesan offices, coordinating committees and councils were established. The diocesan central services had become unwieldy and resources were overextended. After a two year study, the five departments of Administrative Services, Catholic Charities, Diocesan Ministries, Education and Catechesis and Pastoral Formation were created to enhance communication and services. This restructuring took effect July 1, 1986. A re-visioning process in September 1991 led to the elimination of nine offices and the abolishment of thirteen staff positions on July 1, 1992. The offices closed were: Deaf, Graphics, Real to Reel, Properties, Film Impact, Criminal Justice, Women, Poverty and Age, Campus Ministry at Lansing Community College, and the regional coordinator for Parish Social Ministry in Washtenaw County. At the same time five diocesan departments were reduced to four. Later in the fall, responsibility for the deaf was assumed by the Office of Persons with Disabilities. Criminal Justice concerns were added to the duties of the director of the Young Adult Office.

Spiritual Renewal and Continuing Education for Priests

Bishop Povish appointed Rev. William F. Meyers to open the Office of Priestly Life and Ministry in July 1978. The Senate of Priests had requested in February 1978 that an office for priestly life be established. With the support of the Bishop, Fr. Meyers organized two programs for priests, the Doctorate in Ministry program and the Emmaus program. The Emmaus program for the spiritual renewal of the priesthood was launched in May 1979 when nearly 170 diocesan priests met at St. John Provincial Seminary in Plymouth. The priests were asked to sign up for small support groups for discussion of Emmaus program topics. Retreats for the clergy followed that fall at the Portiuncula in the Pines retreat house in DeWitt. The concluding conference at Weber Center in Adrian in May 1980 was attended by 159 priests. An outgrowth of the Emmaus Program was the annual convocation at which the Bishop would give his state of the Diocese address. The 1988 Emmaus convocation was devoted to "The Emmaus Program – A Second Look." Priests were once again asked to sign up for small support/discussion groups and to make a fall Emmaus retreat in DeWitt. A number of our priests participated in another enrichment opportunity, the doctoral ministry program. The sabbatical program was yet another enrichment opportunity for our clergy and Rome, Dublin and Menlo Park in California were among the most popular sites.

During the Povish years the Chrism Mass grew dramatically in importance and was eagerly anticipated by the priests. The Bishop's homily was mostly directed to them and his message challenged, consoled and encouraged them. This was especially true the year that the presbyterate was devastated by the suicide of one of its members.

Diocesan Evangelization Efforts

Evangelization was always a high priority for Bishop Povish. He fostered and encouraged many renewal efforts for the evangelization of the clergy, the faithful, Catholics with special needs, ethnic minorities, lapsed Catholics, and the unchurched.

The Real to Reel program on Channel 6 in Lansing first aired on February 1, 1981. The program was initially hosted by Sr. Monica Kostielney, R.S.M., and Rev. David F. Howell. Rev. Donald L. Eder and his staff in the Communication Office put together quality programs for over a decade. Part of the programming was provided by the National Conference of Catholic Bishops (NCCB) and Fr. Eder's office prepared local features and

Sr. Monica Kostielney, R.S.M., and
Rev. Douglas R. Osborn, cohosts of Reel to Real.

taped interviews with Bishop Povish for each weekly show. Because of budget constraints the last edition was aired December 29, 1991.

One of the largest one time efforts to reach out to lapsed Catholics and the unchurched was the diocesan Open House held March 13, 1983. On that day parishes across the Diocese set up displays and gave church tours. In these and in many other ways our neighbors were invited to *"come and see."*

Bishop Povish encouraged Auxiliary Bishop James S. Sullivan to set the wheels in motion for a weekly Mass to be videotaped at St. Thomas Aquinas Parish in East Lansing. Regular weekly television broadcast began in January 1985. Bishop Povish made it a practice to celebrate the Outreach Mass once a month. Each year Holy Week began with Bishop Povish taping the Palm Sunday Vigil Mass.

Bishop Povish provided for the continued growth of the spiritual lives of many people in the diocese when he decided to purchase the retreat house in DeWitt from the Franciscans. The transfer of property took place on January 1, 1989. Portiuncula in the Pines became

St. Francis Retreat Center. St. Francis provides spiritual nourishment and solace to people of all ages, races and faiths. The spiritual direction internship program began in the fall of 1992. Those trained through the program continue to guide the faithful.

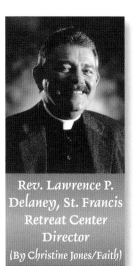

Rev. Lawrence P. Delaney, St. Francis Retreat Center Director
(By Christine Jones/Faith)

Sr. Suzanne Eichhorn, O.P., St. Francis Retreat Center Associate Director

Other diocese-wide evangelism efforts included regional meetings and clergy days to reflect on the NCCB pastorals: *The Challenge of Peace: God's Promise and Our Response* (1984) and *Justice for All* (1987). "Preparing for the Church in the 90's" was the focus of a diocesan long-range planning process. The initial meeting was held in June 1987 and regional meetings began in February 1988. Bishop Povish reported the results at the Chrism Mass in 1990. He felt the Chrism Mass was an appropriate forum because the planning process pointed to the centrality of the priesthood in the life of the Church.

The last diocese-wide program launched during the Povish episcopacy was the three year Stewardship Initiative. At the kickoff in February 1993 Bishop Povish spoke on stewardship as a call to discipleship. Bishop Kenneth E. Untener of Saginaw gave the keynote "To Live and Die the Way Jesus Did." The first year of the initiative focused on *understanding stewardship* and its relationship to daily living. *Stewardship of time and talent* was the focus of the second year. The *stewardship of treasure* was the third year focus.

Parish Evangelization Efforts

The two most important parish evange-lization programs during the Povish episcopacy were Parish Renewal Weekends and the Renew Program. The first Parish Renewal Weekend was held at Cristo Rey in Lansing in 1980. The focus of the Parish Renewal Weekend was to build community within the parish and foster reconciliation of priests and people with one another. Upon the foundation of parish leaders and people becoming more deeply committed to one another, as people and as Church, a renewed spirituality could spark greater evangelization. Recognizing its potential for growth and healing, Bishop Povish participated in the training sessions held at St. Joseph Home in Jackson in February 1981. A number of parishes benefited from these weekends.

In preparation for the Golden Jubilee of the Diocese in 1987 Bishop Povish invested his energies in making the Renew process (for spiritual renewal through small groups of faith sharing) a truly diocese-wide program. On June 7, 1983, Bishop Povish made the decision to launch the Renew Program. The Diocesan Renew Coordinating Team met for the first time in September. Mr. Charles E. Baker headed the team and Rev. Sylvester L. Fedewa served as the spiritual director. Thirteen information sessions on the Renew Program were held across the Diocese in the fall of 1983. Bishop Povish presided over the opening Renew Liturgy at the Cathedral in September 1984. Thousands of Catholics across the Diocese deepened their faith through the Renew experience.

Near the end of the Povish episcopate another parish renewal movement came to the fore. Rev. Matthew J. Fedewa adapted the TEC (Teens Encounter Christ) program and created the Koinonia for adults. Some thirty-five participants celebrated the paschal mystery through meditation, small group discussions and the liturgy at the first Koinonia held in the Diocese at St. Pius X in Flint in April 1994.

Special Focus Evangelization

A wide range of special focus faith development programs were encouraged by Bishop Povish. The first Sons and Daughters Encounter weekend (a retreat designed to foster communication between parents and children) was led by Rev. James G. McDougall in February 1980. With great support from Revs. James A. Murray and Michael D. Murphy, the first Red Mass for Catholic lawyers and judges was celebrated by Bishop Povish in November 1985. The following February the Catholic Lawyers Guild held its organizational meeting. The first president of the guild was Mr. Eugene Krasicky, an assistant attorney general for the state of Michigan and former legal council for the National Conference of Catholic Bishops. In June 1987 Bishop Povish celebrated the inaugural liturgy of the Michigan chapter of Legatus, a group of Catholic chief executive officers headed by Mr. Thomas Monaghan of Domino's Pizza. The Mass was held at Domino Pizza World Headquarters in Ann Arbor. That fall the first remarriage seminar was offered in the Diocese. The first conference for Separated and Divorced Catholics was held at Lansing Catholic Central in the spring of 1988.

Knights of Columbus

Bishop Povish was a very strong advocate of the Knights of Columbus (K of C). When he came to the Diocese there were twenty-six councils. Bishop Povish encouraged the continued establishment of parish K of C councils. In May 1995 when he attended his last state convention on Mackinac Island as our Bishop, there were fifty-eight councils that sent delegates. Bishop Povish was well known to the Knights from across Michigan by his faithful attendance at their annual meetings. In May 1994, he was recognized by the Knights for his distinguished service when he received their new award, Man of the Year.

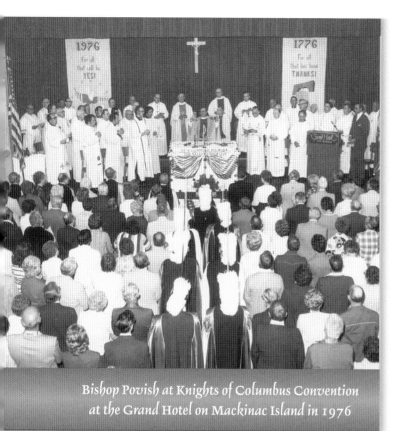

Bishop Povish at Knights of Columbus Convention at the Grand Hotel on Mackinac Island in 1976

Bishop Povish proudly witnessed the presentation of top state awards to councils from the Lansing diocese year after year. During his episcopacy three Lansing men served as state deputy: Thomas Clark of Ann Arbor, James Hayes from Brighton and James Fedewa from Westphalia. Just after the Bishop's retirement, Richard McCloy of Lansing Council #788 served as state deputy during 1996-98. Bishop Povish was asked to serve as state chaplain during that term. His articles in the *Columbian* (the state K of C newspaper) were much appreciated by the membership.

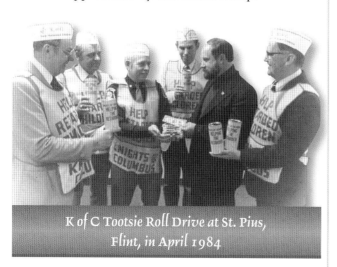

K of C Tootsie Roll Drive at St. Pius, Flint, in April 1984

Pastoral Coordinators

The road to designating pastoral coordinators began with the appointment of Sr. Rita Schaefer, O.P., as pastoral minister of the community of St. Augustine in Deerfield Township in Livingston County in 1980. Her title was pastoral minister but her function was pastoral coordinator. She oversaw the needs of a parish community in the absence of resident clergy. Deerfield was considered a mission of the Fenton parish. Recognizing the success of alternative staffing of parishes, Bishop Povish appointed Kenneth Berger and his wife Patricia Robertson as the first lay couple to administer a parish in the Diocese. In July 1985 they became the pastoral coordinators of Sacred Heart Parish in Flint. Subsequently, St. Joseph in Gaines, St. Mary on the Lake in Manitou Beach, and St. Catherine Labouré in Concord all received pastoral coordinators. Other parishes would soon join their number. Most of the pastoral coordinators have been women religious.

Diocesan Golden Jubilee

In 1983 the diocesan archivist, Rev. George C. Michalek, was appointed by Bishop Povish to chair the diocesan celebration of its 50th anniversary. Rev. David F. Howell served as co-chair. The two priests had developed a proposal for the Golden Jubilee celebration after attending a sesquicentennial exhibit about the Archdiocese of Detroit at Sacred Heart Seminary. A seven member committee met for four years to implement the Golden Jubilee celebration. Workshops were held in the fall for parish historians to begin gathering information.

On December 12, 1985, Bishop Povish issued a proclamation announcing the Golden Jubilee of the Diocese. The "Festival of Faith" opened with a liturgy at the Cathedral and block party on May 25, 1986. At the Mass, jubilee banners were distributed to all the parishes. During that summer the focus was on regional celebrations. Bishop Povish presided at each of the regional celebrations and preached on the centrality of "The Book, The Bread and The Bishop" to Catholic faith. The parish and

Ministry. He came to the Diocese in 1977 after having a similar position with the Genesee Catholic Board of Education from 1972-1977. Under his direction the Youth Congress and Youth Advisory Council began. An outcome of the Youth Congress that was held in 1978 was

Jackson regional celebration of the Diocesan Golden Jubilee November 5, 1986

regional celebrations drew to a close in May 1987. The close was marked by another liturgy at the Cathedral and block party to which parish volunteers were invited. Artifacts and memorabilia gathered by the historians during the previous three years were displayed in the cathedral crypt from May to September 1987. The grand finale was the August 4, 1987, liturgy at St. Mary Cathedral. Bishop Povish presided and Archbishop Pilarczyk of Cincinnati preached. (Our first bishop came from Cincinnati.) Cardinal Dearden and Archbishop (now Cardinal) Szoka were in attendance.

Youth Ministry

Mr. John R. Armstrong was the first individual hired by the Diocese as Consultant for Secondary Religious Education and Youth

the plan to have an annual gathering. A series of annual weekend Youth Convocations were held from 1979 until 1984.

When Mr. Brian Singer Towns assumed responsibility in July 1985, the Office of Youth Ministry became a separate office in the Department of Education and Catechesis. Its main goals were: 1) to provide direction and vision, training and support for parish youth ministry leaders; 2) to provide annual evangelistic and formational events for diocesan youth (13-18 years of age); and 3) to be a strong advocate with parishes and local communities in responding to the concerns of youth.

No convocation was held that year, but youth members across the Diocese were surveyed on future directions. The first Youth Jamboree was held in April 1986 and some 865 students participated in the event. In 1989 the Office began a formal program of certification

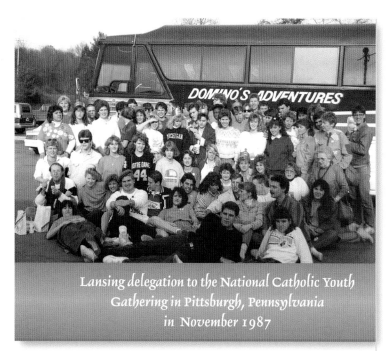

Lansing delegation to the National Catholic Youth Gathering in Pittsburgh, Pennsylvania in November 1987

cation. In the summer of 1986, eighty-six youth and twelve adults participated in the first diocesan youth leadership camp. Bishop Povish was present for the closing day's activities. On May 3, 1991, the first junior high/middle school youth rally was held at Lansing Catholic Central. Mr. Jack Armstrong coordinated the event for the nearly 380 sixth, seventh and eighth grade students.

Bishop Povish led the 640 member Diocese of Lansing delegation to the World Youth Day in Denver, Colorado, in August 1993.

Retirement

In 1995 Bishop Povish was diagnosed with colon cancer. As a result, he submitted his resignation to the Holy Father. On November 7, 1995, the appointment of his successor, Carl F. Mengeling, was announced. The Presbyteral Council then elected Bishop Povish as the Apostolic Administrator of the Diocese until the installation of the new bishop occurred. Bishop Povish continued to serve the Diocese in numerous ways, among them were giving

in youth ministry training. (Training programs for adults had first been held as early as 1981.) These programs later became known as the "Nuts and Bolts". The certification program consisted of three levels: basic, intermediate and advanced. Parish Youth Ministers were required to have the intermediate certification and were encouraged to pursue the advanced certifi-

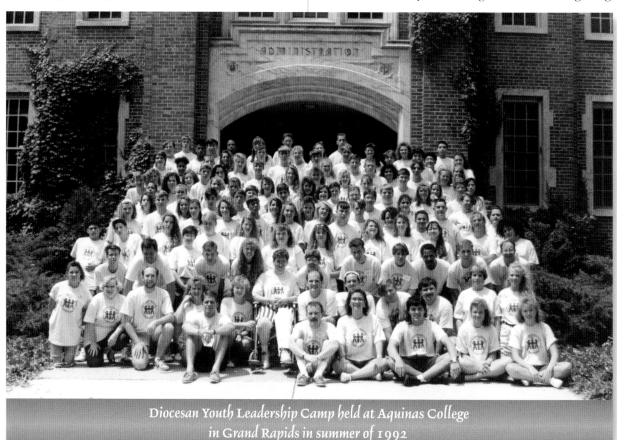

Diocesan Youth Leadership Camp held at Aquinas College in Grand Rapids in summer of 1992

retreats and writing a column in the *Catholic Times*. His courageous eight-year battle with cancer ended on September 5, 2003, when he died in the hospice unit of the former St. Lawrence Hospital. Bishop Povish requested that Bishop Mengeling celebrate his funeral liturgy and that his former chancellor of twenty years, Bishop James A. Murray of Kalamazoo, preach the homily.

To Accomplish His Work

While at the Catholic University of America doing his graduate work Bishop Povish was asked to compile a list of the thirty most important sayings of Jesus. He spent much time researching and praying about the assignment and during his years as a priest he often pondered these key teachings of Jesus. Among the top five on his list was "To Accomplish His Work" (John 4:34). This phrase from John's gospel kept returning to his mind for further meditation. When the episcopal dignity was bestowed upon him while pastoring St. Stanislaus Parish in Bay City, he chose John 4:34 as the embodiment of what he hoped to do as a bishop. When Jesus spoke these words He was speaking to the Samaritan woman at the well. He was seeking to share with her the vision of His Father's Kingdom. In choosing this motto Bishop Povish sought to encourage the flock entrusted to his care and give them hope as they labored with him to build God's kingdom.

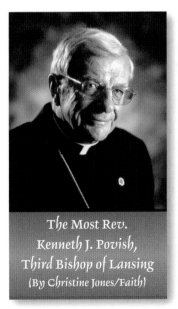

The Most Rev.
Kenneth J. Povish,
Third Bishop of Lansing
(By Christine Jones/Faith)

Carl Frederick Mengeling
S.T.D.

Born: October 22, 1930, Hammond, Indiana

Parents: Carl H. Mengeling and the former Augusta Huke

Ordained a Priest Cathedral of the Holy Angels, Gary, Indiana

May 25, 1957

By Andrew G. Grutka, Bishop of Gary, Indiana

Consecrated a Bishop Cathedral of the Immaculate Conception, Lansing, Michigan

January 25, 1996

Consecrator: Adam Cardinal Maida, Archbishop of Detroit, Michigan

Co-Consecrators: Kenneth J. Povish, Former Bishop of Lansing

Dale J. Melczck, Bishop of Gary, Indiana

Motto: "He Must Increase" John 3:30

Bishop of Lansing January 25, 1996

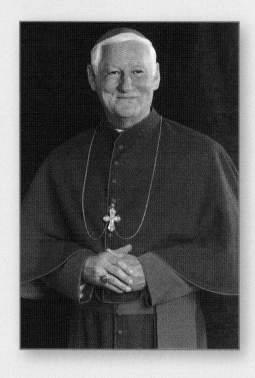

CHAPTER 5

"He Must Increase"

1996-

Consecration of a New Bishop

Episcopal Ordination, January 25, 1996

Bishop-elect Carl F. Mengeling first visited the diocese on November 7, 1995, when the press conference announcing his appointment was held. After the press conference Msgr. James A. Murray, Chancellor of the Diocese, took him on a brief tour of the Cathedral. The Bishop-elect moved to Lansing the following January with all his belongings in his car. His lack of concern for material possessions and his focus on the spiritual life were evident from the moment he arrived in Lansing. His emphasis was on his faith in Jesus the Christ. He proceeded to lead the diocese in the spirit of humility and service consistent with his episcopal motto, "He must increase, but I must decrease" (John 3:30).

Nearly a thousand people filled the Cathedral on January 24, 1996, for the vesper service during which Bishop-elect Mengeling took canonical possession of the diocese. The following day, Adam Cardinal Maida, Archbishop of Detroit, served as principal celebrant of the ordination and installation ceremony which took place before a capacity crowd. Bishop Povish laying hands upon the new bishop was a symbol of passing the torch of leadership to his successor.

Ethnic Ministry

A milestone of Hispanic Ministry during the episcopate of Bishop Mengeling was the first Spanish Koinonia (retreat) which was held at Cristo Rey Parish in June 1996. The Koinonia program has remained a significant source of spiritual renewal in the Hispanic community. Bishop Mengeling has averaged four visits a season to migrant camps to celebrate Mass for the laborers and their families.

The diocesan director of Hispanic Ministry, Serpio Hernandez, led a ten-member delegation to the *Encuentro 2000*. The theme of the conference, which was held in Los Angeles, was "Many Faces in God's House." An outgrowth of the *Encuentro 2000* has been the development of plans for a lay formation program to be conducted in Spanish for the Hispanic Ministry in the diocese. The plans for the lay formation program were further refined in November 2002 when the United States Conference of

Catholic Bishops approved the document *Encuentro and Mission: A Renewed Pastoral Framework for Hispanic Ministry*. It is hoped that the lay formation program in Spanish will be implemented in the near future.

The directors of the offices of Hispanic Ministry and Black Catholics have been purposefully seeking ways to build bridges between Black and Brown. They participated in the VOICES project, a diocesan program established to obtain the input of the laity regarding planning for the future of the diocese. The Hispanic and Black Catholic communities held joint listening sessions for people of color. The Hispanic community also shared the success of the Koinonia experience of reflection upon and immersion in the paschal mystery with the Black community. Black Catholics then held a Koinonia at Christ the King Parish in Flint. St. Martin de Porres is an apt patron saint of these efforts because in his life he united the Black and Hispanic cultures.

The leadership of the Black Catholic Ministry in the diocese was entrusted to Mr. Ronald Landfair in August 1997. He originated the concept of the Blood of the Martyrs Blood Drive to honor Dr. Martin Luther King. The purpose of the project is to provide an evangelistic, concrete method for the Catholic Church to honor the work and memory

Ron Landfair, Head of Black Catholic Ministry
(By Christine Jones/Faith)

of Dr. Martin Luther King, Jr., in a way that is unique, exemplary and in keeping with our Catholic tradition. After just two years, the event spread across the state and nation. The office of Black Catholic Ministry also began a regular series of pilgrimages to the Shrine of the Immaculate Conception in Washington, D.C. These grew out of a call from the Seventh National Black Catholic Congress (held in Washington in August of 1997) for dioceses across the country to design and implement diocesan pilgrimages to "Our Mother of Africa" Chapel, which was dedicated by the Bishops of the U.S. at that Congress. A systematic effort toward increasing awareness within the Catholic community of the role and presence of Black Catholics has also begun, utilizing all

facets of media (radio, television, print) to promote ministries to ethnic peoples.

Although the diocese has a very small number of Native American Catholics, it was the host for the 63rd Annual Tekakwitha Conference which was held at Michigan State University at the beginning of August 2002. The annual conference fosters relations between Native American people and the Catholic Church. The conference theme was "The Spirit of Kateri in the Land of the Great Lakes." The diocesan worship office helped prepare worship aids and Bishop Mengeling celebrated one of the liturgies.

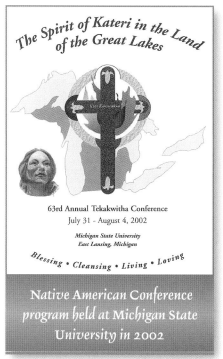

63rd Annual Tekakwitha Conference
July 31 - August 4, 2002
Michigan State University
East Lansing, Michigan

Blessing • Cleansing • Living • Loving

Native American Conference program held at Michigan State University in 2002

Common Conferences

The multiplication of continuing education opportunities for ordained and lay professional and volunteer parish ministers required a reconsideration of how to best provide them. It was decided at the diocesan level to have all the individual office workshops and in-services at the same time. The goal was to reduce scheduling conflicts by offering workshops and inspirational speakers to all parish workers in a concentrated three-day event. Sr. Rita Wenzlick, O.P., was appointed chair of the conference

steering committee which began meeting in October 1994. She has continued in that position. "Building the Kingdom: Many Gifts, One Spirit" was the theme of the inaugural Common Conference held in 1996. Over 2,000 people from six Michigan Dioceses attended the three-day ministry workshop conference held November 21-23 at the Lansing Center. Nationally known speakers and authors as well as local experts were among the presenters. At the closing liturgy, Bishop Mengeling launched the diocesan preparation for the Great Jubilee 2000.

A second Common Conference was held in October 1998 with the theme "We Are Called". The nearly 200 workshops were attended by over 2,000 people. In his opening address the Bishop focused on the need for collaborative ministry. The tradition of honoring lay leaders for their exceptional service began with honoring four people at the Bishop's Banquet. The third Common Conference was held in November 2001 with the theme "Three Powerful Days in One Powerful Mission". Four more lay leaders received outstanding service and leadership awards. At the conclusion of the conference Bishop Mengeling announced the seven diocesan goals which were the result of a diocese-wide planning and listening process. His message focused on the church not *having* a mission but *being* the mission of Christ.

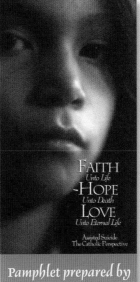

FAITH
Unto Life
-HOPE
Unto Death
LOVE
Unto Eternal Life

Assisted Suicide
The Catholic Perspective

Pamphlet prepared by Michigan Catholic Conference to address the issue of assisted suicide from the Catholic perspective

Constitutional Amendments

Mirroring the experience of the Zaleski years two ballot initiatives came to the fore in the Mengeling years. During both episcopates the issue of protecting the sanctity of life was successfully defended, but the issue of support for private schools failed.

In 1998 "Proposal B", the proposed constitutional amendment to legalize physician-assisted suicide in Michigan, was overwhelmingly defeated by an almost 3-1 margin. The group known as Marian's Friends gathered the signatures to put the proposal on the ballet. A coalition of thirty-two groups formed Citizens for Compassionate Care (C.C.C.). Lt. Governor Connie Binsfeld served as chair of the group. The bishops of the state issued a pastoral letter entitled *Living and Dying According to the Voice of Faith*. An all out campaign of informative literature, small group presentations, sermons, videos and television advertising changed the majority pro-assisted suicide stance that existed

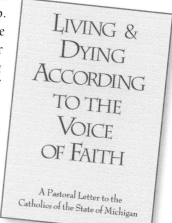

LIVING &
DYING
ACCORDING
TO THE
VOICE
OF FAITH

A Pastoral Letter to the Catholics of the State of Michigan

at the start of the election campaign in September.

Two years later "Proposal 1", the constitutional amendment to allow parents to take their state dollars dedicated to their child's education to a school of their choice, was on the ballot. The Kids First! Yes! Coalition was organized as the pro-voucher group. It was chaired by Richard and Betsy DeVos of Grand Rapids. The Michigan Catholic Conference was a major supporter of

Kids First! Yes! Just as in the 1998 campaign, Paul Long, vice president of public policy for the Conference and a Cathedral parishioner, worked long hours to promote the Conference stance. The bishops of Michigan issued a series of three messages on education and seven sets of homilies resources were prepared. The proposal was defeated on Election Day.

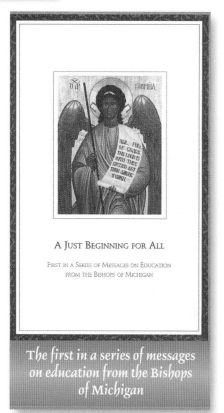

A JUST BEGINNING FOR ALL

FIRST IN A SERIES OF MESSAGES ON EDUCATION FROM THE BISHOPS OF MICHIGAN

The first in a series of messages on education from the Bishops of Michigan

The Great Jubilee 2000

In November 1994 His Holiness Pope John Paul II issued his Apostolic Letter *Tertio Millennia Adveniente* in preparation for the Great Jubilee Year 2000. A fifteen-member Diocesan Jubilee Commission was formed in 1996. Msgr. Steven J. Raica chaired the commission until his transfer to Rome to become superior of the graduate house of studies for the North American College. At that time Sr. Rita Wenzlick, O.P., took over the leadership.

Jubilee banner hanging at St. Paul Parish, Owosso

At the closing liturgy of the Diocesan Common Conference held in November 1996, Bishop Mengeling formally initiated the diocesan preparation for the Great Jubilee. The Holy Father had called for three preparatory years 1997, 1998 and 1999 dedicated to Jesus Christ, the Holy Spirit and God the Father respectively. The bishops of the state of Michigan joined Adam Cardinal Maida for the

Statewide inaugural Mass
for the Great Jubilee held June 22, 1997

and forgiving others. Representatives from many groups, such as the Bishop's Council on Alcohol and Drug Abuse, the Diocesan Tribunal, and Beginning Experience, set up information tables. Large numbers of priests were available for the celebration of the Sacrament of Penance. That same fall the diocese hosted a daylong inter-religious dialogue organized by Rev. Robert T. Kerr, the diocesan Ecumenical Officer. Christians, Jews and Muslims gathered in Ypsilanti to share ideas of God as Father. In December 1999 Bishop Mengeling announced Jubilee gifts for the benefit of the parishes and people of the diocese. Almost 2.5 million dollars, made available through diocesan savings over a period of years, was given in debt reduction, assessment reduction and a Jubilee scholarship endowment fund for diocesan schools. A one-year subscription to *Faith* magazine to over 80,000 registered Catholic households was Bishop Mengeling's favorite gift.

The opening of the Diocesan Holy Year Door at the Cathedral at Midnight Mass Christmas 1999 ushered in the Great Jubilee proper. The door had been blessed the year before at Christmas Midnight Mass. The opening of the Holy Door, a tradition which originated in

formal statewide inauguration of the Jubilee with a liturgy held June 22, 1997, at the Breslin Student Events Center at Michigan State University.

Jubilee activities included a campaign for social justice and peace, a call to reconciliation, an ecumenical program, and Jubilee gifts from the Bishop. During 1998 the diocese joined Catholics across the nation in a "Forgive the Debt" Campaign. Petitions were forwarded to the International Monetary Fund and the World Bank to forgive the debt of the world's thirty-five poorest nations. Individuals were also urged to take the "Jubilee Pledge for Charity, Justice and Peace". In the fall of 1999 hundreds of people attended the "Celebrations of God's Mercy" held in the four population centers of the diocese (Ann Arbor, Flint, Jackson and Lansing) to reach out to fallen away Catholics. Lay speakers addressed topics of racism, divorce/annulments, returning to the church

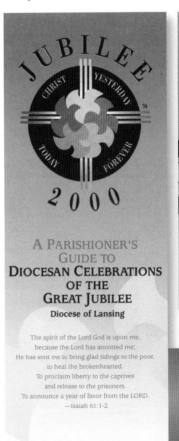

JUBILEE
CHRIST YESTERDAY
TODAY FOREVER
2000

A PARISHIONER'S
GUIDE TO
DIOCESAN CELEBRATIONS
OF THE
GREAT JUBILEE
Diocese of Lansing

The spirit of the Lord God is upon me,
because the Lord has anointed me;
He has sent me to bring glad tidings to the poor,
to heal the brokenhearted,
To proclaim liberty to the captives
and release to the prisoners.
To announce a year of favor from the LORD.
—Isaiah 61:1-2

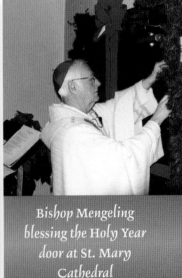

Bishop Mengeling blessing the Holy Year door at St. Mary Cathedral

Parishioner's Guide to Diocesan Celebrations of the Great Jubilee for the Diocese of Lansing

The Jubilee mission held for the Lansing region

Cathedral where they walked through the Holy Door, visited the diocesan museum, and attended Mass which was celebrated by the Bishop. Jubilee Pilgrimage Days were also held for religious, persons with disabilities and lay ministers. Pilgrimages to Mexico and to the National Shrine in Washington were led by Bishop Mengeling. A statewide youth rally held in Lansing and World Youth Day in Rome were also Jubilee 2000 events. The close of the Great Jubilee 2000 took place on the Solemnity of the Epiphany, January 6, 2001, at St. Mary Cathedral.

Secular Carmelites

Rome, is a symbol of the opening of our hearts to Christ. On New Year's Eve, Night Prayer followed by Midnight Mass was celebrated at the Cathedral in expectation of a new millennium of grace. "A Year of Favor From the Lord" was the theme of the downtown churches' ecumenical service at the Cathedral on January 23rd. The diocese held six regional missions to offer the laity an opportunity to deepen their faith by gathering for prayer and reflection on the spiritual life. The Council on Aging sponsored seven regional pilgrimage days which involved travel to historic churches to pray and to hear presentations by the diocesan archivist on the planting of the faith in that region. Seniors from across the diocese also participated in a pilgrimage to St. Mary

The Secular Carmelites began in Flint in 1949. During the last five years they have experienced phenomenal growth. The Flint Secular Order of Discalced Carmelites - Our Lady of Mt. Carmel Community originally met at Marian Hall and then at St. Michael's Parish on a monthly basis. In 1980 Rev. William A. Healy, O.C.D., directed the first of the community's annual retreats. By the mid 1990's the community had nearly 100 members. On the feast of Our Lady of Mt. Carmel in 1994, the Flint Community received canonical recognition in the Diocese of Lansing. The Flint Carmelite Community has given birth to four daughter communities in the Diocese: the Burton Community of The Blessed Sacrament organized September 8, 2001; the Hamburg Community of Our Lady of Mt. Carmel, Spouse of the Holy Spirit organized October 1, 2001; the Lansing Community of Mary, Mother of God, Queen of Carmel organized April 27, 2002; and the Ann Arbor Community of St. John of the Cross organized May 28, 2002. New communities begin as prayer and study groups. An acting council is appointed by the Carmelite provincial once a group has attained at least ten members of whom two must have made their Definitive Promise. Then the group attains the status of

Faith Explosion, a statewide Jubilee youth rally on the State Capital lawn

having a fully self-governing council which must be approved by the local bishop, the Carmelite provincial and the Carmelite generalate in Rome. Outside the Diocese, the Flint community was also instrumental in founding a community in Atlanta, Georgia, and contributed to the foundation of the secular Carmelite community in Clarkston.

Curriculum Guidelines

Bishop Mengeling took a keen interest in the development of the "Curriculum for Catholic High School and Parish High School Religious Programs" which he approved in April 1997. The high school guidelines were based on ten topics with references to the *Catechism of the Catholic Church*. The ten topics were: 1) Fundamentals of the Catholic Faith; 2) Christology; 3) Hebrew Scriptures, the Old Testament; 4) the Christian Scriptures, the New Testament; 5) the Church and Her History; 6) Catholic Morality; 7) Family Life and Vocational Choices; 8) Sacraments; 9) Rational Basis for the Faith; and 10) Prayer. The grade school curriculum guidelines developed under Mary Olive Dion (director of K-12 instructional programs) during the Povish years were all updated during the episcopate of Bishop Mengeling. He requested that a new category, "prayer and doctrine" be developed to encourage memorization of prayers and doctrines appropriate for specific grade levels. These new guidelines were approved in 2000.

Office of Cemeteries

The diocesan cemeteries, New Calvary in Flint and St. Joseph in Lansing, had been established during the Albers episcopate. Each had its own manager, office, sales and ground staff. Each cemetery had its own set of rules, policies and procedures which were at times in conflict with diocesan policy and procedures. A perception arose that the cemeteries had no clearly defined mission and were failing to meet the needs of the Catholic faithful.

In 1997 the National Catholic Cemetery Conference was asked to provide a comprehensive evaluation of the diocesan cemeteries, covering all segments of cemetery operations. The on-site evaluation of cemetery operations was conducted in January 1998 and a final report given to the Bishop in March 1998. As a result of this report, the Office of Cemeteries was created and located in Central Services in Lansing. Mr. Paul D. Garriépy, C.C.C.E., (a Certified Catholic Cemetery Executive) was hired as the first Diocesan Director of Cemeteries to direct and supervise the administration of the consolidated cemeteries. A centralized sales marketing plan was initiated for both cemeteries and administered by Mr. Gerald D. Rice. The Diocesan Director of Cemeteries also became a consultant to individual parish cemeteries.

In 2002 two events affected the Office of Cemeteries. In May at the request of Bishop Basil Schott, Administrator of the Byzantine Catholic Diocese of Parma, the Diocese of Lansing accepted the ownership and administrative responsibility of St. Michael Byzantine Cemetery in Flint, which served Byzantine Catholics of the Flint area. In November the Diocesan Finance Office was restructured, resulting in the Office of Cemeteries merging with the Properties Office of the Finance Department. Mr. Garriépy was named Director of Properties and Cemeteries. Mr. Christopher Root was named Properties Manager and Mrs. Vickie Yankee, Manager of St. Joseph Cemetery in Lansing was named Assistant Director of Cemeteries in Charge of Operations.

Faith Magazine

Shortly after Bishop Mengeling's arrival, discussions arose about the limited circulation of the *Catholic Times*. In 1997 Rev. Donald L. Eder, former communications director for the diocese, convened a committee of people involved in the newspaper business across the diocese. Various newspaper and magazine options were discussed.

That summer Mr. Patrick O'Brien was working at St. Thomas Aquinas Parish in East Lansing. He was helping Rev. J. Thomas Munley, director of seminarians for the diocese, with an ad campaign about the priesthood. Mr. O'Brien questioned where the ten ads they developed would be placed. He lamented that there was no means of communication that reached a majority of the households in the diocese. Mr. O'Brien had previously collaborated with Rev. Dwight M. Ezop on the University of St. Mary on the Lake magazine, *The Bridge*. Fr. Ezop, Fr. Munley and Mr. O'Brien developed a prototype magazine for the diocese. Mr. O'Brien suggested the name *Faith*. He felt it was imperative that the title should be concise, and leave no doubt as to the magazine's content. The *Faith* magazine prototype was presented to the committee and also to the priests at their annual Emmaus Convocation. In October 1998 the committee rejected the magazine proposal and issued a final recommendation to found a newspaper run by the Diocese.

Patrick O'Brien, Managing Editor and Creative Director of Faith magazine

Early in 1999 plans were made to institute an 8-12 page semimonthly newspaper. Rev. Charles E. Irvin was chosen editor in chief of the new diocesan newspaper, Mr. O'Brien was recommended for the position of managing editor. After Fr. Irvin contacted him, Mr. O'Brien shared with him the *Faith* magazine prototype. Fr. Irvin embraced the news-magazine format and lobbied for its acceptance. Msgr. Michael D. Murphy, who had been pastor of St. Thomas Aquinas in 1997 when the *Faith* magazine was first proposed, was now moderator of the curia. Msgr. Murphy and Fr. Irvin encouraged Bishop Mengeling to agree to this new instrument for evangelization, instruction and information. On the feast of Sts. Peter and Paul 1999, Bishop Mengeling announced the inauguration of *Faith* magazine as an official publication of the Diocese of Lansing. In July, Fr. Irvin and Mr. O'Brien assumed their posts as editor-in-chief and managing editor/creative director. In conjunction with the Great Jubilee 2000 Bishop Mengeling announced that one of the Jubilee gifts would be a one-year subscription to *Faith* magazine for every registered Catholic household in the diocese.

On December 8th, the diocesan feast day, *Faith* magazine and its web site, www.faithmag.com premiered at a press conference. The following day a reception and brief program were held in St. Mary Cathedral Hall with a capacity crowd in attendance. Mr. Bill Harris, news anchor of WJRT-ABC12 in Flint, served as Master of Ceremonies for the evening's festivities.

At the Catholic Press Association Convention in Dallas in May 2001 *Faith* magazine won six national awards: two firsts, three seconds and an honorable mention. One presenter of the convention

Monsignor Michael D. Murphy and Bishop Carl F. Mengeling at the Faith magazine launch, December 9, 1999.

described *Faith* as the only Catholic publication that could compete with the secular media.

On July 1, 2001, the team of Ezop and O'Brien was reunited. Fr. Irvin retired as editor-in-chief and he was succeeded by Fr. Ezop, one of the original collaborators on the prototype magazine developed in 1997. Fr. Irvin described his successor as "having talent, ability, vision and knowledge to guide this effort of the New Evangelization of the postmodern culture called for by Pope John Paul II."

Annus Horribilis

The year 2002 was an extremely difficult year for the Church in the United States because of highly publicized cases of sexual abuse by clergy. The horror came home to the diocese when one of our pastors resigned in January and on Good Friday had a statement read in his former parish admitting inappropriate sexual contact with a minor. On March 15th Bishop Mengeling sent a letter to over 80,000 registered households in the diocese addressing the sexual abuse issues. He stressed the policy of "zero tolerance" of abuse and the need to report abuse to civil and church authorities. At the Chrism Mass the bishop reiterated these points and emphasized the importance of following the diocesan sexual misconduct policy adopted two years previously.

The continual national focus on the issue, the large number of clergy in neighboring dioceses who were removed, and the republishing of stories about known abusers who had once served in the diocese necessitated a broad based response. The bishop's staff organized six regional prayer and dialogue sessions to address the problem of clergy sexual abuse from many viewpoints. Bishop Carl F. Mengeling was joined at each of the meetings by Msgr. Michael D. Murphy, Moderator of the Curia, who addressed canonical issues; Richard Strife, Ph.D., a psychologist and the Director of the Department of Diocesan Ministries, who addressed psychological issues; and Judge Marvin Robertson of Clinton County Probate Court, who addressed legal issues. The sessions were held at St. John the Evangelist, Jackson; St. Mary Magdalen, Brighton; Holy Redeemer, Burton; St. Elizabeth, Tecumseh; St. Mary Cathedral, Lansing and St. Francis of Assisi, Ann Arbor. Additional informational and educational sessions facilitated by Msgr. Murphy were held throughout the fall with the priests, seminarians, pastoral ministers, education personnel and pastoral coordinators around the diocese.

Bishop Mengeling at press conference addressing sexual abuse issues in 2002

In July 2002 steps were taken to establish the review board mandated by the U.S. Conference of Catholic Bishops. Throughout the year the Bishop and the curia staff spent countless hours meeting with abuse victims and those claiming to have been abused. Referrals for counseling and spiritual direction were made. All allegations were investigated and other dioceses and religious orders were contacted about accusations against their priests. The year was an extremely traumatic one for the victims and their families. It also took a tremendous toll on the faithful, the clergy and most especially the Bishop.

As a continued response to this tragedy, the diocese in conjunction with several other dioceses in Michigan, has initiated a program called Virtus to provide a safe environment for children. All clergy, lay employees and volunteers who have access to children are required to participate in the training. The first session was held August 13, 2003.

Young Adult and Singles Ministry

Mr. Gary Ashby coordinated the offices of Young Adult and Singles Ministry. Both offices sponsored retreats, conferences, and leadership development programs. The two groups have shared an annual picnic and New Years Eve Dance. In recent years the most successful young adult program has been "Theology on Tap". It is often held at Tripper's Sports Bar in Lansing, but also has been held in Ann Arbor. The semi-annual event is held in the fall and during Lent each year. A featured speaker makes a presentation and then fields questions. Many young adults have found the evenings very meaningful and have deepened their experience by celebrating the Sacrament of Penance following the presentation. The Singles Ministry has sponsored an annual ecumenical event with the First Presbyterian Church in Flint each October since 1999.

Restorative Justice

In 2002 there were approximately 125 volunteers visiting and conducting religious services for Catholic prisoners at about thirty prisons, jails and youth facilities across the diocese. Mr. Gary Ashby, who has directed the restorative justice work since 1992, initiated a pen pal program involving about seventy volunteers and prisoners. The correspondence allowed the prisoners to be supported in their faith, receive encouragement and have contact with someone outside the prison. The diocesan office has collaborated with other dioceses for nearly a decade to sponsor the "Hebrew 13:3" program, which is a day of enrichment for jail and prison ministers.

Pastoral Planning

At the Emmaus Convocation in 1998 a survey was filled out by the priests of the diocese. The results indicated a major concern about the need for planning for the future of the diocese. This planning would address concerns about staffing and the establishment and support of parishes. A day-long workshop was held for the following groups: Priests Assignment Commission, Priestly Life and Ministry Advisory Committee and the Council of Vicars. The day resulted in Bishop Mengeling agreeing to support a diocese-wide strategic planning project. The project was announced to the diocese at the Chrism Mass in 1999. Sr. Rita Wenzlick, O.P., was asked to convene members from the previously mentioned groups to develop a process. At the fall convocation for priests Bishop Mengeling announced that Sr. Rita had been appointed the first director of the Office of Pastoral Planning and the Rev. David F. Howell had been appointed the clergy chair of the Diocesan Strategic Pastoral Planning Commission. A lay chair, Mr. James Rouse from Christ the King, Flint, was later appointed to the planning commission and Ms. Sally Ellis was appointed associate director of the Pastoral Planning Office.

A broad diocese-wide grass roots consultation with the laity occurred during 2000 and 2001. The process was called VOICES. It occurred first at the parish and then at the regional level. For the VOICES process the diocese was divided into ten regions so that each region had no more than ten parishes. The parish representatives were first asked to combine their individual reports into a regional report that stated five goals. A second set of regional meetings occurred to develop strategies for implementation of the developed goals. Of the fifty goals set forth in the regional

Sr. Rita Wenzlick, O.P., Director of the Office of Pastoral Planning and Chairperson of the Department of Diocesan Ministries (Faith)

meetings, forty-nine of them were consolidated into the seven diocesan goals, which were promulgated by Bishop Mengeling at the Common Conference in November 2001. The goals were distributed at the Chrism Mass 2002. The following fall the Parish Assessment Tool (PAT) was sent to the parishes. The PAT was devised by seven task groups formed after the second set of regional meetings. The purpose of the PAT was to help parishes to first determine what was already in place that supported the mission of the church as defined in the seven diocesan goals and, then, to create action plans which would result in the complete implementation of each diocesan goal. The deadline to return the results of the PAT was set for August 1, 2003.

Presbyteral Vocations

The year 2003 was a milestone for the Diocese, as that year the first married priest, Rev. Steven D. Anderson, was ordained. Fr. Anderson had been married to his wife, Cindy, for 25 years. He was ordained a Charismatic Episcopal priest in 1995. Fr. Anderson along with his wife and three sons converted to Catholicism in April 1999. After three years of study at Sacred Heart Major Seminary in Detroit, Fr. Anderson joined Rev. John M. Fain and Rev. Jeffrey Q. Njus (also a convert to Catholicism) for their June 14, 2003 ordination.

In 1996, the year that Bishop Mengeling arrived, there were no ordinations to the priesthood. The Bishop pondered ways to encourage vocations. Bishop Mengeling began the practice of interviewing all suitable candidates for the priesthood and permanent diaconate shortly after their initial entrance into their respective programs. The Bishop's desire was to come to know those who would

The Most Rev. Carl F. Mengeling, Fourth Bishop of Lansing

join with him in serving the faithful of the Diocese of Lansing.

The Bishop read a study which indicated that 78% of priests felt that the invitation of their parish priest played an integral role in nurturing their vocation. After prayer and discernment he proposed that a program be instituted annually in which parish priests invite potential seminarians to consider a vocation to the priesthood. On August 7, 2003 the first event occurred and sixty-seven young men attended the gathering at Bethany House at DeWitt. This initial event was followed by regional gatherings and an invitation from the director of Seminarians, Rev. Gerald L. Vincke, to attend a discernment weekend.

He Must Increase

Bishop Mengeling chose as the motto for his episcopate the words of John the Baptizer "He Must Increase" (John 3:30). He has enthusiastically focused his energies on placing before the faithful of the Diocese of Lansing the person of Jesus Christ. The centrality of Jesus Christ in every activity we undertake has been repeatedly stressed in his homilies at Common Conferences, ordinations, Chrism Masses, and lay minister commissionings. Each year at Christmas he has given books on the spiritual life to clergy and diocesan staff. Bishop Mengeling has held himself accountable to his motto. His example has challenged the faithful to do likewise. His motto provides a vision of hope in which our personal relationship with Jesus the Christ increases. Imitating Our Blessed Lady's deep faith in Jesus Christ we live in joyful hope reflecting on the blessings of the past and awaiting future glory with God.

Part II

Centers of Hope

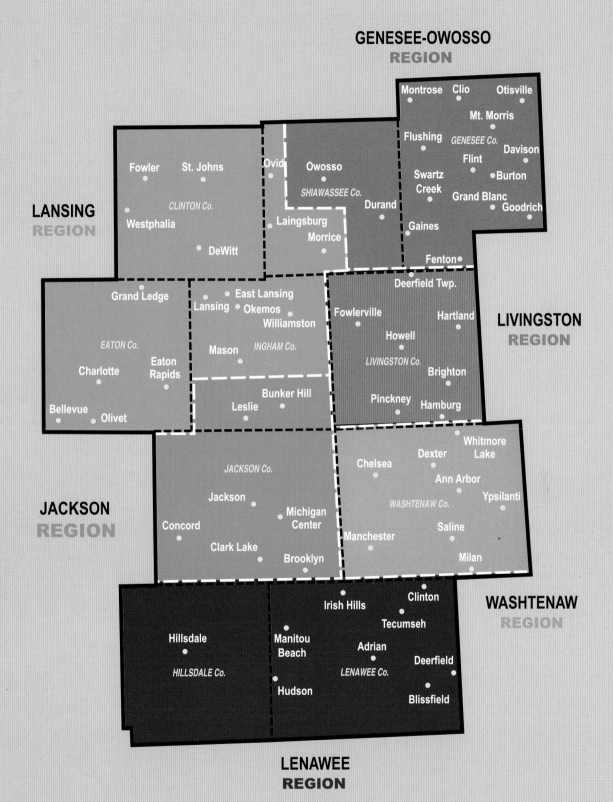

GENESEE-OWOSSO
REGION

Montrose   Clio   Otisville

Mt. Morris

Flushing   *GENESEE Co.*   Davison

Flint

Swartz   Burton
Creek

Grand Blanc   Goodrich

Gaines

Fenton

LANSING
REGION

Fowler   St. Johns   Ovid   Owosso

CLINTON Co.   *SHIAWASSEE Co.*

Durand

Westphalia   Laingsburg

Morrice

DeWitt

Deerfield Twp.

Grand Ledge   East Lansing   Fowlerville   Hartland

Lansing   Okemos

Williamston   Howell

EATON Co.   Mason   *INGHAM Co.*   *LIVINGSTON Co.*   Brighton

LIVINGSTON
REGION

Charlotte   Eaton
Rapids

Bunker Hill   Pinckney   Hamburg

Bellevue   Leslie
Olivet

Whitmore
Lake

Dexter

JACKSON Co.   Chelsea   Ann Arbor

Ypsilanti

Jackson   *WASHTENAW Co.*

JACKSON
REGION

Concord   Michigan
Center   Saline

Manchester

Clark Lake

Brooklyn   Milan

WASHTENAW
REGION

Irish Hills   Clinton

Tecumseh

Hillsdale   Manitou
Beach   Adrian

Deerfield

HILLSDALE Co.   *LENAWEE Co.*

Hudson   Blissfield

LENAWEE
REGION

95

SIENA HEIGHTS UNIVERSITY

ADRIAN

Siena Heights University evolved from St. Joseph Academy for girls, which opened in 1896. Many of the young women desired to continue their education. Mother Camilla Madden, prioress general of the Adrian Dominican congregation, also felt it would be very beneficial to have a college to educate the order's numerous sisters. This would cut back the amount of funds that were being paid to Catholic University of America and DePaul University in Chicago. Mother Camilla founded St. Joseph College in 1919. The school conferred its first bachelor's degree in 1924. To overcome the confusion between St. Joseph Academy and St. Joseph College, the name of the college was officially changed in April 1939 to Siena Heights College, in honor of the Dominican tertiary St. Catherine of Siena. This occurred during the presidency (1933–1957) of Mother Mary Gerald Barry, O.P.

A graduate school was added to the Siena Heights curriculum in 1958. Mother Gerald had laid the foundation, which Sr. Benedicta Marie Ledwidge, O.P., brought to fruition during her presidency from 1957 until 1964. The graduate school was open to both women and men. The undergraduate division remained female only until 1969.

Sr. M. Jeanine, O.P., of Studio Angelico at Siena Heights College, completes work for a convent chapel in 1959.

His Eminence, Edward Cardinal Mooney, Archbishop of Detroit, dedicated Lumen Ecclesiae Chapel and blessed Angelicus Hall in May 1957. The capacity of the chapel at its opening was 1,000. In addition to summer sessions, evening classes were offered beginning in the 1960s to better serve adult students. The last Adrian Dominican Sister to serve as president was Sr. Petronilla Francoeur, who served from 1965 until 1969. In the 1970s Siena inaugurated weekend classes and opened degree completion centers. There are now degree completion centers in Benton Harbor, Battle Creek, Jackson, Kalamazoo, Monroe and Southfield.

The college underwent its second name change in July 1998 when it became Siena Heights University. Since August 1994 Richard B. Artman has served as president of the University, which now has a student body of over 2,000.

AVE MARIA LAW SCHOOL

Ann Arbor

On April 7, 1999, pizza magnate, Thomas Monaghan announced that he was founding the Ave Maria School of Law, the 26th Catholic law school in the United States. A transition staff was put in place. Joseph L. Falvey, Jr., served as acting dean and Michael Kenney served as dean of admissions. Within one week of the announcement of the school there were applications received from 120 individuals who sought possible faculty positions. The first professor to be hired was Judge Robert Bork. By the end of June five libraries (four of them personal libraries of lawyers) had donated more than 10,000 volumes as a starting point for the new law library. Later that summer an eleven-acre site with an 84,000 square foot building was purchased and renovated. The first dean, Bernard Dobranski came on staff full time in September. He had experience as dean of the law schools at Catholic University of America and the University of Detroit Mercy. The first Ave Maria law lecture was given in November by United States Supreme Court Justice Clarence Thomas.

The school actually opened on August 21, 2000, with seventy-seven students, which was well over the goal of forty. The students were chosen from 218 applicants from forty states. The yearly tuition was $19,750. Bishop Carl F. Mengeling dedicated the St. Thomas Aquinas Chapel at the law school on November 9, 2000. Bishop Mengeling returned to the school for the Oath of Fidelity Mass on May 14, 2001.

The administration immediately set out to receive accreditation from the American Bar Association. By the time the school opened, the library held over 225,000 volumes. This was well over the requirement set in the accreditation standards. The library had seating for 281 with twenty-two computer terminals. In addition, every study table and carrel were wired for direct network access.

■ *The Law Library*

Francis Cardinal George, Archbishop of Chicago, came to Ann Arbor for the dedication of the law school building. He preached on the inextricable link between law and culture. The school's student body of 135, four justices of the State Supreme Court, Lieutenant Governor Richard Posthumus, and founder Thomas Monaghan were on hand for the dedication in April 2002.

AVE MARIA COLLEGE

*Y*PSILANTI

Ave Maria Institute was formally established on March 19, 1998. During that summer the Institute received state authorization to recruit students and offer non-degree course work. Affiliation agreements were worked out with the Franciscan University of Steubenville, Ohio, and Madonna University in Livonia, Michigan. Bishop Carl F. Mengeling celebrated the Institute's opening Mass on the Feast of the Assumption of Mary. The liturgy was held at Holy Trinity Student Chapel in Ypsilanti. At that celebration the first provost, Dr. Ronald P. Muller, and the first dean of students, Dr. Madeline Wright, took their oath of fidelity to the teaching authority of the church. After Mass a Knights of Columbus honor guard led the procession to the new Institute's campus, a few blocks away. There Bishop Mengeling blessed the building. In September the first semester of the core curriculum was taught by a faculty of five professors to forty students.

The joining of St. Mary College in Orchard Lake and Ave Maria College in Ypsilanti to create Ave Maria University came about in the year 2000. The schools maintained their separate identities but shared many resources. Nicholas Healy, Jr., became president of Ave Maria College and Dominic A. Aquila became provost. In 2001 it was announced that the college would move to Domino Farms pending zoning approval. Because of continuous obstacles placed by local authorities, the move never took place. The first graduating class comprised the seven members of the class of 2002. Bishop Mengeling was the celebrant and homilist of the Baccalaureate Mass, which was held in conjunction with commencement on May 3. Honorary degrees were awarded to Mother Mary Angelica, foundress of the Eternal Word Television Network, and to Rev. Michael Scanlon, T.O.R., chancellor of the Franciscan University of Steubenville.

Plans are now being implemented to relocate Ave Maria College to Florida within the next few years. Rev. Joseph Fessio, S.J., has been made the school's first Chancellor to fulfill this vision.

Dynamic, faith-filled campus life

Preparing students academically and spiritually for the 21st century

Joyful fidelity to Christ

Young, committed Catholics living, learning, and praying together

Integrating Faith & Reason for Life

AVE MARIA COLLEGE

Premier Catholic Liberal Arts Education

10-1 average student-to-teacher ratio

Challenging Academic Program

Modeled on Pope John Paul II's vision for Higher Education

AVE MARIA COLLEGE

BETHANY HOUSE

DeWitt

A "dream come true" is the way Bethany House has been described. The dream was that of Bishop Carl F. Mengeling. The idea took shape shortly after the shooting at Columbine High School in Colorado. In May 1999 at the State Knights of Columbus convention on Mackinac Island, Bishop Mengeling shared his dream of a retreat facility dedicated to youth with the leadership of the Lansing Councils. Everyone recognized the critical need for Christ-centered youth programs. The dialogue between Bishop Mengeling and the Knights continued.

In March 2000 Bishop Mengeling was privileged to announce that plans for a facility dedicated to the spiritual formation of youth was going to become a

reality. The Knights pledged to undertake a three million dollar fundraising program to assist in the construction of the new retreat center. Bishop Mengeling announced that the center would be named Bethany House. It was to Bethany that Jesus went for rest and renewal at the home of Martha, Mary and Lazarus. Past State Deputy Richard F. McCloy of Lansing was designated chairman of the fund raising program.

On July 6, 2000, ground was broken for a 40,000 square foot retreat facility. Rev. Gerald L. Vincke was appointed program director of Bethany House in June 2001. Deacon Richard J. Savage, business manager at St. Francis Retreat House, oversaw the five million dollar project. The new building was attached to the former Franciscan friary, which was extensively renovated as well. On September 9 an open house was held for the faithful to inspect the facility designed with the help of youth members from around the diocese. In late October the center opened.

December 8, the Diocesan feast day, was chosen as the day to bless the facility and consecrate the altar in the renovated chapel. Youth from Holy Redeemer parish in Burton were the first to use the facility.

■ *Bishop Carl Mengeling breaks ground for Bethany House with the Knights of Columbus July 6, 2000. (Faith)*

ST. FRANCIS RETREAT HOUSE

DeWITT

The gospels often describe Jesus as going to a desert place to pray. To provide such a place for prayerfully encountering God was a concern of Bishop Joseph H. Albers. The superiors of Hungarian Franciscans who served at St. Joseph Parish in Flint approached Bishop Albers to establish a new friary. These two factors combined and Bishop Albers gave permission for a retreat house and friary to be established. In 1954 the thirty-five acre Surratt property in DeWitt was purchased by the Franciscans. Sixty adjoining acres were purchased in 1967.

Rev. Julian Fuzer, O.F.M., was sent as the first provincial superior of the DeWitt friary and Fr. Maximus Mandl, O.F.M., was appointed the first retreat master. The retreat house was named the Portiuncula in the Pines. Bishop Albers blessed the finished retreat house on October 9, 1955. The complex was able to accommodate thirty-four retreatants. The first retreat was given in November. The old Surratt home served as the friary until a friary was built and dedicated in September 1960. The twenty-fifth anniversary of the retreat house was observed with a series of events in 1980.

In January 1989 the Diocese of Lansing took possession of the retreat house, which had been purchased from the Franciscans the previous fall. Rev. Lawrence P. DeLaney was appointed the first diocesan director. The following fall Sr. Suzanne Eichorn, O.P., accepted the position of associate director. The new leadership expanded the programming to include: AA retreats for men and women; singles retreats; Retrouvaille retreats for troubled marriages; and the annual Mother/Daughter retreat on Mother's Day weekend.

In September 1994 the Dominican Center for Religious Development and the retreat center began offering a two-year internship in spiritual direction. This program has trained many individuals to help others in their search for God.

The tree-lined Stations of the Cross are part of the Retreat Center's heritage and four-season beauty.

The Retreat Center bookstore offers a wealth of fine books, music, and gifts. (Faith)

CATHOLIC OUTREACH

FLINT

Flint Catholic Outreach

Sr. Claudia Burke, S.F.P., has often been called the Mother Theresa of Genesee County. In January 1977 Sr. Claudia, a Franciscan Sister of the Poor, founded Catholic Outreach. The purpose of Catholic Outreach is to assist families in time of emergency crisis. Catholic Outreach seeks to help with emergency financial aid. When individuals or families receive eviction notices because they can't pay their rent or shut off notices for electricity or water, they come to Catholic Outreach. There is a three member staff that interviews clients to assess their needs and respond as best they can.

The food pantry at 509 North Grand Traverse sees to the needs of the hungry. It is also the place where client interviews occur. A diaper program assists mothers of new borns with food and diapers on a monthly basis. The St. Christopher transportation program now has three full time vehicles. The program focuses on children who require medical attention not available in Genesee County. Children under twelve needing dialysis currently have to go elsewhere. About 600 children a year are helped through the St. Christopher program.

The programs are funded through donations from individuals, Protestant and Catholic Church groups, civic organizations, and state and federal grants. Catholic Outreach has been a recipient of funds from Genesee County Lenten Appeal for many years. In 1997 the agency relied on bingo six nights a week for

Food Pantry at Outreach East

seventy-seven percent of its budget. The agency has often had to close for two weeks at a time until more funds come in to pay the debts and start again.

In 1987 Sr. Claudia founded a branch, which is now known as Outreach East in Davison. Now an independent agency, Outreach East serves the M-15 corridor from Otter Lake to Goodrich. Sr. Rita Berby, S.S.J., has served as director since July 1994.

Sr. Claudia and Sr. Rita seek to bring the Good News by reaching out to those St. Matthew describes in his gospel as the "least of my brethren".

Sister Claudia Burke, S.F.P., Founder and Director of Catholic Outreach

CRISTO REY COMMUNITY CENTER

𝓛ANSING

The beginnings of the Cristo Rey Community Center are closely intertwined with the founding of Cristo Rey Parish in October 1961. The social services agency can be traced to the establishment of the Cristo Rey Legal Aid Clinic in the fall of 1962. The building of the I-496 expressway claimed the first Cristo Rey site and necessitated a move. The Cristo Rey Community Center at 1314 Ballard in North Lansing became a reality in 1968. Rev. Kenneth Faiver was the pastor at the time and Benjamin Kennedy was named the first director of social services programs. There

◼ *The Chapel*

were three programs - Direct Assistance, Health Services and Legal Aid - and three staff people at the time. The following year Mr. Kennedy was replaced by Antonio Benavides. Mr. Benavides served as director for over thirty years before becoming mayor of Lansing. The Center on Ballard Street strove to meet the spiritual and social needs of the Spanish-speaking and of the North Lansing neighborhood. In 1973 the Community Center became a United Way Agency but continues to also be supported by the Diocese of Lansing.

The Ballard Street chapel became too small for the parish and in 1978 a new site on South Washington was purchased. The social services side of Cristo Rey expanded into the available space. Soon that, too, was not enough to provide for growing programs. For example, the Community Kitchen began in January 1983. The same year an agreement was reached with

the Lansing Food Bank to provide foodstuffs for the Direct Assistance program. In the summer of 1987 Cristo Rey Community Center moved into the former High Street Elementary School. By its twentieth anniversary the agency sponsored ten different programs. By its twenty-fifth anniversary in 1993 there were fifteen different programs including adult learning, health services, after school care, substance abuse counseling, community kitchen, self esteem workshops, direct emergency assistance and employment training. Its budget was $1.5 million.

In 1991 and 2000, major capital fund drives were held to update the facilities to enhance the providing of services. In May 2002 Bishop Carl F. Mengeling blessed the new 2,800 square foot addition. The new medical clinic facilities included ten exam rooms, two treatment rooms, a laboratory, a nurse's station, five offices, a break room and a medical supply closet.

◼ *The Health Center*

ST. JOSEPH

ADRIAN

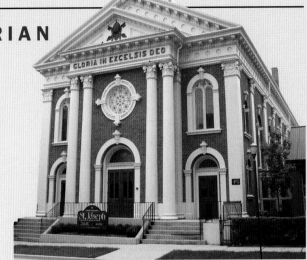

"Dutch Hill" (probably a corruption of Deutsch) in Adrian had a thriving German community by the 1850s. By 1860 there were about 50 Catholic families and in April 1862 they petitioned Bishop Lefevere in Detroit for a German congregation separate from the Irish one organized in 1852. The German Catholic Society began to meet and gather funds. Bishop Lefevere assigned their care to the German Redemptorists at St. Mary Parish in Detroit in 1863. A frame school was built and opened that year.

■ *First Communion, May 29, 1910*

With the appointment of Rev. John G. Ehrenstrasser, C.SS.R., as pastor on July 8, 1865, the German-speaking Catholics achieved parochial status. While Rev. Anthony Kullman was pastor (1872-1875) eight acres on Oakwood Road were purchased for a cemetery.

Rev. P. Casimir Rohowski, C.PP.S., was a great builder. During his pastorate, 1876-1889, the present rectory, church and a school (the present activities center) were built. At the request of Fr. Rohowski the Dominican Sisters came in 1880 to teach in the school.

Rev. Frederick W. Schaepen, C.PP.S., a native son of the parish, shepherded St. Joseph parish from March 1903 until July 1915. The

school financing was changed by Fr. Schaepen from tuition to a monthly collection envelope. The parish golden jubilee was celebrated October 12, 1913, with a Mass at which Bishop Edward D. Kelly presided.

St. Joseph High School was opened in 1924 during the pastorate (1923-1951) of Rev. Anthony C. Schneider. Establishing a library and upgrading the facility to house the high school taxed an already tight budget. Fr. Schneider served as a fulltime teacher in the new high school to save money. The high school closed in 1945.

From 1947 till 1961 and since 1985 there has been a Guadalupe Society at St. Joseph. The society celebrated the Hispanic culture and sought to address their specific needs.

Rev. Harold E. Wolf was pastor when the parish celebrated its centennial in 1963. For the 125th anniversary in 1988 Rev. Francis E. Williams was pastor of the parish. The 1884 school was renovated and dedicated as an activities center in June 1992. The renovation of the church and building of a magnificent baptistery were completed during the pastorate of Rev. James W. Lothamer, S.S. The building renovations are complete but the renewal of the Spirit among the parishioners is ongoing under the leadership of Rev. Craig G. Carolan.

ST. MARY OF GOOD COUNSEL

Adrian

The Catholic community in Monroe was the source of evangelization in Lenawee County. It was to Monroe in 1843 that Patrick Stanton went on a handcar to bring a priest back to Adrian to administer the sacraments to his ailing wife. In August 1844 the Redemptorist Congregation committed themselves to St. Anthony (later St. Mary) parish for a period of 360 years, but they remained only until 1855. In 1846 Rev. Simon Saenderl, C.SS.R., went on a missionary journey to Lenawee County to conduct a census of Catholics. Adrian was found to have enough to warrant a quarterly visit. Under the direction of Rev. Aegidius Smulders, C.SS.R., a frame church was built on the corner of Erie and Center Streets and dedicated to the Immaculate Conception. Rev. Peter Joseph Kindekins was appointed first resident pastor in 1852.

Rev. Kindekins opened the first school in 1855. When it was felt sisters should teach in the school it was again to Monroe the St. Mary Catholics turned. The Sister Servants of the Immaculate Heart of Mary staffed the school from 1863–1864 and 1867-1877. When fire destroyed the church and school, the operation of the school was disrupted. The "Wigwam Cathedral" was erected as a temporary church.

One of the leading church architects of the day, Gordon Lloyd, was engaged by Rev. Ernest Van Dyke to design a new

■ *Fr. Tom Helfrich and his liturgical ministers enter for the 11:45 Sunday bilingual Mass.*

church. The present Romanesque church was dedicated Thanksgiving Day 1871 by Bishop Casper H. Borgess.

The Adrian Dominicans staffed the parish school for ninety years beginning in August 1879. A new school was built in 1913, and a high school begun in 1929. The first graduates were the Class of 1933. In 1952 St. Mary's and St. Joseph High Schools merged. Adrian Catholic Central was later formed and remained open until 1968.

Hispanics became an integral part of the parish during the pastorate of Rev. William J. Carolin (1967–1977). When the parish school was demolished in 1982 to make way for the new activities center, the chapel in the center was dedicated to Our Lady of Guadalupe. Mass is celebrated in Spanish as well as English.

■ *St. Mary High School Youth Group*

Since 1977 the pastoral care of the parish has been entrusted to the Oblates of St. Francis de Sales. The first Oblate pastor was Rev. Louis A. Komorowski, O.S.F.S., (1977–1984 and 1991–1997) and the present is Rev. Thomas J. Helfrich, O.S.F.S.

CHRIST THE KING

ANN ARBOR

The origins of Christ the King parish are to be found in the origins of the charismatic community in Ann Arbor.

Four young Catholic men, Steve Clark, Ralph Martin, Jim Cavnar and Gerald Rauch, came to Ann Arbor in 1967 to work on an informal basis at St. Mary's Student Chapel as campus ministers. All four had been active members of the Cursillo movement. In their search for a deeper relationship with God, they found themselves in a new renewal movement, the charismatic.

The prayer meetings, first held in the young men's apartments, attracted so many that they were later held at St. Mary or St. Thomas parish facilities. Much growth necessitated a formal organization and the name "The Word of God" was adopted for this ecumenical group.

Originally the Word of God members retained membership in their local parishes in Ann Arbor and Ypsilanti. As more and more members married and had families, it became obvious that the advantages which a parish provided were desired.

The Coordinators of the Word of God began to deal seriously with this issue in 1976. Rev. Robert D. Lunsford, the bishop's liaison to the Word of God Community helped develop a Catholic "fellowship" within the community.

The Catholic Fellowship of the Word of God was constituted as an official association in the diocese of Lansing in January 1979. On Pentecost Sunday 1981, the over 800-member Catholic Fellowship began. Rev. Frank Mc Grath served as chaplain from 1981-1993. On Pentecost in 1986 the group received a new name and status – The Christ the King Catholic Association. Under its statutes the presiding lay coordinators were the heads of the Word of God community.

On the Feast of Christ the King, November 24, 1991, Bishop Povish announced a further step in Christ the King parish being created. All formal ties between Christ the King and the Word of God Community were severed. The Association was restructured as the Christ the King Catholic Center. On November 16, 1997, Rev. Edward O. Fride was installed as the first pastor of Christ the King Parish. The personal parish (rather than territorial) had 350 families at the time of its creation, September 9, 1997.

Ground was broken for a church on January 22, 2000, with the dedication held in June 2001. On October 1, 2001, a perpetual adoration chapel was opened in the new church.

ST. FRANCIS OF ASSISI

ANN ARBOR

The parish grew rapidly and an assistant was assigned to St. Francis in December 1955.

Rev. Francis P. Screbernak arrived in 1959 and quickly set out to enlarge the school and build a permanent church. John Cardinal Dearden of Detroit dedicated the present structure on March 29, 1969. An activities building was constructed during the pastorate (1976–1987) of Rev. Raymond M. Rademacher. Further development was highlighted in the pastorate (1987–1997) of Rev. Charles E. Irvin when in December 1994 a new Létourneau organ, school addition and renovated gymnasium were dedicated.

The Great Jubilee 2000 in the universal church coincided with St. Francis parish's golden jubilee. The parish fiftieth anniversary celebration was observed in October. A University of North Carolina study found St. Francis Parish to be among the best 360 Catholic parishes in the nation. The report was released in November 2001 during the pastorate of Rev. James G. McDougall.

The postwar boom was the impetus for the founding of St. Francis of Assisi Parish. In December of 1945, Msgr. G. Warren Peek, pastor of St. Thomas Ann Arbor arranged for the purchase of eight acres of the Tuomy farm on East Stadium Boulevard for a future parish. The Tuomys donated another two acres. Sunday Mass was first offered by religious order priests at the Pittsfield School in 1947. A European trained Sacred Heart Seminary professor, Rev. Leon O. Kennedy, was assigned as the first resident pastor in June 1950. Before the end of the year a rectory with a daily Mass chapel had been built.

Children's Christmas Concert, 2001

The first Mass in the original church was held Easter Sunday, 1951. The school opened in the fall of 1952. For many years the Adrian Dominican Sisters staffed the school. The original church soon was converted to classrooms when a new gymnasium-auditorium was built as the second church.

Celebrating new life

ST. MARY STUDENT PARISH

ANN ARBOR

The Catholic connection with the University of Michigan has its origins in 1817 when the University was founded in Detroit. The cofounders were the Rev. John Montieth, a Presbyterian minister, and the saintly Rev. Gabriel Richard who, until his death during the cholera epidemic in 1832, was the pastor of St. Anne Parish in Detroit.

Catholics at the University were ministered to by St. Thomas Parish, which was begun in 1835. After an 1889 visit from Bishop John S. Foley of Detroit to Ann Arbor, the Foley Guild for Catholic Students at the University was organized. The Auxiliary Bishop of Detroit, Edward D. Kelly (who was also pastor of St. Thomas) arranged for the appointment in 1914 of a priest, Rev. Michael P. Bourke, to work solely with university students. A facility was purchased in 1915 and became independent of St. Thomas parish in 1919. The present church was dedicated to the Immaculate Conception in 1925.

Following Fr. Bourke's death in 1928 the chapel reverted to being a mission of St. Thomas. Rev. (later Bishop) Allen J. Babcock was the assistant in charge from 1928– 1936. During this time the site for the Richard Center was acquired. Fr. Babcock laid the foundation for the Newman Club Chapter to be established.

The building of the Richard Center occurred during the pastorate (1942–1956) of Rev. Frank J. McPhillips. Fr. McPhillips was an avid supporter of the Newman movement and had been appointed national chaplain in 1946. The Richard Center was dedicated November 22, 1953.

■ *The University of Michigan Catholic Student Club Annual Ball, 1912*

The pastorates of Rev. John F. Bradley (1956–1967) and Rev. Charles E. Irvin (1968–1979) saw the changes and implementation of the Second Vatican Council. Folk liturgies, a weekly midnight mass, a chapel constitution, classes in the foundation of Catholic Doctrine and the beginning of the charismatic movement in Ann Arbor were all events which took place at St. Mary after the Council.

The pastorate of Rev. William J. Stevenson was one of renewal. The church and Gabriel Richard Newman Center were rededicated by Bishop Kenneth J. Povish on October 29, 1995. Rev. Thomas M. Firestone has led this very vibrant community since 1997. Since his arrival St. Mary Student Parish celebrated their 75th anniversary with a yearlong celebration from December 8, 1998, to December 8, 1999.

ST. PATRICK

ANN ARBOR (WHITMORE LAKE)

The first parish in the State of Michigan where the primary language was English is located in Northfield Township and was begun in 1831. Fr. Gabriel Richard sent Rev. Patrick O'Kelly from St. Anne's in Detroit to minister to scattered Irish Catholics in Washtenaw and Livingston counties. A log church was constructed in the spring of 1831 where St. Patrick rectory now stands. In September eighty acres of land were purchased for one hundred dollars cash. Fr. O'Kelly stayed in Northfield until 1835 when he moved to Ann Arbor. Fr. O'Kelly's successor, Fr. Thomas Morrissey, ministered to several groups of Catholics in Livingston County from his base at the log church. In 1837 a frame church was built in the present cemetery and dedicated to St. Bridget. St. Bridget's was enlarged in 1850.

After a lapse of almost twenty-five years a resident pastor, Rev. Peter Wallace, came to St. Bridget's on January 1, 1864. St. Bridget's had been attended from St. Thomas Ann Arbor since 1840. Rev. J. Joseph Van Waterschoot, pastor from 1874 until 1884, recognized that a new church was in order. To raise funds he promised the Germans it would be dedicated to St. Joseph if they raised the most money and to the Irish he promised a dedication to St. Patrick. The Irish must have raised most of the $10,000 cost because Bishop Caspar H. Borgess of Detroit dedicated the edifice to St. Patrick on October 30, 1878.

During Rev. Louis P. Goldrick's pastorate (1889– 1924), a new rectory was built in 1890. Both the rectory and the church had to be repaired after a cyclone in 1917. The parish picnics were an important source of financial support. During the early part of Fr. Goldrick's tenure, the festivals were held at Whitmore Lake on the Fourth of July. Later the picnics were held Labor Day Weekend.

Victorian holy water font

Old St. Patrick Cemetery (By Christine Jones/Faith)

While Rev. Patrick A. Jackson was pastor (1971–1980) the centennial of the parish church in 1977 was observed by building a parish center. Tragedy by tornado struck the Labor Day festival in 1980 and the parish center was destroyed. Fortunately no one was hurt. The parish center was rebuilt and used for the parish Sesquicentennial celebrations on May 24, 1981. This was during Rev. Joseph A. Immel's pastorate. Since June 1994 Rev. Terrence J. Dumas has pastored this historic Catholic faith community.

Old St. Patrick Church, built in 1878

ST. THOMAS THE APOSTLE

ANN ARBOR

The pioneer priest to Washtenaw, Livingston and Ingham counties, Rev. Patrick O'Kelly first visited Ann Arbor in 1831 when he moved to Northfield Township. He moved from Northfield in July 1835 and placed a notice in the Ann Arbor paper that he would be holding regular services in "Mr. Harrigan's large room". Fr. O'Kelly left Ann Arbor early in 1839 for Milwaukee, Wisconsin.

During Rev. Thomas Cullen's pastorate (1840–1862) the first St. Thomas church was built (1842–1845) and the parish cemetery begun (1843).

■ *Church dedicated in 1899*

At the age of 28, Rev. Henri Delbaere began his pastorate (1866–1872), a very significant one for St. Thomas. In 1868, Fr. Delbaere applied to the motherhouse in Monroe for sisters to begin a Catholic school. They arrived on September 1 to find neither a permanent convent nor school, but with great faith and a deep desire to pass it on. The old Fourth Ward public school was purchased on September 21, but a convent was not bought until the next year.

The old Fourth Ward school building on Kingsley Street became inadequate. Rev. William J. Fierle (1878-1891) spent most of his energy purchasing land, building and paying for a new school and convent. The new school opened in 1886 and the first class of three students graduated in 1887.

A golden era occurred at St. Thomas during the pastorate of Bishop Edward D. Kelly. Fr. Kelly came from Dexter in 1891 and left Ann Arbor in 1919 as the Bishop of Grand Rapids. The parish bulged and the pastor built a new hall (1891), a new church (1897–99), a

new rectory (1902) and a new convent (1911). In 1911 he became auxiliary bishop of Detroit.

Monsignor G. Warren Peek's pastorate lasted almost thirty years. He had a tremendous memory for names and could call almost any child in the school by his or her first name.

The struggle to keep the high school ended with its closing in 1977. During Monsignor Robert O. Lunsford's pastorate the parish celebrated its sesquicentennial on July 14, 1985. Rev. Timothy M. Crowley was pastor in 1993 when the sanctuary was renovated and new restrooms and bridal room were added to the church. Rev. Roger L. Prokop has pastored the St. Thomas community since 1993. He presided over the 1998-99 year-long centennial celebrating the dedication of the present church.

■ *A block party was held to celebrate the 100th anniversary of the present church.*

ST. ANN

*B*ELLEVUE

Bishop Mengeling joined the congregation in celebrating the 75th anniversary in 1999

It was the request of two devout Catholics on their wedding day that brought about the first Mass in Bellevue in the log cabin of Mr. and Mrs. James Sharkey. The Sharkeys had to travel to Marshall early in 1855 to find a priest to marry them. They then prevailed upon Rev. James Hennessey to come to their home in Bellevue. Fr. Hennessey's transfer to Detroit in May 1855 brought the regular visits to a halt.

It seems that the Marshall pastors cared for Bellevue until St. Philip's in Battle Creek became a parish in 1869. While Rev. John Linskey was the assistant at St. Philip's from 1904 until 1909, he began monthly visits to Bellevue. Mass was celebrated in the Dyer Opera House (on which site later stood the Lothamer Market).

The monthly visits were continued by the following St. Philip assistants: Rev. Raymond T. Fleming (1909–1913); Rev. Maurice Walsh (1913–1916); Rev. William J. Flanagan (1916–1917); and Rev. Frank J. McQuillan (1917–1918).

In 1919, the connection between Bellevue and Charlotte was forged. On August 16, 1918, Rev. Peter J. Jordan had been appointed the first pastor of Charlotte. Fr. Jordan came to Bellevue twice a month for Mass.

His successor was Rev. John M. Duffy. With twenty-five families, on a lot donated by the Sharkeys and Lennons, they received permission from Bishop Gallagher in 1923 to build a $5,000 wood structure. On March 4, 1924, about 200 people attended the dedication of St. Ann Church.

In 1965, the parish house was bought. It had been the home of William Lennon and Mass had been held there monthly from about 1915 until 1921. The ordination to the priesthood of James Lothamer in June 1968 was the first for the parish family. The church basement was finished off and the church redecorated in the 1970s.

In 1970 St. Ann elected its first parish council. The first chair was James E. Mathias. On July 22, 1973, he became the first layperson to distribute Holy Communion in the parish. On June 13, 1981, Mathias was ordained a permanent deacon. He served the parish in that capacity for many years.

In 1995 St. Ann was designated a quasi parish with Rev. Steven J. Raica as the pastor. Since 1997 priests from Immaculate Heart in Lansing and Resurrection in Lansing have provided the sacraments for the Bellevue community. Msgr. Raymond Goehring currently serves as administrator of St. Ann.

ST. PETER THE APOSTLE

*B*LISSFIELD

The parish at Blissfield first celebrated the Eucharist together on January 10, 1910, in the home of Julia Plunkett. Rev. Clement T. B. Krebes of Clinton celebrated the liturgy on a square rosewood piano, which served as the altar.

During 1910-11 and 1915-16, Clinton was the parish which had charge of the Blissfield mission. Blissfield was counted among the St. Mary missions of Manchester the rest of the time until 1917.

Rev. Edwin A. Fisher served as pastor of Manchester (1909–1917). During that time he oversaw the construction of several

the community for nearly twenty years, Fr. Philbin was appointed the first resident pastor in 1933.

A parish credit union was begun in 1959 with thirteen parishioners each giving $100. In April 1971 ground was broken for a hall, which was completed in September. The first parish event in the new hall was the annual chicken dinner. (The chicken dinners were first held in 1910 to begin raising funds for the first church). The parish had a splendid celebration of its 75th anniversary in 1985 while Rev. Carl A. Simon was pastor.

More recently, in 1992, the church basement was completely renovated for meetings and religious education class use. For the Great Jubilee 2000 the parish renovated the church, restoring the statues to the sanctuary and refurbishing the pews. A last element was the new lighting system installed in 2002. Since June 2000 Rev. Vincent H. Van Doan has led the congregation.

■ Epiphany Ethnic Potluck, January 7, 1990

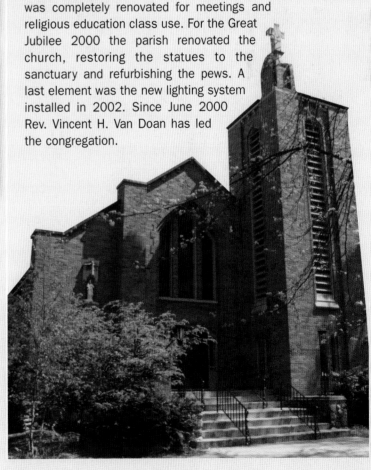

cobblestone churches. At Blissfield, Fr. Fisher had the local families take their horses and wagons and draw stones from as far away as the Irish Hills (another part of the Manchester missions at the time). The cobblestone church was dedicated November 28, 1912, Thanksgiving Day. This structure was destroyed by fire Pentecost Sunday 1927. Bishop Michael J. Gallagher dedicated the second church August 5, 1928.

The pastoral care of the St. Peter congregation was entrusted to the chaplains of St. Joseph Academy in Adrian in 1917. It was while serving there that Rev. Anthony F. Philbin first came to Blissfield. After serving

ST. MARY MAGDALEN

BRIGHTON

The significant population growth in Livingston County necessitated the founding of a new parish in Brighton Township. On March 18, 1993, the Diocese closed on the purchase of twenty acres of land on Old US 23. On June 29, 1993, the parish known as the "New Catholic Community of Brighton", or NCCB for short, was formally established by Bishop Kenneth J. Povish. Rev. David F. Howell was sent as the founding pastor. At first he resided at the St. John Hartland rectory. He helped out there and at St. Patrick in Brighton. A list of Catholics in Brighton Township was compiled and Fr. Howell met these people in small groups, seeking their vision of the new parish. He took notes on the comments of over 400 people. The first Eucharistic celebration of the new community was held November 28 in the Farms Middle School in Brighton Township. Later two groups were asked to draft vision statements from Fr. Howell's notes. After review these were merged into one statement. The revised vision statement is still presented to each person who seeks to register. They are asked to agree to make that vision a reality and sign the statement as part of registering.

In July 1994 Marilyn Pence became the first pastoral minister in the parish and Kay Thurmon became the first secretary/bookkeeper. The religious education program began under the direction of Sr. Marietta Churches, O.P., in September 1994. The same month, on the Feast of the Triumph of the Cross, the daily Mass chapel opened in the former garage of the parish house on Old US 23. Bishop Povish confirmed the

selection of St. Mary Magdalen as the patron saint of the NCCB, which had about 375 registered families.

In February 1995 the parish newsletter "The Visionary" made its first appearance. The following June the first twelve member pastoral council was chosen by lot from sixteen nominated. In August 1995 Harry David Scharf and in May 2003 James Maurice Chevalier were ordained to the permanent diaconate. Their wives Judith and Linda support their service to the parish.

■ *The flame of faith*

The groundbreaking for the church was held in conjunction with the third annual parish picnic and ice cream social on September 8, 1996. Bishop Carl F. Mengeling dedicated it on June 28, 1998. That fall a parish Knights of Columbus Council and Ladies Auxiliary were organized. Fr. Howell continues to guide the parish community.

■ *Children gather for the Journey with Jesus Bug Safari during summer Vacation Bible School in 2002.*

ST. PATRICK

*B*RIGHTON

The origins of the Catholic community in Brighton go back to the 1831 visit of Rev. Patrick O'Kelly to Green Oak Township. A structure was begun in that year but its fate is now unknown. In 1838 Rev. Thomas Morrissey of St. Bridget at Northfield directed the building of a log church in Green Oak. The Old Irish Cemetery there still remains. Fr. O'Kelly then returned as pastor of Livingston County from 1843 to 1856. The Green Oak Mission dwindled after his departure and finally closed in 1875.

An acre of land was purchased in Brighton in March 1861 under the direction of Rev. Francis X. Pourret from Holland. The first subscription to build a church was taken in December 1862 and amounted to $17.50. The cornerstone was laid in 1864. After being attached to the parishes at Hartland, Deerfield and then Fenton, Brighton was assigned its first resident pastor, Rev. James Wheeler, on September 1, 1876. The rectory built that year was destroyed by fire in October 1916. Much of the parish's early history went up in smoke.

In 1946, while Rev. Maurice Kissane was pastor, the old public high school was purchased. The services of the Adrian Dominican Sisters were secured to staff the school that had opened in 1947. The last Dominican principal, Sr. Mary Margaret Pachucki, left in 1986. The parish has maintained a strong Catholic school tradition with an enrollment in the fall of 2002 of 266 children in grades one to eight.

While Rev. Leo McCann served Brighton (1949–1971) the parish took on a new look. The present school was built in 1951, a new church and rectory were built in 1961, and a new convent in 1963. Bishop Joseph H. Albers blessed the new church on May 13, 1962.

Upon Fr. McCann's death in October 1971, Rev. Michael D. Murphy, the associate pastor, became the administrator. He later

■ *First church, begun in 1864*

returned as pastor from 1977–1985, when new offices and a multi-purpose building were constructed.

Rev. Thomas W. Thompson pastored St. Patrick's from 1985–1999. The enlargement and renovation of the church were necessitated by substantial growth in the area. Bishop Kenneth J. Povish dedicated the new worship space on September 22, 1991. Since 1999, Rev. Dan J. McKean has pastored St. Patrick's, which has remained the largest parish in the Diocese for the last decade. The registration in the fall of 2002 was 3,923 households.

ST. JOSEPH SHRINE

BROOKLYN (IRISH HILLS)

The first step in organizing a parish in the Irish Hills was the deeding of an acre and a half of land to Bishop Peter Paul Lefevere on October 14, 1851. The Metropolitan Catholic Almanac from 1852 recorded that the area known as Springville was visited once a year by the Redemptorists of Monroe.

The pastoral care of St. Joseph parish was later given to Hillsdale (1879–1890) and Manchester (1890– 1944). Rev. John R. Hackett was pastor at Manchester 1917 to 1921 when Mass began to be celebrated every Sunday during the summer months at St. Josephs.

The Irish immigrants struggled to clear the land, survive the many hardships of pioneer life and nurture a faith community. This was facilitated in 1853 when the first resident pastor, Rev. Peter Kindekins, was appointed in Adrian. The pastor of Adrian supervised the growth of St. Joseph Parish for a decade.

St. Joseph Parish was completely made over during Rev. Joseph V. Pfeffer's pastorate (1924–1938). The church was enlarged, taking the shape of a cross. The outdoor Stations of the Cross were begun in 1931. Succeeding pastors brought Fr. Pfeffer's work to completion.

Construction of a church was begun in 1854 but it was not used for Mass until late 1863. Rev. Edward Van Lauwe had been appointed pastor of the new Clinton Parish on November 14, 1863, and he celebrated the first liturgy in the St. Joseph Church.

Part of the shrine's original Way of the Cross

On June 25, 1954, Rev. Henry T. Hengehold was appointed the first resident pastor. His appointment necessitated the building of a rectory.

For over a century the St. Joseph community remained a mission attached to various parishes. When Clinton lost its parochial status in 1873 the newly appointed pastor of St. Mary Adrian, Rev. Peter Wallace, took charge. St. Joseph (then known as Cambridge) became a mission of the newly formed parish in Freedom Township in 1874.

A parish hall was built during Rev. James Fitzgerald's pastorate (1965–1975). A storage area was added during Rev. William McKeon's pastorate (1975–1982). While Rev. Edward F. O'Grady was pastor (1988–1991) the parish was listed on the state register of historic sites and a marker was unveiled on September 14, 1991. Rev. Carl A. Simon has led the St. Joseph congregation since 1999. The parish looks forward to its sesquicentennial in 2004.

BLESSED SACRAMENT

BURTON

While the rest of the State was preoccupied with the opening of the Mackinac Bridge in 1957, the Catholics in Flint were more excited by the founding of three new parishes: Our Lady of Guadalupe, St. Leo the Great and Blessed Sacrament.

A census had been taken in 1955 of the Lapeer Heights area of Holy Redeemer parish and eighty acres of land was purchased in June 1956. On June 20, 1959, the parish of the Most Blessed Sacrament was created. The first pastor, Rev. Howard J. Noeker, was appointed six days later. A home for Fr. Noeker was purchased in August. The Bentley Community School was the site of the new congregation's first Mass. Daily Mass began being held in the rectory in October. Confraternity of Christian Doctrine classes were begun that month and were taught by Oxford Dominican Sisters for a period of two years.

■ *The First Annual American Hungarian Ethnic Festival, 1978. Rev. Matthew Kiss, O.F.M., compares notes with Harry Martinbianco, chairman, while Patricia Jurasek looks on. Standing, in Hungarian costume, are James and Eva Puppan.*

■ *Judy LaBeau welcomes Rev. Joseph Kim at his installation as pastor of Blessed Sacrament Church, 2000.*

During the pastorate of Rev. Matthew Kiss, O.F.M. (1975–1984), Blessed Sacrament became well known for its Hungarian Festival. The 25th anniversary of the church was celebrated on Easter 1983 with a special liturgy presided over by Bishop Kenneth J. Povish. Rev. Phillip Schweda, O.F.M., who was the associate pastor, succeeded Fr. Kiss as pastor.

Rev. Denis R. Spitzley pastored Blessed Sacrament parish from 1994 to 2000. Fr. Spitzley is well known for his devotion to Blessed Pauline Von Mallinckrodt. A Mother Pauline Guild meets monthly at Blessed Sacrament. Since June 2000 Rev. Joseph Sy Kim has led the Blessed Sacrament congregation.

Ground was broken for a church/gymnasium and six classrooms in June 1958. The church was first used on the following Easter Sunday. Bishop Joseph H. Albers dedicated the complex in May 1959.

The school opened in the fall of 1959 with 120 children in three grades. The Dominican Sisters from Adrian staffed the school from its opening until its closing in 1970. Adrian Dominicans continued to serve in the parish for several years in the religious education program.

Upon Fr. Noeker's transfer in 1972, the parish was entrusted to the care of the Hungarian Franciscans. In 1973 St. Joseph Hungarian Parish was merged with Blessed Sacrament Parish. Rev. Albin Thum, O.F.M., who had served St. Joseph's since 1967, became pastor of Blessed Sacrament.

One of the parish organizations that came from St. Joseph Parish was the Secular Franciscans, which are still a very active part of Blessed Sacrament Parish.

■ *First Mass, Easter, 1959*

HOLY REDEEMER

BURTON

In September 1938 some of the families in the south end of St. Matthew's parish organized a census in that area to ascertain if there were enough Catholics there to form a new parish. The results indicated some 300 Catholic families were located in the area. Genesee County had become a part of the Diocese of Lansing in May 1938, so it was to Bishop Joseph H. Albers that a petition for a new parish was addressed. Bishop Albers commissioned his own survey in June 1940. Ten acres of land were purchased and on September 7, 1940, the parish of Holy Redeemer was inaugurated. Rev. Louis P. Gauthier was assigned as founding pastor. The first mass was held in the Burton Theatre on Saginaw Street on September 22. The following year a temporary church-hall was constructed. Once the War in Europe was over, plans were made to start building a school, convent and rectory. The rectory and convent were built by men laid off and hired to work for $1.00 an hour.

In September 1946 the Sisters of The Holy Cross from Notre Dame, Indiana, opened the parish school for 410 children. The school blossomed. A high school addition was completed in 1950 and a new grade school was built in 1956.

The death of Fr. Gauthier on Passion Sunday 1957 brought Rev. John A. Blasko to Redeemer. Fr. Blasko, during his three years at Redeemer, turned Fr. Gauthier's dream of a new church into a reality. The present church was built, but the dedication occurred after Fr. Blasko's death in January 1960.

The pastorate of Rev. Raphael R. Dunigan (1960–1969) saw the dedication of the new church in September 1960, the present convent built in 1966 and the present rectory built in 1967.

The pastorate of Rev. Sylvester L. Fedewa (1970–1988) saw the parish continue to grow and remain one of the largest in Genesee County. Stained glass windows were installed in the church between 1982 and 1984. The sanctuary was totally redecorated in 1985 and 1986.

■ *Bingo*

■ *(By Dean Peterson/Faith)*

During the pastorate of Rev. Vincent A. DeLorenzo (1988–2003) the parish celebrated its 50th anniversary and on January 1, 1993, the Perpetual Adoration Chapel opened in the old daily Mass chapel. People from all around Flint come to pray. A Family Life Center was dedicated in February 1997. Rev. William F. Wegher assumed the helm of Holy Redeemer in June 2002.

■ *Rev. Gauthier leads a procession of busses at the end of the school day (c. 1950).*

116

St. Mary

Charlotte

Charlotte became a station of the newly created parish in Marshall in 1852. The first recorded Mass celebration in Charlotte occurred in the Patrick and Mary McDonald home in 1859. The couple had recently moved from Marshall and they prevailed upon their pastor, Rev. Peter C. Koopmans, to come to Charlotte. Two lots were bought and a frame church erected in 1868. Charlotte remained a mission of St. Mary Marshall (1868–1877), St. Philip Battle Creek (1877–1886), St. Rose of Lima Hastings (1869–1899), St. John Albion (1899–1917) and St. Mary Lansing (1917–1918).

While attached to Hastings, land was purchased in 1893 at the corner of Washington and Seminary for a new church. The old church was raffled off and won by the pastor Rev. Peter Loughran. Bishop John S. Foley of Detroit dedicated the new place of worship on November 12, 1893.

Rev. Peter J. Jordan went to Charlotte as the first resident pastor in August 1918. Charlotte, which had been a mission for so long, became a mission center. Grand Ledge, Eaton Rapids and Bellevue were assigned to its care. With the hope of opening a school during the pastorate of Msgr. Michael J. Mleko (1950–1957) the parish was relocated to eighteen acres. The Seminary Street property was sold and the buildings were to be moved. The moving equipment broke down and the church sat in the middle of the street for some time. The church was relocated upon a full basement to be used as a

■ *"Our Lady of Charlotte" has been with the parish over the 135 years of its history. She now greets those who enter the new Family Life Center.*

parish hall. A fund drive was held and a school was opened in the fall of 1960. For a number of years the school was staffed by the Sisters of St. Joseph from Nazareth. It celebrated its silver jubilee during the 1985-86 academic year.

The present church was built in 1976 and dedicated May 1, 1977, during Rev. Francis B. Wahowlak's pastorate. Since Rev. Denis R. Spitzley arrived in 2000, dreams of a Family Life Center with a social hall seating 500, four meeting rooms dedicated to the four evangelists, and parish office space have become a reality. Bishop Carl F. Mengeling dedicated the facility on June 11, 2002.

■ *Fr. Denis Spitzley breaks ground for the Family Life Center, August 15, 2001. (Faith)*

■ *The second church, built in 1893, and convent.*

ST. MARY

CHELSEA

The Catholic faith was brought to the Chelsea area by Irish immigrants in the 1830s. A two-acre site in Sylvan Township was purchased in November 1844. The Sylvan Mission Church built the following year was used until destroyed by fire in 1903. Rev. Thomas Cullen, pastor of St. Thomas the Apostle in Ann Arbor, celebrated the sacraments for God's people from 1844 until 1854.

Rev. James L. Pulsers became the first resident pastor of Dexter in 1854 and was also responsible for the missions at Bunker Hill, Stockbridge and Sylvan Township. Dexter cared for the Sylvan Mission for many years. Land was purchased in the village of Chelsea four miles from the original site and a church was erected there in 1869. The first resident pastor, Rev. Patrick Duhig, arrived in 1878 from Hillsdale.

The much-loved Rev. William P. Considine pastored Chelsea from 1885 until 1917. In laying plans to open a school, he precipitated a major diocesan crisis. Bishop John S. Foley favored the Sisters, Servants of the Immaculate Heart of Mary in Monroe. The Sisters of St. Dominic in Adrian were favored by Fr. Considine and the Chelsea congregation, since about sixty of their young ladies had attended the St. Joseph Academy in Adrian. After the Apostolic Delegate in Washington, D.C., was contacted, the bishop gave in to Fr. Considine's wishes stating that the I.H.M.s had declined to staff the school. The school, which opened in such conflict, closed in 1968 (the high school portion having closed in 1934).

In 1961 the old church was beyond repair and torn down. Mass was held in the school gym until a new church was built on Old US 12. The congregation moved into the new church in December 1966.

The pastorate of Rev. D. Philip Dupuis (1972–1998) was one of consolidation and building facilities at the new parish site. A rectory was built in 1977. Bishop Carl F. Mengeling dedicated the addition to the church consisting of a large gathering space, a small day chapel, a bridal room, a cry room, a cloakroom and restrooms in August 1996. Plans were immediately put forth for a parish center to contain offices, a parish hall, meeting rooms and classrooms for the religious education program. On Fr. Dupuis' last Sunday in the parish before his retirement, the new parish center was dedicated. Since 1998, Rev. William J. Turner has pastored the St. Mary community.

■ *The Bell Tower, Stations of the Cross, and Right to Life Memorial*

■ *In September 2002 the youth group gathered for a service remembering those who suffered and died in the terrorist attacks of September 11, 2001.*

St. Rita

CLARKLAKE

The pioneer priest to the Clarklake area was the Rev. Edwin A. Fisher. In the early teens he visited the residents at Clark Lake and made inquiries about purchasing land on which to build a Catholic church. On October 5, 1914, land was obtained from Ben and Eliza Graziani.

The Graziani estate was known as Kentucky Park (they were from Covington, Kentucky) and the road on which a small wooden chapel was built was called Kentucky Drive. The chapel was built no later than 1916 and the sections were hauled from Manchester and assembled on the site.

St. Rita's remained one of the St. Mary (Manchester) Missions until the creation of the Diocese of Lansing in 1937. The mission was located in the new diocese and the mother parish in the old diocese of Detroit. Msgr. Eugene M. Cullimane, at St. Mary Star of the

In 1966, fifteen acres on Hayes Road were purchased as a future parish site. The following year a new church was constructed. By 1974 a forty by eighty foot addition was needed. A parish hall followed in 1975. Ten more acres and a house were bought in 1978. Bishop Kenneth J. Povish elevated the Clarklake Mission to parochial status in May 1982. The founding pastor was Rev. James J. Prentice, O.S.F.S. The much-loved Fr. Prentice led the congregation in doubling the seating capacity of the church to 820. The new church was created by removing the north and south walls of the previous worship space. The parish social center was converted into eight religious education classrooms and a new social hall, with a capacity of 500, was built. Bishop Povish dedicated the new facilities in August 1987.

Since Fr. Prentice's death in 1991, Rev. Lehr Barkenquest, O.S.F.S., has served as pastor of the St. Rita congregation.

■ *Stained glass window of the Baptism of Jesus (Artist: Richard Handley, of Omnibus Studios, New Era, Michigan)*

Sea in Jackson, was given the pastoral care of the Clarklake Mission. The assistants at St. Mary's continued to celebrate Mass there each Sunday during the summer until 1955. At that time Msgr. Frank J. Hardy was instructed that the pastor of the parish at Michigan Center would now be responsible for the chapel on Clark Lake.

■ *The stained glass window of Noah's ark features native American animals. (Artist: Richard Handley, of Omnibus Studios, New Era, Michigan)*

ST. DOMINIC

$\mathcal{C}$LINTON

(By Dean Peterson/Faith)

Longing to receive the sacraments in late 1852, Edward and Margaret Gillan purchased the Baptist meeting hall to provide a place for the celebration of the Eucharist.

When Rev. Peter Joseph Kindekins was sent to St. Mary's Adrian in 1853 as its first resident pastor, Clinton was included in his mission charge. That same year the former Baptist Meeting House, which had been built in 1839, was moved and refurbished. It stood on what is now the old portion of the cemetery and served as the parish church for twenty years.

pastors of Adrian and Hillsdale who had to travel a farther distance.

From the time Manchester became a parish in 1889, the area missions of Freedom, Irish Hills, Clark Lake, Clinton and Tecumseh became known as the St. Mary's missions. Rev. Joseph V. Pfeffer was appointed pastor of these missions in 1924. Beginning in 1935, Fr. Pfeffer assigned one of his assistants, Rev. Lambert M. LaVoy, to live in Clinton itself.

The St. Dominic community again became a parish on July 5, 1944. Rev. Herbert F. Weier was the resident pastor at Clinton with missions at Tecumseh and the Irish Hills.

During the pastorate of Rev. Chester V. Tomaszewski, the Driscoll car dealership on Michigan Avenue was purchased and renovated. This building provides a suitable parish hall, which was dedicated by Bishop Kenneth J. Povish on January 17, 1982.

Rev. Donald Rausch, after a fifteen-year pastorate, retired in 2001. The pastoral care of St. Dominic was entrusted to Rev. Daniel F. Wheeler, the pastor of St. Elizabeth's in Tecumseh.

After attempts to build a brick church failed, the present frame structure was begun in 1872 under the direction of Rev. Ferdinand Allgayer. Fr. Allgayer left just two months before the church was dedicated on March 21, 1873. Bishop Caspar H. Borgess preached the dedicatory sermon.

St. Dominic's remained a mission (except for 1904-09, 1910-11, and 1915-16) from 1873 to 1944. The Clinton Catholics were successively attended from St. Joseph Dexter; St. Mary, Adrian; St. Francis, Freedom; St. Anthony, Hillsdale; and St. Mary, Manchester. At times, the responsibility was shared by a couple of parishes. The pastors of Freedom frequently filled in for the

■ *St. Dominic Hall*

SS. CHARLES AND HELENA

Clio

In 1946 Bishop Joseph H. Albers received a petition from Mrs. Margaret Carlton requesting a new parish be established in Clio. The Bishop's reply indicated that it was because of the shortage of priests that he was unable to grant her request. In October 1952 Bishop Albers again looked into establishing a parish in Clio. At that time, he wrote Rev. William M. Gannon, pastor of St. Mary in Mt. Morris, requesting information on the number of Catholic families in the Clio portion of his parish. Bishop Albers already had his eye on Fr. Gannon's assistant, Rev. Frederick C. Horton, to become the founding pastor of the new parish.

Word circulated of the new parish and Mrs. Mary Hughes Mann offered a sizable nest egg to get the new parish off the ground. Bishop Albers, in gratitude for the gift, named the parish SS. Charles and Helena. Charles was name of Mrs. Mann's son and Helena was her other baptismal name.

The decree of establishment of the new parish was issued by Bishop Albers on June 30, 1954. Fr. Horton

was appointed as the first pastor. Vienna Township Hall was the site of the first Mass celebrated on July 25, 1954. The groundbreaking for the new church was held in September. Until it was completed the congregation continued to meet in the Vienna Township Hall. A rectory and office building were begun in 1956. Upon Fr. Horton's retirement in 1970, Rev. C. Robert Stockwell began his twenty-year pastorate. More land was acquired and a parish center opened in October 1973. The church was extensively remodeled in 1981.

Since Rev. Gerald J. Ploof became pastor in 1997, a welcoming Christ statue was placed near the entrance to the parish property. A major renovation project was dedicated in November 2002 by Bishop Carl F. Mengeling. The seating of the church was expanded to 620 and a daily Mass chapel as well as a reconciliation chapel were constructed. The parish center was also expanded and six new classrooms were built.

Fr. Gerald Ploof and Deacon David Pigott with the First Communion class, 1999

A new church and altar were dedicated November 24, 2002. Bishop Mengeling presided at the concelebrated Mass.

St. Catherine Labouré

Concord

The Concord Opera House, which was built in 1900, was the home of the St. Catherine Labouré parishioners from 1953 until 1996. In May 1953, thirty-nine families attended the first Mass in the Opera House. Rev. John H. Dougherty, C.M., pastor at Queen of the Miraculous Medal in Jackson, was the celebrant. Several men of the parish agreed to work winter weeknights cleaning, plastering and painting. The ladies brought in a meal and cleaned up the mess on Saturday mornings so that Mass could be celebrated on Sunday. These same women spent one fall day before the dedication making and hanging drapes.

Many of the furnishings came from Queen's old church. Statues of St. Joseph and St. Therese of Lisieux and an organ came from there. The folding chairs were eventually replaced by pews from the Fort Custer military chapel in Battle Creek.

Bishop Joseph H. Albers celebrated the dedicatory Mass on the stage of the old opera house on May 16, 1954. The Queen's choir sang the High Mass from the balcony, which had now become the choir loft.

In 1982 the last in a series of requests was submitted to the Bishop for a resident pastor. A parish council was organized in April 1984 and its first job was to purchase a house for use as a rectory because on June 27, 1984, Rev. Edward O'Grady began his pastorate of the newly created quasi-parish.

With Fr. O'Grady's retirement in 1988 the leadership of the parish was entrusted by Bishop Kenneth J. Povish to a lay couple, Ken Berger and Pat Robertson. Mr. Berger was ordained to the permanent diaconate in 1990. After his departure in 1992, Ms. Robertson continued to foster the parishioners' dream of a new church. Groundbreaking ceremonies were held in 1995. A community-wide open house of the new facilities was held in February 1996. Later that month Bishop Carl F. Mengeling dedicated the new worship space, social hall and catechetical classrooms. Since July 1999 Mrs. Ellen Joyce Rochow has served the parish as pastoral coordinator.

■ *(By Dean Peterson/Faith)*

■ *Exercise room in St. Catherine Labouré (By Dean Peterson/Faith)*

ST. JOHN THE EVANGELIST

DAVISON

In the early 1860s the first Catholic families moved into Richfield Township, Genesee County. The priests from St. Michael Flint visited these Catholics and celebrated Mass in the home of George Walk and A. Balser Conrad. In March 1871, Mrs. Madaline Conrad deeded one and a half acres to Bishop Peter Paul Lefevere for a church and burial ground. A twenty by forty foot frame church was built that same year. In 1882 the pastoral care of the St. John the Divine community was transferred from St. Michael Flint to Immaculate Conception Lapeer. In 1890 Rev. William J. Sinn of Lapeer began offering Mass one day a week in Richfield Township.

It became apparent that the church should be located in Davison so a building committee was organized in 1893. In August 1894, Rev. Francis Clement Kelley, pastor in Lapeer (later second Bishop of Oklahoma),

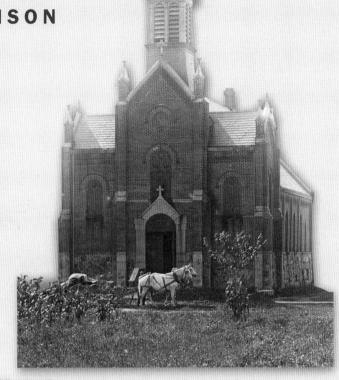

■ *The old church, built in 1894*

(1950–1960) a new church with attached rectory and a new eight-room school were built.

Since Rev. Andrew A. Czajkowski became pastor in 1983 the parish has been completely transformed. In 1984 three permanent deacons, Neil Huiskens, Robert Poulson, and Claude Spencer, were ordained from the parish. A new parish hall costing 4.9 million dollars was dedicated in March 1990. There were 1,600 registered families and continued growth led to the need for the new church, which was dedicated in May 1993. A 55,046 square foot Family Center, including a gym, track and wellness area, was dedicated by Bishop Carl F. Mengeling on September 15, 2001.

celebrated the first Mass in the church. In 1926 a rectory was built and one of the assistants for Lapeer lived there until a resident pastor (Rev. Henry M. Mayotte) was appointed in October 1928.

During the pastorate of Rev. Earl V. Sheridan a school was opened in the fall of 1946 with 175 students. Sisters of Joseph from Nazareth initially staffed the school. During Rev. Edward G. Donahoe's pastorate

■ *Exercise room in the Family Center*

ST. ALPHONSUS

DEERFIELD

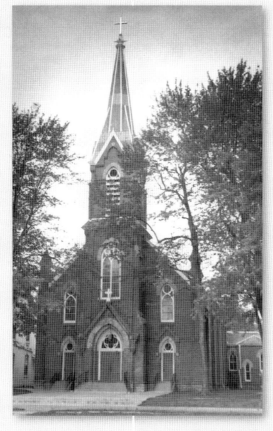

T under the direction of one of the Redemptorists, Rev. Louis F. Gillett. The Redemptorists in Monroe nurtured the Deerfield Catholics until 1855. In the early 1860s land was purchased in the village of Deerfield where an edifice was dedicated to the glory of God on October 12, 1864. Land for a cemetery was acquired the next year.

A rectory was built in 1882 with the expectation that a resident priest would soon be assigned. In March 1884 Rev. Louis Van Straelen came as the first pastor. During the pastorate (1892–1896) of Rev. Frank J. Broegger the present church was built. In 1914 a school was built. The Adrian Dominican Sisters staffed the school until its closure in June 1969.

To mark the 100th anniversary of the dedication of the first church in the village of Deerfield, a year-long centennial celebration was organized in 1964. Rev. William Griffith was pastor at the time. The church was renovated for the occasion.

In more recent years meeting space has been a priority. Beginning in 1976 a committee was formed to look into having a hall, bathrooms and a kitchen put in the church basement. The new facilities were dedicated by Bishop Kenneth J. Povish in January 1984.

A St. Peter (Blissfield)-St. Alphonsus (Deerfield) K of C chapter was organized in 1983. In 1990 the church was placed on the Michigan Register of Historic Buildings. During the pastorate (1995– 1998) of Rev. James F. Eisele the parish celebrated the centennial of the dedication of the present church. Rev. John Loughran, O.S.F.S., is the current pastor.

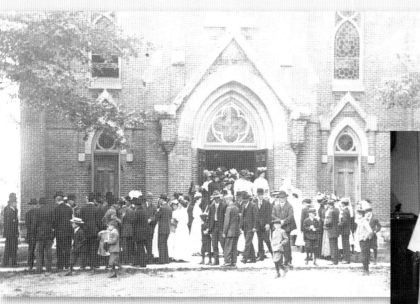

■ *Confirmation, 1910*

■ *Confirmation, 2001*

CATHOLIC COMMUNITY OF ST. JUDE

DeWITT

While Rev. Robert T. Palmer served as pastor (1967–1968) of St. Therese Parish in Lansing he was approached by parishioners from DeWitt about the possibility of organizing their own parish. He encouraged them.

Bishop Alexander M. Zaleski had previously been informed of possible sites and of the potential growth of the DeWitt area. In July 1964 Bishop Zaleski authorized the purchase of 9.6 acres of land on North Bridge Street in DeWitt. The DeWitt Catholics approached Fr. Palmer's successor, Rev. John Shinners, about celebrating Mass for the community.

■ *The Our Lady of Fatima Grotto (By Dean Peterson/Faith)*

the church. He celebrated the Sacrament of Confirmation for the community for the first time at the dedication Mass.

The community continued to develop during the pastorate (1977–1990) of Monsignor David W. Stotenbur. When Rev. Bernard L. Reilly arrived it was evident a new church needed to be built. In October 1992 a design committee for a new church and renovation of existing facilities was set up. Ground was broken in September 1995 and Bishop Carl F. Mengeling dedicated the new church on February 2, 1997. During the Great Jubilee year 2000, Rev. Dwight M. Ezop came to DeWitt as pastor.

Furestenau School was the site chosen for the first eucharistic celebration. Some 300 people participated in the September 28, 1969, inaugural liturgy of the Catholic community in DeWitt. The community rapidly developed. The servers were formed into the Knights of the Altar before Christmas. In January 1970 the first meeting of the parish council took place and in May a unit of the Legion of Mary was organized.

■ *(By Dean Peterson/Faith)*

On the same day (July 1, 1970) that Rev. John M. Grathwohl was appointed administrator of St. Therese parish, the Catholic community in DeWitt was officially designated a mission of St. Therese parish. The support and cooperation of the parishioners were tremendous, so much so that on June 30, 1971, the mission achieved parochial status.

Rev. Jerome I. Schmitt was appointed the first resident pastor. He served for almost five years. He oversaw the purchase of a rectory in August 1971 and the groundbreaking for a temporary church/activity center in August 1973.

The first Mass was held in the community building/church in July 1974. Bishop Zaleski came in November to dedicate

ST. JOSEPH

DEXTER

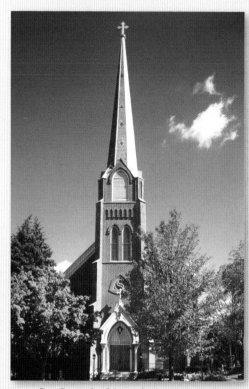

St. Joseph Church, built in 1872

In 1829 and 1830 several Irish Catholic families (Lacey, McGuire, McGuiness, Rabbitt, and Sullivan) settled near Dexter. During 1835 Rev. Patrick O'Kelly from Ann Arbor visited these families. It was arranged for Mass to be held on January 1, 1836, at the home of Rose and Patrick Lavey. In 1840 the first church edifice was constructed in Dexter Township at the northeast corner of Dexter Townhall and Quigley Roads. A cemetery was established on the northwest corner. When the frame building burned in 1854 it was decided to build the next church in the village of Dexter. It is evident that Rev. James A. Hennessey of Marshall, who cared for Dexter from 1852 until 1854, organized the building of the second edifice.

The Sisters, Servants of the Immaculate Heart of Mary were invited to open a parish school in September 1920. It was closed for three years during the Depression. The sisters returned in 1936 and stayed until the school's final closure in 1968. The I.H.M. sisters continued to serve the parish as religious educators and pastoral ministers for many years.

The school was converted into a parish center during Rev. Kenneth C. McDonald's pastorate (1977–1985). During Rev. David F. Howell's pastorate (1985–1990) the church, parish center and rectory were all thoroughly renovated. Space was still at a premium and the Dexter area continued to grow rapidly. Since Rev. Brendan J. Walsh came as pastor in 1998, various options have been pursued. The Diocese has purchased a forty-six acre site in Webster Township. Plans for a 1,200 seat church, a parish center, a multipurpose facility and a parking lot for 400 cars are being implemented.

Children 5-8 take part in the Liturgy of the Word for their age level and return to the church for the Liturgy of the Eucharist.

In the fall of 1854 Rev. James L. Pulsers arrived as the first pastor of Dexter and its missions at Pinckney, Sylvan (later Chelsea), Unadilla and Bunker Hill. The third and present Gothic revival church was begun in 1872 during Rev. John F. Van Gennip's pastorate (1859–1874). The present rectory was built during the pastorate (1899–1912) of Rev. John P. Ryan.

Middle school and high school youth portray the Passion through mime on Palm Sunday, 2003.

ST. MARY

DURAND

CATHOLIC CHURCH AND PARSONAGE — DURAND, MICH. SH-6

■ *The first church, built in 1899,
and rectory built in 1903*

Rev. Franklin D. Hay, pastor from 1949 until 1970, saw the need for relocating the parish to a larger site. Land was purchased and a new church was dedicated on May 30, 1957. A new rectory was built in 1960. An eight room educational center was erected in 1965 and expanded with four additional rooms in 1972.

The first Mass celebrated near Durand was led by Rev. Joseph Kraemer, of Owosso, in 1876 on the farm of John Shield. Twenty years later, in 1896, Durand was designated a station of Gaines. The Ann Arbor Railroad had located its headquarters in Durand in the 1890s. This had brought many Irish Catholic laborers to Durand. Two lots were deeded to Bishop John S. Foley in July 1897. Beginning in 1898 services were held in various store buildings on Saginaw Street. The first church was begun in 1899. Pope Leo XIII authorized midnight Mass on December thirty-first that year to welcome in the new century. This was the first Mass held in the Durand church. Since the church was not quite complete it was not formally opened until the Feast of the Annunciation in March 1900. On October 21, 1901, Rev. Dennis A. Hayes was sent to Durand as its first pastor. For the next quarter of a century St. Mary Morrice was attached to Durand as a mission. After the Ann Arbor railroad relocated its headquarters to Owosso in 1904, twenty-four railroad families (mostly Irish) left for Owosso.

The pastorate of Rev. Francis A. O'Connor ended on December 3, 1918, when he laid down his life for his sheep. During the flu epidemic he was tireless in ministering to the sick and dying in Durand and Morrice. His resistance became low and he succumbed to the disease.

The parish centennial year, 2000–2001, occurred in the pastorate (1983–2002) of Rev. Joseph E. Aubin. Centennial events included eucharistic adoration, a parish mission. The celebration culminated in the dedication on March 25, 2001, of the newly built gathering space. Since Fr. Aubin's retirement in June 2002, Rev. J. Thomas Munley has been the spiritual leader of the parish.

PARISHES

ST. JOHN THE EVANGELIST STUDENT PARISH

EAST LANSING

In 1923 Rev. John A. Gabriels, from Resurrection, began visiting the Catholic students at Michigan Agricultural College. A student organization was set up in 1924. When Rev. Cecil M. Winters became Fr. Gabriels' assistant in 1928, he began to care for the college students. In 1933 the Catholic students organized a Newman Club with Fr. Winters as chaplain. The club remained under his leadership until his transfer in 1939. Bishop Joseph H. Albers had recognized Fr. Winters' talents at working with young adults and decided to found a new parish in East Lansing that would have a large focus on the students at MAC. On October 1, 1940, Fr. Winters became the founding pastor of St. Thomas Aquinas parish in East Lansing. (St. Thomas Aquinas is patron saint of students.) Fr. Winters taught the first credited courses in religion at any public college in the State. A man of frail health, he died in May 1943.

Rev. Jerome V. MacEachin (Fr. Mac) succeeded as pastor. The Newman Club secured a house for their activities and grew to be the largest Newman Club in the nation in 1950. Fr. Mac was a very outgoing person and he took on raising funds for a new student parish in 1954. He traveled the state. In 1956 ground was broken and the building was open for use in August 1957. Fr. Mac decided to stay with St. Thomas and Rev. Robert E. Kavanaugh, who had worked with Fr. Mac at St. Thomas from 1951 until 1954 and again since 1955, was assigned as the first

■ *Catholic Student Organization Activity Carnival, 1958*

pastor of the student parish. The President of Notre Dame, Rev. Theodore Hesburgh, C.S.C., preached the dedicatory sermon of the new facility on June 12, 1958.

■ *St. John Pastoral Team, November 1987, left to right: Sr. Elizabeth Walters, Christian Service Coordinator; Rev. Thomas McDevitt, Parish Priest; Marjan Helms, Director of Music; Elizabeth Schweitzer, Parish Administrator; Rev. Mark Inglot, Parish Priest; Nancy Seubert, Director of Liturgy and Catechumenate; Rev. John Foglio, Parish Priest*

In 1966 the first Weekends in Christian Living began to be held. The first Saturday night Mass was held November 1, 1969. During the pastorate (1971–2000) of Rev. Thomas D. McDevitt, St. John East, on Hagadorn Road, was sold and the main facility on M.A.C. was entirely refurbished. Bishop Kenneth J. Povish rededicated it on April 14, 1991. Following Fr. McDevitt's retirement, Rev. Mark J. Inglot (previously associate pastor) returned to St. John parish, this time to serve in the capacity of pastor.

ST. THOMAS AQUINAS

EAST LANSING

The first meeting of St. Thomas parishioners was held October 1, 1940 in the Spartan Room of the Union Building on the Michigan State University campus. Rev. Cecil M. Winters celebrated the first Mass in the State Theatre on Abbott Road. The house at 601 Abbott had been purchased by the Diocese in September for use as a rectory. On Easter Sunday 1942 the first Mass was held in the basement church which became known as the catacombs of East Lansing. The basement church was also located on Abbott Road.

At the Newman Hall in 1951, Fr. MacEachin addresses campaign leaders raising funds for building additional classrooms and gymnasium facilities.

present church in April 1968. At the time of its dedication the church contained the largest faceted glass window in North America.

St. Thomas Aquinas Parish is known across mid-Michigan for the weekly Outreach Mass that originates there. The first Outreach Mass was televised on WSYM, TV-47 Lansing, on Easter Sunday 1984. The Outreach Mass was spearheaded by Bishop James S. Sullivan, pastor of St. Thomas from 1978 until 1985. In July 1997 the viewing area was expanded when broadcast began on WSMH, TV-66 Flint.

During the pastorate (1985–1998) of Rev. (later Monsignor) Michael D. Murphy the parish held a year-long semi-centennial celebration in 1990. The Corpus Christi procession was re-instituted as a part of the observance. The church was re-roofed and the school was enlarged also during Fr. Murphy's pastorate.

Rev. David J. Speicher, a graduate of St. Thomas school, returned to St. Thomas as pastor in July 2000.

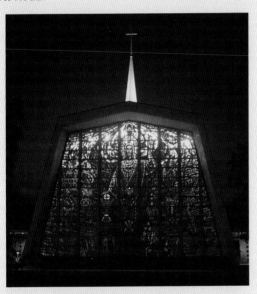

The Grande Window

Rev. Jerome V. MacEachin was appointed to St. Thomas after Fr. Winters' untimely death in May 1943. Fr. Mac, as he was fondly known, foresaw the need to expand the parish. Twenty-four and three-quarter acres were purchased on Alton Road in February 1948. A school was opened in September 1949 with ninety-five pupils in six grades. For many years the Adrian Dominicans staffed the school. Besides the school, Fr. Mac oversaw the building of a convent, school additions including a gym that served as the temporary church, the present church and rectory. Bishop Alexander M. Zaleski dedicated the

The parish TV control room is the production hub for videotaping the Outreach Mass each Saturday for Sunday morning broadcast. (Faith)

ST. PETER THE APOSTLE

EATON RAPIDS

■ *Old St. Peter Church, which was an Episcopal mission purchased in 1891. Mrs. Bromling, a parishioner, had a fieldstone exterior added in 1935.*

The first visitation of a priest to Eaton Rapids took place in 1852 when Rev. James H. Hennessey from Marshall came to celebrate Mass. The 1878 annual report from St. Mary Lansing lists Eaton Rapids as a station attended by Rev. Louis Van Driss. Mass became a monthly occurrence in the home of Frank Birney on Dexter Street. With Fr. Van Driss' transfer from Lansing, the care of the Eaton Rapids Catholics was entrusted to the parish in Hastings. In April 1891 the former Episcopal church was purchased by Rev. Francis J. Broegger, the pastor of St. Rose of Lima in Hastings.

In December 1898 Rev. Henry D. Sullivan was appointed the first resident pastor of St. John, Albion. Fr. Sullivan also received the care of the missions at Eaton Rapids and Charlotte. The Albion priests cared for the Eaton Rapids mission for twenty years.

When Rev. Peter J. Jordan became the first resident pastor in Charlotte in 1918, Eaton Rapids and Grand Ledge were attached to the new parish. While Rev. Wilshire J. Lockwood was pastor of Charlotte (1929–1938) he guided the Catholics of Eaton Rapids in their endeavors to enlarge the church. An eighteen foot addition, entry way and sacristy were added to the frame church which was then faced with fieldstone. The parishioners brought in wagonloads of stone to complete the new exterior.

In June 1940 the care of the Eaton Rapids congregation was turned over to a priest who worked in the Chancery office in Lansing. A house next to the church was purchased in 1952 during Rev. (later Bishop) Paul V. Donovan's tenure as administrator of St. Peter from 1951 until 1955.

To celebrate the Diocesan Silver Jubilee of the Diocese in 1962, Bishop Joseph H. Albers decided to raise the St. Peter mission to the status of parish. Rev. Charles J. Crowley arrived on August 1, 1962, as the first resident pastor. Fr. Crowley immediately saw the need for a new church for the growing community. A new church and catechetical center were dedicated May 9, 1965. Rev. Bennett P. Constantine came to Eaton Rapids as pastor in 1990. He oversaw the efforts to build the present church, which was dedicated by Bishop Kenneth J. Povish in October 1994.

In June 1994 a day care with pre-school, entitled "St Peter's Rainbow Child Development Center", was begun. Two years later the house bording parish property on Knight Street was procured for a rectory. The former rectory was transformed into the day care with an additional building erected in 1997.

Another milestone was the opening in September 2003 of an elementary school from K-6th grade. The first principal of St. Peter School was Mr. Matthew Vokoun.

■ *(By Dean Peterson/Faith)*

ST. JOHN THE EVANGELIST

FENTON

The first mention of Fentonville in the Official Catholic Directory is in the year 1857 among the stations of St. Michael in Flint. Rev. Charles De Ceuninck came to St. Michael in 1855 and began visiting the outlying Catholics in Genesee County the following year.

In June 1868 two acres of land in Fenton were bought for $400. A five-member building committee was soon established. That summer a frame church was erected. In 1871 Rev. Thomas Rafter, who as pastor of St. John the Baptist in Oceola had overseen the building of the church, had a rectory built at Fenton. He moved in upon its completion.

Rev. David L. Dillon pastored Fenton from 1906 until 1920. Fr. Dillon, aware of the need to build a large church, in 1911 began a building fund, which amounted to $220. It was up to Fr. Dillon's successor, Rev. Maurice Walsh, to build the new church. In August 1928 the parish rejoiced at the dedication of its new church and rectory. The $50,000 Tudor Gothic structure had a cobblestone exterior. All the stone and timber used in the construction came from the farms and yards of parishioners. Mr. Frank McKeon fashioned the altar out of granite and fieldstone. On this same altar his grandsons, Revs. William and Robert McKeon, celebrated their first Masses.

Rev. Dennis P. Tighe arrived in Fenton in 1932. He secured in 1933 the services of the Immaculate Heart of Mary Sisters at St. Michael Flint to come to Fenton on Saturdays to teach C.C.D. This continued until the school opened in September 1950. The I.H.M. sisters staffed it until 1974.

The present Romanesque church was dedicated by Bishops Alexander Zaleski and M. Joseph Green on April 17, 1966. It has an exterior of Amherst sandstone, a Vermont slate roof and a 105-foot bell tower and spire.

The old stone church became a gym until it was refurbished, under Rev. David Harvey's leadership, and rededicated by Bishop Kenneth J. Povish as St. John Parish Center in August 1981. The parish center includes offices, an assembly room and a beautiful chapel.

Bishop Povish returned to Fenton for the dedication of the activity center and gymnasium complex on the Feast of St. John the Evangelist in 1989. A new 35,000 square foot addition to the school, including a cafeteria, was dedicated by Bishop Carl F. Mengeling on November 25, 2000.

Fieldstone chapel

ALL SAINTS

*F*LINT

Bishop John S. Foley of Detroit, in February 1910, appointed Rev. Boleslaus Stefanski to found a new parish for Polish and other Slavic Catholics. Before his departure in September, Fr. Stefanski oversaw the purchase of eight lots and the laying of the foundation for a church. Rev. John B. Hewelt, in his ten-year pastorate, saw the completion and enlargement of the church and the purchase of five acres of land for a cemetery. The school was staffed for many years by the Franciscan Sisters of St. Joseph from Cleveland, Ohio. The school was open from 1915 until 1957. It had a high school department from 1938 until 1954.

During Rev. Stanislaus Bortnowski's pastorate (1932–1955) the 25th anniversary of the parish was observed by remodeling the church. Bishop Gallagher and Auxiliary Bishop Plagens of Detroit blessed the renovated church in November 1935. Bishop Plagens preached in Polish and Bishop Gallagher in English.

After the Second World War, the automobile industry expanded. The area around the Industrial Avenue parish site became very sparsely populated as more and more property was turned over to factory use. It became necessary to relocate the parish. Rev. Anthony P. Majchrowski, who still serves as pastor, was appointed pastor in 1955. The following year the Buick Motor Division of General Motors purchased the Industrial Avenue property. The relocation site was 12.7 acres on West Pierson Road. The school was closed in June of 1957. After that time the children of All Saints attended Sacred Heart.

■ *The renovated All Saints Church in 1936*

■ *Lottie Slonczka tempts us with trays of paczki made for the Rosary Society's 71st annual bingo social at Powers High School February 14, 1988.*

Ground was broken for the present church and rectory in September 1957. The congregation celebrated Mass for the first time in the new church in August 1958.

Fr. Majchrowski has seen the 50th and 75th anniversaries of the parish during his pastorate. Bishop Kenneth J. Povish was principal celebrant of the 75th anniversary liturgy, which took place on November 3, 1985.

In November 1989 All Saints became the home of the Tridentine Mass in the Flint area. Over 700 signatures were gathered requesting Bishop Povish to grant permission for this weekly celebration of the old Latin Mass.

■ *The new All Saints Church relocated to West Pierson Road in 1958*

CHRIST THE KING

FLINT

■ *The new Christ the King Church, dedicated April 7, 2002, with the previous church in the background.*

Just a month before the stock market crash of 1929, Rev. Norman A. DuKette had been sent to Flint to found a parish for Black Catholics.

Four people (the priest, the server and two communicants) attended the first Mass offered by Fr. DuKette in St. Joseph Hungarian Church. The Mass was celebrated on the Feast of Christ the King and, because of that, the "Colored Catholic Mission", as it was known, took Christ the King as its patron. At first, Mass was offered in the parishioners' homes. Soon, a former Methodist parsonage on Kennelworth Avenue was rented for Mass and used as a rectory.

■ *Rev. Norman DuKette (right) concelebrates with Rev. George Zabelka. Knight Joseph Rowlery, of the St. Martin de Porres Assembly No. 11 Fourth Degree Knights of Peter Claver, Detroit, assists Fr. DuKette.*

After a few years the rent became too high for the congregation. Within the first ten years, the congregation moved half a dozen times because of rent increases.

To help the struggling community build a church, Fr. DuKette founded the Christ the King Aid Society in October 1933. The subscription rate was one dollar. The membership benefited from the Mass celebrated every Wednesday for the living and deceased members.

With deep faith in God and invoking the intercession of the Blessed Mother, a house and lots on Clifford Street were purchased in 1937 at a cost of $4,500. The congregation had forty-five dollars in the bank, but God provided. The house was renovated and the chapel served as the parish worship center until 1946. The Diocese purchased a former National Youth Administration building that was moved to Clifford Street. Half of the building was used as a church and the other half as a parish hall. A brick façade was later added to the building.

The parish faced destruction with the building of the I-75 expressway in 1969. Pride in their parish led to a new birth. A new rectory on Seymour Street was purchased and the first Mass was offered there on the Feast of Christ the King in 1969. Fr. DuKette retired the following year and was succeeded by Rev. Michael P. Matarazzo. He oversaw the building of a new church and the first commissioning of Ministers of Service in 1972.

Since 1989 Sr. Joanne Fedewa, S.L.W., has served the parish as pastoral coordinator. In 1990 the community sponsored its first African American Festival. The continued growth of the parish led to erection of a beautiful new church, which was dedicated by Bishop Carl F. Mengeling on April 7, 2002.

HOLY ROSARY

Flint

On the Feast of the Nativity of Mary, in 1951, Holy Rosary parish was carved out of territory formerly belonging to St. John the Evangelist, Davison, and St. Mary, Flint. The first parish liturgy was celebrated at the Kearsley Theatre on September 23 by the founding pastor, Rev. William J. Malewitz. A twelve and one-half acre site on Richfield Road was purchased and ground was broken for a temporary church in March 1952. The present church was blessed by Bishop Joseph H. Albers in March 1955. Fr. Malewitz invited the Oxford Dominicans to staff the parish school that opened in September 1953 with six grades. A high school department was opened in 1964 and remained open until June 1992. The Holy

The first Holy Rosary Church in 1951

Rosary Education Center was built next to Kearsley High School with which it had a unique shared time program. It was the last parish high school to remain in the Diocese.

The longest serving pastor of Holy Rosary parish was Rev. Joseph R. Robb who served from 1968 until his death in March 1988. In 1971 a daycare center

was opened in the parish. The parish silver jubilee was observed with Bishop Kenneth J. Povish celebrating Mass with a dinner following.

The church underwent major renovations during the pastorate of Rev. James G. McDougall. The newly refurbished church and altar were dedicated in October 1991 in observance of the parish's 40th anniversary. Since June 1993 Rev. Paul J. Schwermer has led the Holy Rosary community.

OUR LADY OF GUADALUPE

FLINT

The uniqueness of the Hispanic culture and the Spanish language were the reasons why Bishop Joseph J. Albers established a Spanish-speaking parish in Flint.

The first pastor had the very non-Hispanic name of Reikowsky. Rev. Carl B. Reikowsky, C.PP.S., who had been the assistant at St. John Vianney since 1954, received notice of appointment as administrator of the newly created parish in June 1957. Fr. Reikowsky was appointed at the same time the Diocesan Director of the newly formed Office for the Mexican Apostolate.

Rev. Richard Simons with First Communion class, April 1, 1962

With the arrival of Rev. Eduardo Lorenzo in December 1966, the community began to rapidly grow. The old church on Carpenter Road became too small. A building drive was begun and the old church was left in July 1971. Until the new church was completed in 1973, Sunday Mass was held at Powers High School and weekday liturgies at St. Francis of Assisi. On July 28, 1973, Bishop Alexander Zaleski dedicated the first Catholic Church in the state built solely by the Spanish-speaking community.

In 1982 Bishop Kenneth J. Povish led the 25th anniversary celebration of the parish. A Mariachi band and the lively parish choir provided music.

Bishop Albers directed Fr. Reikowsky to use the old St. Francis of Assisi church and rectory on Carpenter Road as the home of the new parish. (In 1956 St. Francis parish had built a new church in Saginaw.) The Hispanics (both Mexican and Cuban) soon felt at home in the small frame church where the congregation celebrated its first Mass on June 30. The first parish fiesta was held that year.

Fr. Reikowsky's association with St. John Vianney helped in securing as C.C.D. teachers the Sisters of St. Joseph of Nazareth, Michigan, who taught in the school of St. John Vianney. They continued in this capacity until the late 1960s.

Rev. Eduardo Lorenzo receives the gifts at Mass December 12, 1976

During the late 1980s Fr. Lorenzo was able to secure the services of the Passionist Sisters from Mexico. From 1987 until 2001 they served the parish in religious and adult education. Upon Fr. Lorenzo's retirement in June 2002, Rev. Timothy A. Nelson was sent to Our Lady of Guadalupe as pastor.

Fiesta!

SACRED HEART OF JESUS

FLINT

■ *Christmas Midnight Mass, c. 1958*

At a christening party at the home of Mr. and Mrs. Michael Popovich on November 29, 1925, the idea of a Slovak parish was discussed and a collection of fifteen dollars was raised. A petition was sent to Bishop Michael J. Gallagher in Detroit. Many early members of the parish were already members of the Catholic Slovak Union. A building committee and the Altar Society were organized in 1926. In April 1928 ground was broken for the church then the spade used was auctioned off for $300. The first pastor, Rev. John J. Tresbock, arrived in July and held services in Fr. Murphy Hall at St. Michael's downtown. Bishop Gallagher laid the cornerstone for the church July twenty-eighth and the first services were held in September.

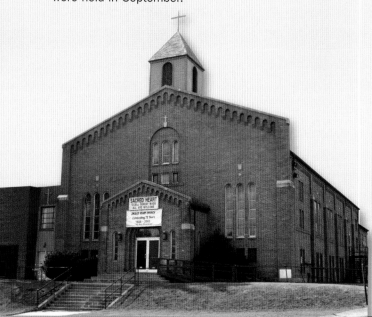

The first eleven years were very trying. The economic crash did not help the tense situation that existed between certain laymen and the eight priests assigned during those eleven years. At one point, foreclosure proceedings were begun on the land on which the $5,500 combination church and rectory had been built.

The golden era of Sacred Heart Parish dawned with the arrival of Rev. John A. Blasko in 1939. After refinancing the $75,000 parish debt, Fr. Blasko looked forward to someday opening a school for the rapidly growing parish.

The Dominican Sisters from Pontiac (later Oxford) came in 1942 and opened the grade school. They taught the 285 students in the six classrooms into which the parish hall had been converted. The Oxford Dominicans were still a part of the school staff when it was closed.

■ *Learning about the faith at the CCD Home Mission Bible School, summer of 1965.*

The former assistant pastor, Rev. George B. Zabelka, returned to Sacred Heart in July 1955 as pastor. The recreation center was begun in 1957 and dedicated in March 1958. The high school, which had opened in 1946, was closed in June 1967. In June 1970 the grade school closed as well. The church basement was remodeled into a hall after the recreation center was rented out in 1971.

Throughout the 1970s and 1980s the parish population continued to dwindle. The last resident priest, Rev. Alan Wakefield, was transferred in June 1985. The parish was then entrusted to the care of a lay couple, Ken Berger and Patricia Robertson. This was a first for the Diocese. Since the retirement of Dr. Connie McClanahan as pastoral coordinator, in June 2001, the pastor of St. Michael Flint has also been appointed pastor of Sacred Heart.

ST. AGNES

FLINT

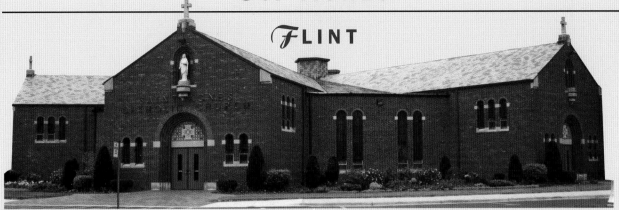

In 1928 General Motors, in the northwest section of Flint, began a housing development for its workers known as Chevrolet City. Bishop Michael J. Gallagher of Detroit was made aware of this and he authorized the purchase of eleven acres on Pierson Road. The new parish was to be dedicated to St. Agnes and Rev. Louis Hammer was sent as the founding pastor. The first Mass was held on July 1 in the Photoplay House on the grounds of the Flint Amusement Park. The altar was a board across two sawhorses.

A temporary frame building was soon built but was destroyed in a windstorm. It was agreed to construct a two-story structure, the second floor serving as a rectory and hall. The first floor was dedicated as a church October 29, 1930. The upper floor was converted to classrooms and the lower floor became the parish hall when a new church was dedicated in 1943.

A school was opened in the fall of 1942 and was staffed by the Sisters of St. Joseph from Nazareth. During Rev. Maurice Olk's pastorate (1944–1968) a further ten rooms were built and, a decade later, a new high school. The first high school graduating class was in 1954. In 1970 the high school consolidated with other parish schools to form Luke M. Powers High School. In 1971 St. Agnes Grade School closed. In the fall the high school building opened as Donovan North Middle School and the grade school as Maurice Olk Elementary School. Donovan and Olk combined in 1977 and closed in 1980. Since August 1980 DuKette Catholic Elementary School has been located at St. Agnes.

The urban exodus of the early seventies left St. Agnes greatly reduced in population. Joining other urban parishes in 1977 to form the Flint Catholic Urban Ministry (FCUM) was a turning point for the better. St. Agnes parish hosted many of the FCUM's revivals and missions. The theme of the 60th anniversary celebration held in 1988 was "This Far by Faith". Bishop Kenneth J. Povish rededicated the renovated church in 1993 as the parish celebrated it 65th anniversary during Rev. John P. Klein's pastorate (1984–1998). Rev. James F. Eisele, who has led the St. Agnes community since 1998, presided over the parish's 75th anniversary in 2003.

Tashara Fields is baptized at Easter, 2001.

St. Joseph Guild members Ken Sanborn, Bob Stoutenburg and Dalton Blackwell

ST. JOHN VIANNEY

FLINT

As World War II overshadowed Europe, Bishop Joseph H. Albers looked forward to establishing new parishes before all materials were dedicated to the war effort. He directed that a survey in the area of the proposed parish take place in September 1939. Land was purchased in December 1940 for a new parish which was canonically established January 20, 1941. Msgr. William J. Flanagan came to Flint as the founding pastor. A cornerstone for the new parish church was laid by Bishop Albers in November. The facility was dedicated the following May. Fr. Flanagan was transferred to St. Mary Cathedral in 1944 and Msgr. Henry W. Mayotte served the parish until 1969. He oversaw the establishment of the school, present church and the growth of the parish to about 1,000 families.

Ground was broken for a grade school in 1947. The school opened the following year and was staffed by the Sisters of St. Joseph from Nazareth. The high school was open from 1955 until 1970. The parish grade school closed in 1971. The facilities were then used for inter-parochial schools. The high school building opened in the fall of 1971 as Donovan South Middle School; the grade school became Mayotte Primary School. Eventually the schools became known as Donovan-Mayotte with one principal. Since July 1988 the sponsorship of Donovan-Mayotte has been that of St. John Vianney parish alone.

Msgr. Mayotte oversaw the construction of the present church, which cost $625,000. Bishop Albers dedicated the edifice in October 1960. Msgr. Walter E. Mehm led the parish from 1969 until 1985. These were times of great change with the renewal following the Second Vatican Council. Population shifts out of the city and new configurations of the schools brought about other changes.

The 50th anniversary of the parish was observed on the feast of St. John Vianney in 1991. A banquet and program followed the semi-centennial Mass. Rev. Douglas R. Osborn has led the St. John Vianney community since 1985.

▬ *Theatre where first Mass was celebrated*

▬ *The RCIA class around the altar, Easter 2002*

ST. LEO THE GREAT

FLINT

St. Leo garage chapel, 1957

Almost 200 people attended the first Mass of St. Leo the Great parish at the Potter School on August 25, 1957. Bishop Joseph J. Albers had established the new parish in the Thrift City area of Flint in June and assigned Rev. Paul J. DeRose as the founding pastor. The next year the cornerstone for a parish church was laid. The "Titan" club for men and the "Immaculata" club for women were also organized in 1958.

Bishop Albers dedicated the present church in September 1959. The second story of the church was constructed for classroom use. In September 1961 a school with 148 children in grades four through seven was opened. The Adrian Dominican Sisters staffed the school for the decade of its existence. Grades one through eight were all opened in the fall of 1963. Enrollment peaked in the fall of 1964 with 458 students. The Diocese implemented a forty-pupil limit per classroom in the fall of 1966.

Fr. DeRose supervising in the kitchen, c. 1960

Fr. DeRose was forced because of ill health to retire after twenty-two years as pastor. He was well known for his concern for those alienated from the church. During the pastorate of Rev. Philip P. Gallagher, the parish celebrated its 30th anniversary in 1987 by burning its mortgage. In April 1989, ten St. Leo parishioners were commissioned as Stephen's Ministers. They were among the first Stephen's ministers in the diocese. Since June 1991 Rev. James B. Bettendorf has been entrusted with the care of souls in St. Leo Parish.

ST. LUKE THE EVANGELIST

FLINT

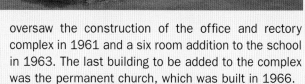

The post World War II years in Flint were boom years. In November 1949 Bishop Joseph H. Albers met with the pastors of St. Agnes and St. John Vianney to discuss the possibility of another parish in the northwest of Flint. On July 9, 1950, the parish of St. Luke the Evangelist was canonically erected and Rev. Raphael R. Dunigan was sent as the founding pastor.

■ *Everybody pitches in at St. Luke, May 1954. (Photo courtesy of The Flint Journal)*

The first Mass offered for the St. Luke community was held at the Haskell Community Center on January 7, 1951. After completing a census, Fr. Dunigan reported to Bishop Albers in August 1951 that he found 490 homes with Catholics in them. He found 65 unbaptized children and 746 children twelve years of age and younger. With all these children, efforts were directed toward a school. A six-classroom school was begun in September and opened in the fall of 1952. The Sisters of St. Dominic of Adrian staffed the school and remained there until the school closed in June 1971.

The fifties were a time of great expansion. Mass was first celebrated in the second temporary church in August 1954. A social hall, kitchen facilities and four classrooms were added to the school in 1956. The convent had a four-room addition built in 1959.

Even after Fr. Dunigan was transferred in March 1960 the building spree continued. Rev. Edward G. Donahoe

oversaw the construction of the office and rectory complex in 1961 and a six room addition to the school in 1963. The last building to be added to the complex was the permanent church, which was built in 1966.

Rev. Donald Eder succeeded as pastor at St. Luke. From 1969 to 1973 St. Luke was part of the tri-parish team ministry which served St. Luke, Sacred Heart and Christ the King parishes. The team ministry concept was dissolved in 1973 and Rev. Robert Kolenski became pastor and remained for five years. On October 12, 1975, Bishop James S. Sullivan celebrated the 25th anniversary Mass.

The year 1990 was very significant for St. Luke parish. In June the last resident pastor, Rev. Bernard L. Reilly was transferred. Sr. Jean O'Conner, I.H.M., became the parish's first pastoral coordinator. Bishop Kenneth J. Povish presided over the parish's 40th anniversary Mass in October of that year. Since July 1994 Sr. Judith Blake, S.S.J., has cared for the needs of the St. Luke parish family.

140

ST. MARY

FLINT

In 1919 Rev. Laurence Soest celebrated the first Mass for the parish, which is dedicated to Our Blessed Mother under her title as the Immaculate Conception, in the Franklin Avenue Chapel that had been established by the Diocese the previous year in an attempt to start a second Polish parish in Flint.

On June 25 the builder came to stake out where the church and rectory would be built. Farmers were expected to bring their teams and implements and city dwellers their shovels. Thus, the basements were dug. The first Mass in the new building was held Christmas Day, 1919.

In the spring of 1920 a rectory was purchased and the trio who came from Whittaker in 1919 were once again under the same roof. Miss Rose Polzin and her brother, Frank, had worked for Fr. Soest for several years before he came to Flint. Rose served as cook and housekeeper of St. Mary's parish for forty-two years. Frank served as chauffeur, custodian, school patrolman, boiler man and all around fix-it man for the parish.

Once the church had been dedicated in 1921 and the rectory in 1923, Fr. Soest directed parish efforts toward building a school. The school opened in September 1925 with four grades taught by four Sisters of St. Joseph from Nazareth, Michigan. When four more classrooms and a gymnasium-auditorium combination were added in 1928, the school was ready for a full high school program including athletics. The first class to graduate from St. Mary's High School was in 1930. The high school closed in 1970, the sisters left in 1988, and the grade school closed in 1992.

By the early fifties the church had become inadequate for the more than 800 families. It was decided to build a new church. The new church was dedicated on December 4, 1955, by Bishop Joseph H. Albers.

The year 1959 saw the erection of a new convent on Delaware Avenue, the golden jubilee of Fr. Soest's ordination, and the 40th anniversary of the parish. Fr. Soest was named a domestic prelate and invested as a monsignor on December 15, 1959.

During Rev. Henry Berkemeier's pastorate (1961–1987) a bell tower, stained glass windows and a new Baldwin organ were purchased. The parish was under Rev. Francis J. Faraci's leadership from 1991, until his 2003 retirement. Rev. Robert F. Copeland then came to St. Mary Parish for his first pastorate.

Rev. Henry Berkemeier blesses the statue of St. Francis of Assisi, October 1985.

ST. MATTHEW THE EVANGELIST

FLINT

■ *St. Matthew Church, c. 1919*

Bishop John S. Foley of Detroit announced the founding of a new parish in Flint on September 29, 1911. The founding pastor, Rev. Michael J. Comerford, served St. Matthew parish for five years. For the celebration of the Divine Liturgy on October 8, 1911, a vacant store building on South Saginaw was rented and chairs were borrowed from St. Michael's. The first year over $27,000 in debt was incurred to purchase four lots, two houses, one garage and a barn.

Ground was broken on August 16, 1913, for a school. The red brick building on Beach Street was to serve as a temporary church as well as a school. Mass was held on the first floor and the second floor of the building, completed in May 1914, served as a school. In August, four Sisters, Servants of the Immaculate Heart of Mary from Monroe arrived to staff the school.

During the pastorate of Rev. Thomas G. Hennessey, in November 1919, the cornerstone for the present Romanesque structure was laid. The first services in the new church basement were held on Ash Wednesday 1920. Due to ill health, Fr. Hennessey was forced to resign in 1920. To his successor, Rev. Francis W. McQueen, fell the task of completing the church, building a new school, and purchasing a larger convent on Church Street.

Bishop Michael J. Gallagher contacted the Augustinian Fathers in Chestnut Hill, Pennsylvania, in early 1926 requesting that they take over St. Matthew parish. A parish with a half-million dollar debt was a lot to accept. Rev. Mortimer A. Sullivan, O.S.A., was up to the challenge as was his successor, Rev. Luke M. Powers, O.S.A.

The school continued to grow and to everyone's delight St. Matt's defeated St. Mike's in football for the first time in 1930. This great inter-parish rivalry ended only when both high schools were closed in 1970.

Fr. Powers celebrated his 25th anniversary as pastor of St. Matthew in 1954. At the time, there were 1,100 families in the parish. Before his retirement, a new convent (1955), a new field house (1958) and a new rectory (1960) were built.

A wonderful parish history was published to observe the 75th anniversary of the parish in 1986. To mark the Great Jubilee 2000 the parish placed a new roof on the church and installed air conditioning and new carpet. Rev. Frederick Taggert, O.S.A., has served as pastor since 1995.

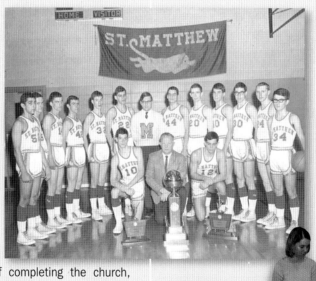

■ *The 1968 Class D State Champions*

■ *Children's Liturgy of the Word*

ST. MICHAEL

FLINT

St. Michael parish has often been referred to as the "Mother Church" of Genesee County because St. Michael was the first parish in Genesee County. The parish's origins are traced to Mr. Daniel O'Sullivan, a devout Irish Catholic schoolteacher, who first taught religion classes in the fall of 1834. Rev. Martin Kundig of Detroit stopped in Flint in May 1841 and April 1842 on missionary trips to the Saginaw Bay Area. Rev. Laurence Kilroy succeeded Fr. Kundig as pastor of Holy Trinity Detroit in 1842. He encouraged the beginning of the first church in September 1843. The first resident pastor, Rev. Michael Monaghan, was appointed May 20, 1847. The church was finally completed in 1848.

St. Michaels Catholic Church, Flint, Mich.

■ *The old church, c. 1910*

1871. From 1877 until 1951 this building was used as the convent. A new school was built in 1872. Rev. Robert M. Haire procured the services of the Sisters, Servants of the Immaculate Heart of Mary who came in the fall of 1877. The school closed in 1970.

During the pastorate (1880–1919) of Rev. Timothy J. Murphy the second St. Michael's church was built. The brick and stone church with its tall spire served as the center of worship from 1883 until 1964.

Rev. Patrick R. Dunigan came to Flint after serving as a World War I Army Chaplain. While he was pastor

During the tenures of Fr. Monaghan (1847–1850), Rev. Joseph Kindekens (1850–1854), and Rev. Charles L. De Ceuninck (1854–1869) St. Michael had a large missionary territory with stations in Genesee, Lapeer, Shiawassee, Livingston and Saginaw Counties. Fr. De Ceuninck found time to organize a one-room school in 1856. The school remained open until 1870.

Ten acres of ground were purchased in 1871, during Rev. James Gillespie's pastorate, and consecrated as Calvary Cemetery. Fr. Gillespie built a new rectory in

■ *Commissioning of the Sisters of Judith*

(1919–1934) a new school was built and forty acres for New Calvary Cemetery were purchased. Msgr. Maurice W. Chauke's pastorate (1934–1950) is remembered for the annual missions and the daily rosary, which he promoted. The face of St. Michael parish changed during Msgr. Earl V. Sheridan's pastorate (1950–1975). A new church, convent and rectory, as well as a school addition, were constructed. The St. Michael facilities were used during the pastorate of Rev. Matthew J. Fedewa (1975–1991) to house the Flint Newman Center and the DuKette Intercultural Center. Since June 2002 Rev. Philip P. Gallagher has served as the parish's sixteenth pastor.

■ *Sanctuary, 1987*

ST. PIUS X

$\mathscr{F}$LINT

In August 1953 Bishop Joseph H. Albers wrote to Rev. Luke M. Powers, O.S.A., pastor of St. Michael Flint, requesting that a survey be made of the west Court and west Corunna Road areas.

The results of the survey led to an eleven and one-half acre site being purchased in December 1954. Rev. John A. Blasko was given the charge to be founding pastor of the new parish on June 2, 1955. He celebrated the congregation's first liturgy in the C.I.O. Labor Temple in August 1955. In October a house and garage adjoining the parish property were purchased. The garage was remodeled and used as a chapel for daily Mass until the church was built in 1956. Within a year after the dedication of the church by Bishop Albers in September 1956, Fr. Blasko was transferred.

St. Pius X school children select books to read under the federally funded R.I.F. (Reading is Fundamental) program, December 1978

Rev. Anthony G. Brakora came to St. Pius parish and was its pastor for the next seventeen years. By 1960 the parish debt had been significantly reduced and plans for a school were begun. The ten-room building was completed in November 1961 and opened the following September. The Sisters of the Precious Blood from Dayton, Ohio, staffed the school along with lay teachers. Sisters of St. Joseph and Sisters of Charity have also taught at St. Pius. From June 1971 until June 1977 the school was under the control of the Genesee County Catholic Board of Education.

The growing parish received its first assistant pastor in 1962. So the assistant did not have to sleep in the school, a new rectory was completed in 1964. A large convent was completed in 1967.

Within months of Rev. Vincent DeLorenzo becoming pastor in June 1976, a major renovation of the church and a hall addition were undertaken. In February 1980 faceted glass windows depicting themes of children and the family were dedicated by Bishop James S. Sullivan.

With the appointment in February 1979 of Rev. Steven J. Raica as associate pastor and chaplain for the deaf ministry in the diocese, St. Pius became the home for the deaf community until 1992.

The 25th anniversary of the parish was celebrated on June 29, 1980, with a Mass and dinner at the Sons of Italy Hall. Bishop Kenneth J. Povish returned to celebrate the 40th anniversary Mass in February 1995. Since June 1985 the St. Pius X faith community has been led by Msgr. Richard J. Groshek.

This section of stained glass windows depicts a spring scene of sacraments (Baptism, First Eucharist, Confirmation)

ST. ROBERT BELLARMINE

FLUSHING

It was in the home of Irish immigrants that the first Mass in the Flushing area was celebrated. Rev. Charles L. De Ceuninck was assigned to St. Michael Flint in October 1854. He was determined to visit the Catholics living far from Flint. The Peter McCartney family hosted Fr. De Ceuninck in their home for that first Eucharist. Land was acquired in 1865 in Hazelton Township, Shiawassee County, from Henry and Ann McCarthy. A building was not constructed for several years. It is presumed that the church was dedicated to St. Robert because Rev. Robert W. Haire was pastor (1875–1880) of St. Michael at that time.

When St. Joseph Gaines became a parish in 1892, two missions were assigned to it: St. Robert, Hazelton and St. Mary, Antrim. As the Catholic population grew, thoughts of building a new church were raised. The question was where. A petition was sent to Bishop Michael J. Gallagher in Detroit that the new church be built in Flushing. Groundbreaking for the church in Flushing was held in the fall of 1919. The Frawley

(By Dean Peterson/Faith)

■ *Students at St. Robert's release balloons on Ascension Day 1985*

Fackler was pastor (1972–1983) an activities center was constructed and stained glass windows were installed in the church. Fr. Gerald J. Ploof (1988–1991) organized the Fr. Jacobs Educational Trust Fund to ensure Catholic education. The St. Robert Bellarmine parish has been led by Rev. Steven F. Makranyi since 1992.

family had donated the lot. The first resident pastor was Rev. David Cunningham who was assigned in the fall of 1927.

The pastorate (1953–1972) of Rev. Charles E. Jacobs was one of much building. A school was built and opened in September 1954 and staffed by the Sisters of Charity from Cincinnati, Ohio. The present church was dedicated in May 1963. While Rev. John M.

■ *The school baseball team, 1989*

MOST HOLY TRINITY

*F*OWLER

Holy Trinity Church, Fowler, Mich.

The roots of the faith in Fowler can be traced to 1857 when Rev. George Godez, pastor of St. Peter's (now St. Mary's) in Westphalia, came to the Fowler area to celebrate the Eucharist. Fr. Godez continued to visit Fowler from time to time until he left Westphalia in 1873.

Holy Trinity Church, c. 1910

The 1877 National Catholic Directory listed the Fowler congregation for the first time under the category of station as "Dallas, Clinton Co., attended from Hubbardston". Fowler is in Dallas Township. Rev. Peter De Smedt was pastor in Hubbardston. He encouraged the fledgling Catholic community.

In 1878 John and Elizabeth Fowler gave land for a church provided one was built within three years. In October 1879 a meeting was held at the Bengel's furniture store in Fowler to discuss building a church. Two months later, a building committee consisting of John Kissane, William Henderson, Conrad Martin and Charles Bengel was appointed to begin soliciting funds.

Interior of the church, circa 1930

In June 1880 Bishop Casper H. Borgess of Detroit designated the Fowler Catholics a mission of St. John Hubbardston. The care of the Fowler mission was entrusted to pastors of St. Joseph, St. Johns from 1880 until 1886. During this period a church was built in 1881 at a cost of $2,293.45. The Racine Dominican Sisters staffed the school, which opened in the fall of 1888. They remained in the parish until 1976.

Parochial status was achieved when Rev. Bernard H. Holthaus was appointed the first resident pastor in June 1886. The growing parish necessitated an addition be built to the church in 1889, but additional space was again soon needed. The cornerstone for the present church was laid by Auxiliary Bishop of Detroit Edward D. Kelly on July 4, 1916. He returned to dedicate the edifice in 1918.

In June 1939 the first Diocesan Eucharistic Day was held in Fowler. Rev. George J. Esper, pastor of Fowler from 1923 to 1958, was host and Bishop Joseph H. Albers presided over the impressive ceremonies. Rev. Albert J. Schmitt (pastor from 1958 to 1980) oversaw the building of a new rectory in 1959. The parish centennial was observed in 1981 when Rev. Denis R. Spitzley was pastor. A spacious activities center was dedicated in 1988 while Rev. Arthur F. Bosse was Fowler's spiritual leader. Rev. Timothy E. MacDonald assumed the Fowler pastorate in 2002.

Eucharistic Day, June 11, 1939.
It featured an outdoor mass with
Bishop Joseph Albers as celebrant
and a eucharistic procession.

ST. AGNES

FOWLERVILLE

Bishop Carl F. Mengeling dedicated the new facilities in June 1998. Rev. James W. Lothamer SS. was entrusted with the care of souls in St. Agnes Parish in August 2003.

Family records indicate that the first Mass in the bounds of St. Agnes parish was celebrated in the McCarthy home in Iosco Township by Rev. Patrick O'Kelly from Ann Arbor. The first record in diocesan archives of a Catholic presence in Fowlerville is the 1876 annual report of St. Patrick parish in Brighton. Fowlerville remained a station of Brighton until 1887. After a year under the care of the Williamston parish, Fowlerville was entrusted to Howell for the next seventeen years. While Rev. John P. Ryan was pastor in Howell a stone and brick church was built in Fowlerville in 1891. In October 1901 the original Mt. Olivet cemetery site was purchased by three Irish families for $500.

From 1905 to 1954 the St. Agnes community was assigned to the pastoral care of the pastor of St. Mary Williamston. Tragedy struck the St. Agnes parish family when the church was destroyed by a cyclone in May 1909. In May 1911 the succeeding edifice was dedicated by Auxiliary Bishop of Detroit, Edward D. Kelly.

A house was purchased for a rectory in 1953 and the first resident pastor was Rev. Martin M. Walker. During the pastorate (1966–1971) of Rev. George A. Higgins the parish relocated. A new church and catechetical center was constructed east of town on Grand River Road. A rectory was built the year after Fr. Higgins left. The Centennial of the parish was celebrated in 1991. An open house/ice cream social in June, a parish picnic in August, a new pictorial directory and a closing Mass followed by a dinner/dance in October rounded out the festivities.

The pastorate (1992–2000) of Rev. Francis George was very eventful. Additional acreage was purchased. The worship space was expanded and renovated.

■ *The second St. Agnes Church, 1934*

■ *Pentecost, 2003*

ST. JOSEPH

GAINES

The Catholic presence in Gaines is first attested to in the Metropolitan Catholic Almanac of 1857 when Gaines is listed as a station of St. Michael Flint. This entry indicates that Rev. Charles L. De Ceuninck visited in 1856. In July 1857 Gaines is among the stations assigned to the newly erected parish of the Annunciation in Corunna. It was under the direction of Rev. Ignatius B. Rickert, of Corunna, that in May 1869 two lots were purchased in the village of Gaines for a future church. Rev. Joseph Kraemer, who moved the parochial residence from Corunna to St. Johns and then to Owosso, oversaw the construction of the present church in 1871 at a cost of $2,000.

When Rev. William Kilroy became pastor of Fenton in September 1876, the Gaines mission was placed under his care. Fr. Kilroy continued to celebrate the sacraments for the mission until it achieved parochial status in 1892. The new parish was given the care of missions in Antrim Township (later Morrice) and Hazelton Township (later Flushing).

The Marshall home was bought to serve as a rectory for Rev. George O'Sullivan. After his arrival in March, Fr. O'Sullivan immersed himself in work. The church in Gaines was then moved three blocks to its present location across the street from the rectory. Fr. O'Sullivan fostered the development of the Catholic community in Durand which was regularly attended from 1896 until it became a parish in 1901.

For a brief period (1927–1929), Gaines became a mission of Swartz Creek. When it was re-established as a parish, St. Augustine in Deerfield was attached as a mission until 1980.

■ *Easter season, 2000*

The parish celebrated the centennial of its beloved church in 1971 during the pastorate of Rev. D. Philip Dupuis. A two day celebration included a concelebrated Mass, a parade and a chicken dinner for over 1,200. A parish center was completed in 1976.

The Gaines parish was entrusted to a pastoral coordinator in July 1988. Sister Ann Marie Petri, O.P., followed Sister Geraldine Maloney, O.P., as pastoral coordinator in July 1995. Sr. Ann Marie is leading the parish in a relocation process. Since ordination in 1990, Deacon Currie T. Cormier and his wife, Donna, have served the Gaines parish.

ST. MARK THE EVANGELIST

*G*OODRICH

On the universal level three popes held the chair of Peter in 1978. Ten men were ordained priests for the Diocese of Lansing that year. The Catholic families of Goodrich petitioned Bishop Kenneth J. Povish for a parish of their own. There were enough Catholic households to begin a parish separate from St. John the Evangelist in Davison.

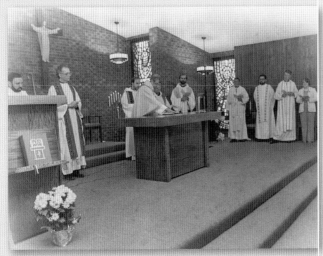

■ *Bishop Povish anoints the altar at the dedication of the new church, April 1982*

The first Mass for the Goodrich Catholics was celebrated in August in the Goodrich library. Bishop Povish formally established the mission of St. Mark the Evangelist on November 26, 1978. A religious education program and the Altar Society were also organized that fall.

The response to the mission was better than expected and soon the library was too small. The Goodrich High School cafeteria became the temporary site of worship. Rev. Joseph Aubin, pastor of St. John's in Davison (1977–1983), oversaw the formation and organization of the Goodrich mission.

The year 1979 was extremely important in the life of the community: the first parish council was established in June; First Holy Communion and Confirmation were celebrated for the first time in May; and land was purchased and a building drive for a new church was begun. Ground was broken for the new church in June 1981. Bishop Povish dedicated the church in April 1982.

A decade of growth necessitated more on-site leadership. On the Feast of SS. Peter and Paul in 1989, Sister Joan M. May, S.S.J., came to St. Mark as pastoral coordinator. She has led the Catholic community for over a decade. Ground was broken for a parish center in May 1993. Bishop Povish dedicated the center the following May. The center includes offices, classrooms and a kitchen. This doubled the size of the parish facilities for this vibrant Catholic community.

■ *The Goodrich Library, where the first two Masses in Goodrich were held in 1978.*

CHURCH OF THE HOLY FAMILY

GRAND BLANC

Sixty-eight Catholic residents signed a petition that was sent to Bishop Joseph H. Albers in February 1945. The petition requested a new parish be established in Grand Blanc. Once World War II was concluded, Bishop Albers could begin to make plans for the future parish. In October 1945 several lots were purchased by the Diocese. Further land was purchased the following January. The acreage included the site of the first trading post between Detroit and Saginaw. On July 20, 1946, Bishop Albers canonically established the parish of the Holy Family. Rev. John H. Bush was the founding pastor. Fr. Bush remained at Holy Family until his retirement in 1983.

The first church, referred to by parishioners as the "White Hall", had been built for the National Youth Administration Camp on Dort Highway. The cornerstone for the second church was laid in 1952. Bishop Albers came to Grand Blanc for its dedication. The Sisters of St. Joseph from Nazareth opened the school in the fall of 1956. The school has continued to grow and has been added on to several times.

Within a decade of being built the second church was exceedingly cramped. A two-wing addition was dedicated by Bishop Albers in September 1964. Fr. Bush's last building project, a parish center, was named for him when it was dedicated by Bishop Kenneth J. Povish in December 1983. Fr. Bush had retired the previous June and had been succeeded by Rev. James R. Swiat.

Fifth grade Jeopardy-Quiz Bowl, Holy Family School, 1988

(By Dean Peterson/Faith)

Shortly after the parish golden jubilee was celebrated in 1996, it was evident that the educational facilities of the parish once again needed expansion. In 1998 a 2.3 million dollar fund drive saw the construction of eight classrooms, a science lab, a computer lab, a preschool room and expanded school and religious education offices.

(By Dean Peterson/Faith)

St. Michael the Archangel

Grand Ledge

Rev. Louis Van Driss, pastor at St. Mary Lansing, listed Grand Ledge as a station for the first time on his 1870 annual report. During that year he offered Holy Mass at the McMullen family home on Jefferson Street in Grand Ledge. Visits were infrequent and the next time Grand Ledge appears on an annual report is in 1880.

Continuity in the Grand Ledge community begins in 1901. Rev. Lafayette I. Brancheau listed Grand Ledge as a station that year and thereafter. Fr. Brancheau, pastor of St. Mary Lansing, went to Grand Ledge once a month and celebrated Mass at the Campbell, Rossman or Juenker homes.

■ *Rev. Brancheau from St. Mary, Lansing, visits parishionersin Grand Ledge, c. 1905*

When Charlotte became a parish in 1918, Grand Ledge and Eaton Rapids both became its missions. In 1924 the care of the Grand Ledge Catholics was given to the newly created parish of Holy Cross in Lansing.

Mr. Joseph Gleason, a prominent Lansing Catholic, purchased the George Berry home in Grand Ledge in 1929. The following year he deeded the house and adjacent property to the parish. Mr. Gleason requested that the new community be dedicated to St. Michael in memory of his father. The renovated house was soon outgrown and a new $30,000 building was dedicated in 1941. A resident priest, Rev. George P. Horkan, was assigned to St. Michael the following year.

■ *St. Michael Church, 1957*

The pastorate (1949–1966) of Rev. Anthony E. Csaky will long be remembered by the people of St. Michael as a time of great growth and development. Fr. Csaky invited the Adrian Dominican Sisters to staff the school that opened in September 1961.

Rev. Charles J. Crowley came to Grand Ledge in 1966 and set about building the present church. When it opened in 1970 it seated 800 people. Administration and activity rooms that were added to the school were blessed by Bishop Kenneth J. Povish in February 1987. The school celebrated its 30th anniversary in 1991 with an all-alumni dance. Since 1995 Rev. Robert H. McGraw has led the congregation. He oversaw the complete renovation of the church which was rededicated on Pentecost Sunday, 1999. Most recently the parish celebrated the school's 40th anniversary and the parish's centennial in 2001.

HOLY SPIRIT ROMAN CATHOLIC CHURCH

ℋAMBURG

With St. Patrick parish in Brighton bursting at the seams and development in the Township of Hamburg and Green Oak continuing, a new parish was organized on June 29, 1979. Rev. Charles E. Irvin was appointed the founding pastor. In August the first meeting of a parish advisory board was held. The new Catholic community was united around the Lord's Table for Mass for the first time on September 16. The Eucharist was participated in by about 420 people in the Hamburg Veterans of Foreign Wars Hall. Balloting began in late September for a name for the new parish. It was inconclusive until Bishop Kenneth J. Povish celebrated mass with the parishioners on October 14. He proposed three names. Church of the Holy Spirit won by a landslide when the results were tabulated at the end of the month.

In August 1980 the first pastoral assistant/ religious education director in the person of Sr. Donna Hart, I.H.M., was hired. That same month the rectory was finished and the first parish festival was held.

Rev. Charles Irvin and Bishop Kenneth Povish break ground for the new church in April 1981.

Director of Religious Education Sean Lavell and members of the youth group

permanent church, which had been constructed during the pastorate (1987–1996) of Rev. Paul J. Cummings.

Fifteen acres of land were purchased in March 1980 and ground was broken for the parish center in April 1981. This building was dedicated by Bishop Povish in December. Just over a decade later Bishop Povish returned, in September 1992, to dedicate the

Since Rev. William W. Thomas became pastor in June 1999, plans to open a parish school developed rapidly. On September 3, 2002, the school opened with preschool, kindergarten and first grade. Bishop Carl F. Mengeling dedicated the school building on All Souls Day 2002.

St. Anthony of Padua

Hillsdale

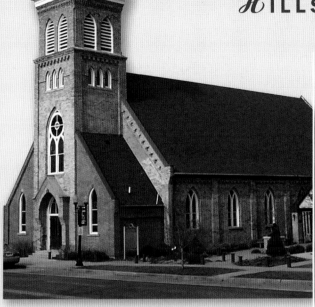

Vatican II leaders, c. 1966

help pay for the church a huge St. Patrick's Day festival had been held the previous March. Among the items raffled off were a cow and a gold watch and chain. The gaslights were removed from the church in 1922 when it was wired for electricity.

Rev. Francis L. Sharp's pastorate (1949–1952) laid the foundation for the opening of a grade school, which was realized in September 1956 during Rev. Norbert B. Wheeler's pastorate (1951–1960). The Sisters of St. Joseph from Nazareth, Michigan, staffed the school for many years before its closure in June 1985.

Bishop Kenneth J. Povish came to Hillsdale in May 1987 for the blessing of a new altar and in August 1991 for the dedication of the state historical marker recognizing the architectural value of the church. With the arrival of Rev. Thomas W. Butler in 1993 hopes for a parish center became a reality. The new facility was dedicated in January 1995.

The Redemptorists from Monroe were the first clergy to visit Hillsdale Catholics in 1846. The names of the early families, Murphy, Regan, Donahoe, Connelly, McCabe, Cavanaugh, McIntyre, Burns and Sullivan, attest to the thoroughly Irish makeup of the congregation. When St. Mary Adrian achieved parochial status in 1853, Hillsdale was among the missions of the new parish. Rev. Joseph Kindekins oversaw the purchase in 1856 of the old Presbyterian Church. It is reported that the following Easter 100 faithful received Holy Communion. Rev. Charles Ryckaert was sent to Hillsdale as the first resident pastor in May 1858. Fr. Ryckaert also had responsibility for nurturing the faith of Catholic families in Coldwater, Jonesville and Palmyra. A parish cemetery was begun in 1863 with the purchase of two acres from Mr. Ferris for $203.

A new church became necessary and in June 1884 Bishop Casper H. Borgess of Detroit dedicated the present church. The dedicatory sermon was preached by the well know orator, Rev. Dr. Ormond O'Reilly. To

The bronze sculpture "Holy Mary, Mother of God" by Anthony Frudakis, graces the courtyard.

ST. AUGUSTINE

HOWELL (DEERFIELD TOWNSHIP)

During the 1830s Irish Catholic families settled in Deerfield Township, Livingston County. When Fr. Patrick O'Kelly was assigned pastor of Livingston and Oakland Counties in February 1843, he found thirteen families to organize into a faith community. Of these, the Bennett, Carr, Conklin, McCarthy, McGuire, McKeon, Murphy, Ryan, Scullin and Sweeny families had their roots in Counties Longford and Clare in Ireland. Fr. O'Kelly first dedicated the community to St. Andrew. The first church was begun in late 1843. It was probably finished in 1846 when the community became known as SS. Peter and Paul. While a mission (1860–1870) of St. John Oceola (Hartland), land was purchased for a rectory to be built and two additional acres were bought for the cemetery. From 1870 to 1871 Rev. Thomas Rafter was the resident pastor of St. Augustine (as it is now known). When Fr. Rafter moved to Fenton in 1872 the Deerfield community became a mission of Fenton. It remained a mission of Fenton until 1929.

■ *Historical marker dedicated October 1997*

While Rev. George J. Mauer was pastor of Fenton (1893–1899) the present St. Augustine church was constructed. The Detroit architect Harry J. Rill designed the building. The five member building committee was all Irish. Deep faith in the community was evidenced by the fourteen young women who entered religious life from St. Augustine.

From 1929 to 1980 Deerfield was a mission of St. Joseph Gaines. In 1980 the mission was again given to Fenton. New life came to the parish when Sr. Rita Schaefer, O.P., came to reside in Deerfield Township as the parish pastoral minister. Sr. Rita was the first sister to administer a congregation in our Diocese. In May 1983 ground was broken for a family center. It was dedicated the following October. Sr. Rita left St. Augustine's in 1984 when the Deerfield mission became a quasi-parish with Rev. William J. Carolin as the first resident priest in over one hundred years. The church and cemetery have been placed on the state register of historic sites. Since 1999 Rev. Gregg A. Pleiness has served as pastor.

■ *Groundbreaking for St. Augustine Family Center took place May 6, 1983.*

ST. JOHN THE BAPTIST

HOWELL (HARTLAND)

In 1837 the home of James Gleason was where the first liturgy was held in the present day Hartland parish. Local tradition records Rev. Thomas Morrissey of Northfield as celebrating the first Eucharist. Later that year Rev. Bernard O'Cavanaugh (pastor of Holy Trinity, Detroit) purchased forty acres in Hartland Township. On July 1, 1840, Fr. O'Cavanaugh deeded the site to Bishop Frederic Rese of Detroit. The Brophy Road Cemetery still marks that site.

The old St. John the Baptist Church in Osceola Township begun in 1868

A pastor was assigned to Livingston and Oakland Counties in February 1843. Rev. Patrick O'Kelly had returned from the Wisconsin portion of the Diocese of Detroit the previous fall. He oversaw the purchase of another piece of property in 1844. There, a church was erected in 1846. This land was located in Osceola Township and for more than a century the community was know as the Osceola Mission.

From 1860 until 1871 the Hartland community had a resident priest. The west end of the little brick church was laid on the Feast of St. John the Baptist in 1868 and the east end was completed in 1873. In September 1876 Rev. James Wheeler became the first pastor of Brighton. The St. John the Baptist community began a ninety-eight year period as a mission of Brighton. While still a mission, seventeen acres were purchased in 1970 for future expansion.

St. John regained its status as a parish on October 14, 1974, when Rev. Allen J. Theis was appointed the first resident priest in more than a century. Rev. Thomas W. Thompson succeeded him in July 1976. It fell to Fr. Thompson to lead the parish during a period of great growth. Well over 400 families had joined the parish between 1974 and 1979. The weekend Mass schedule had to be expanded and services were held in Hartland High School. A parish center consisting of a 720-seat worship space and parish offices was erected and was ready for use in April 1979.

Continued rapid growth led Fr. Thompson's successor, Rev. David J. Speicher, to begin planning for a larger permanent church. His transfer left the challenge of the actual building of the present church to Rev. Francis M. George. Bishop Carl F. Mengeling dedicated the new church on October 27, 2002.

The altar at the first Christmas in the new church, 2002.

These are chair people and area coordinators for the annual Lenten Fish Fry. As many as 1,000 meals are served each Friday in Lent.

ST. JOSEPH

*H*OWELL

■ *The old
St. Joseph
Church (1878)
and rectory*

The pioneer priest of the Diocese, Rev. Patrick O'Kelly, was the first to visit the Catholic families in Howell. His first visit was probably in 1843. After Fr. O'Kelly's departure for Livingston County in 1856, the care of the Howell area was given the following year to the newly opened parish in Corunna, headed by Rev. Edward Van Paemel. It was not until

■ *St. Joseph School*

June of 1871 that land was purchased by Bishop Casper H. Borgess for a future church. The cornerstone for a forty by seventy foot structure was laid in August 1878. A decade later the first resident pastor, Rev. James J. Gore, was assigned to Howell.

In the first decade of the twentieth century the church was enlarged by adding on a new sanctuary and sacristy. In 1914 land was purchased for a parish cemetery.

Rev. Herman P. Fedewa arrived in Howell in 1929. He led the parish through the Depression. A long-delayed goal of opening a parish school occurred in September 1940. The Sisters of Mercy from Farmington opened

grades one through five with forty-seven pupils. The last Mercy principal, Sr. Mary Carlos Knight, R.S.M., left in 1986.

Between 1954 and 1963 the parish totally relocated from its Grand River location to the present site on Washington Street. What Rev. John R. Day began by building a new school in 1954, Rev. Joseph E. Wieber finished by building a new church and rectory.

During the pastorate of Rev. Gilbert O. Rahrig the school facilities were significantly expanded and the large parish center, including a daily mass chapel, were constructed. The Fall Fun Daze were annual events and everyone looked forward to purchasing one of Fr. Rahrig's famous jams.

Rev. William A. Ashbaugh was sent to Howell in January 2001. There was a renovation of the rectory to create much needed office space for staff.

■ *Easter, 1996*

SACRED HEART OF JESUS

ℋUDSON

School children perform for Grandparents Day.
The main altar of Carrara marble, in the
background, was imported from Italy in 1906.

The first house of worship in the present Hudson parish was built in 1853 in Medina Township in an area noted for the fervent practice of Catholicism. The "Catholic Hill" church served the community until land was purchased in Hudson five years later. The barn on the village property was remodeled into a church. The first resident pastor was Rev. Francis J. Van Erp who served from 1859 until 1872. To accommodate the growing parish, the barn was added on to in 1863. That same year land was purchased for a Catholic cemetery. Fr. Van Erp felt a proper church was needed to replace the barn. Bishop Peter P. Lefevere of Detroit laid the cornerstone for a new church in 1866. The church was completed enough for services to begin being held there in May 1869.

While Rev. Joseph F. Hallissey was pastor (1899–1922) a new church and rectory were built and a new cemetery site was purchased.

Bishop Michael J. Gallagher of Detroit dedicated the school when it opened in September 1929. The school was staffed by the Sisters of St. Francis of Rochester, Minnesota, from 1929 until 1937. The Adrian Dominican Sisters replaced them in 1937. A high school department operated from 1933 until 1946. The parish's native son, Auxiliary Bishop Henry E. Donnelly of Detroit, returned to the parish to celebrate its centennial liturgy in 1959.

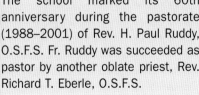

During Rev. Jonathan W. Wehrle's pastorate (1982–1988) the parish's 125th anniversary was celebrated. To mark the anniversary the church was completely renovated and the basement was transformed into a social hall with a full kitchen. The organ was rebuilt to reveal the rose window.

The school marked its 60th anniversary during the pastorate (1988–2001) of Rev. H. Paul Ruddy, O.S.F.S. Fr. Ruddy was succeeded as pastor by another oblate priest, Rev. Richard T. Eberle, O.S.F.S.

(By Dean Peterson/Faith)

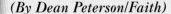

157

QUEEN OF THE MIRACULOUS MEDAL

JACKSON

In the midst of the Depression, Bishop Michael J. Gallagher wrote to the Vincentian Fathers to organize a new parish in Jackson. The new parish was carved out of territory formerly belonging to St. Mary, Star of the Sea. Rev. Arthur J. Keegan, C.M., was the founding pastor. He was also appointed chaplain for Mercy Hospital and for the Michigan State Police post. When he arrived in Jackson he first resided at Mercy Hospital. The Knights of Columbus building at Wildwood and Michigan hosted the weekend Masses for the parish from 1934 until 1938.

The World Peace Prayer Club was formed by seven to ten year old girls from the parish in spring 1960.

A temporary church was not begun until 1938. The parish school began in the convent purchased in November 1939. The school was staffed by the Adrian Dominicans for many years. Sr. Mary Raymondo was the first superior (1939–1945). In January 1941 the eight classrooms, built atop the basement church, were opened. For a number of years, Queen's had the largest school in the Diocese. Additions to the school happened during the pastorates of Rev. John H. Dougherty, C.M., and Rev. Francis X. Desmond, C.M. In the fall of 1963 there were 1,181 students in the eight-grade school.

The present church was dedicated by Bishop Joseph H. Albers on May 21, 1950. During the Marian Year of 1954 a solemn novena in honor of Our Lady, Queen of the Miraculous Medal, was held.

In 1981 the convent was remodeled into parish offices and a rectory. The rectory was sold. The parish's 50th anniversary was celebrated with a Mass and parish picnic in June 1984. On Monday of the First Week of Lent, March 1, 1993, the parish opened the second perpetual adoration chapel in the diocese.

The Sixty-two year Vincentian tradition came to an end in 1996 and diocesan clergy have carried on the leadership of Queen's. Rev. Thomas D. Nenneau has pastored the congregation since June 2000.

(Faith)

ST. JOHN THE EVANGELIST

JACKSON

That the first mass in Jackson County was celebrated in 1836 in Jackson is agreed upon. Who the priest was, is in question. About 1842 a log church was built under the direction of Fr. Thomas Cullen of Ann Arbor. In November 1853 John and Mary Guinine deeded land to Bishop Peter Paul Lefevere on the condition that a church be built upon the lots within five years or the property would revert to them. Bishop Lefevere in 1856, laid the cornerstone for a church. This building, although enlarged several times, is the oldest church building in the Diocese of Lansing in continuous use. Rev. Cornelius Moutard was the first pastor of the parish serving from 1856 until 1870.

■ *St. John's Academy, c. 1920*

Rev. Theophilus Buyse shepherded the St. John congregation from 1871 until 1895. He sought the help of the Sisters, Servants of the Immaculate Heart of Mary to open a school for 200 children in the fall of 1873. A high school department was opened in 1888. The first graduates were three young ladies in 1892. In 1903 a three-story school was opened and known as St. John Academy. Rev. C. M. B. Schenkelburg was pastor at the time. Fr. John Wall served the St. John's parish family for twenty-eight years (1914–1942). He oversaw the remodeling of the church when its red brick exterior was replaced with the present Indiana limestone.

■ *Former pastors at the 125th Anniversary celebration: Rev. Francis Murray (1979 - 1990); Rev. Leo Ramer (1971-79); Rev. Adolph Oser (1962-69); Rev. George Higgins (1956-1962)*

A new high school was dedicated in 1955. It had been built on twenty-five acres of land purchased by Rev. Joseph V. Coyle. The last graduating class was in 1968. That fall the high school began to be used as Jackson Catholic Middle School. The last I.H.M. principal, Sr. Rose Ange Leddy, left the grade school in 1985 ending a 112-year tradition.

During the pastorate (1979–1990) of Rev. Francis J. Murray the parish celebrated its 125th anniversary and the church was redecorated in 1984. The old convent was torn down and an administration building erected in 1986. It contained offices, a library, two meeting rooms, a garage and rooms for the Knights of Columbus and St. Vincent de Paul Society.

Since June 1995 Rev. James R. Shaver has led the congregation.

ST. JOSEPH

JACKSON

The first initiative for a Polish language parish occurred in 1895. As a result the St. Joseph Society was organized. A priest was sent to Jackson in 1901 but was removed only months later. There was a tremendous controversy over the location of the parish. Rev. Joseph F. Herr, considered the first pastor of the parish, was assigned to the community in the fall of 1902. The first Mass for the parish was offered in White Hall at Columbus and Michigan Avenue.

The following September two Felician sisters taught forty-five pupils in a converted brick barn. In 1908 a four-room school was built. Eight more rooms were added in 1914. The Felician community celebrated their centennial of service to the parish in 2003.

The first St. Joseph church was completed in the fall of 1904. The Polish native, Rev. Joseph Przybylski, pastored St. Joseph parish from 1925 until 1963. A

new convent and rectory were built. Fr. Przybylski celebrated the 50th anniversary of his ordination on July 6, 1963. He retired the same month and Rev. Marian J. Lesniak began his thirty-nine year pastorate.

■ *Fresh paczki!*

Fr. Lesniak immediately began plans for a new church. Bishop Alexander M. Zaleski dedicated the present parish church in May 1968.

One of the St. Joseph parish traditions is the annual paczki sale. It is one of the parish's largest fundraisers. In the parish centennial year, 2002, about seventy-five volunteers made 800 dozen paczki. The centennial celebration concluded with a Mass on October second. It was a bittersweet affair because the retirement of Fr. Lesniak was observed at the same time. The care of souls was entrusted to Rev. Louis Madey in June 2003.

■ *The 2002 Pastoral Committee: Back row: Brian Millen, Joe Ziepiela, Howell Wynne, Fr. Mike Petroski, Raymon Gorczyca, Steve Job; Middle row: Linda Bush, Deacon Al Kreiger, Shelley Page; Front Row: Stasia Kistka, Val Davidowicz, Rita Konopka, Dave Zemer, Sr. Josephine Lechowicz, Ed Szczepanski*

ST. MARY, STAR OF THE SEA

Jackson

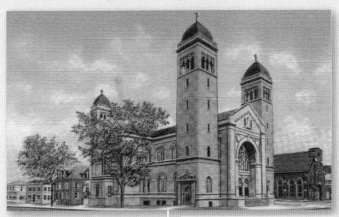

In September 1880 a petition was sent to Bishop Casper Borgess in Detroit signed by 124 people who requested a new parish in Jackson. Rev. John W. Maloney, who was temporarily filling in for the vacationing pastor of St. John parish, encouraged the petition drive. On November 29, 1880, Bishop Borgess appointed Fr. Maloney the pastor of the new parish. Fr. Maloney remained at St. Mary parish until his death in May 1908.

The first church was built in the Gothic style and completed in 1881. A school consisting of ten classrooms and a convent were built in 1880. The school opened with a high school department and the first graduation took place in June 1892. The Sisters of Charity from Cincinnati, Ohio, staffed the school for over eighty years.

While Rev. Eugene M. Cullinane was pastor (1908–1944) the St. Mary parish was almost entirely rebuilt. A new convent was built in 1912 and the capacity of the school was doubled in 1913. The present three-story rectory was built in 1915. The present church was begun in 1923. The twenty-two stained glass windows and mosaic Stations of the Cross were created in Innsbruck, Austria. The last edifice Fr. Cullinane constructed was a new high school erected in 1931 on the site of the old church.

The parish debt was only paid during Monsignor Frank J. Hardy's pastorate (1944–1966). He could,

■ *St. Mary High School, Class of 1898. Left to right: Mrs. Felder Cook, Elizabeth McGraw, Gertrude Doyle Murphy, Margaret Hennessey*

in 1949, turn attention to decorating the church. St. Mary was the site of the presbyteral ordination of four Jackson men in 1949. Among them was native son Gilbert Rahrig. Monsignor Hardy continued to add to the school throughout the 1950s.

As part of the parish centennial celebration, the organ was rebuilt and the 1889 school sandblasted. Bishop Kenneth J. Povish celebrated the centennial Mass in December 1980. The centennial liturgy of the school was held in July 1989. Rev. Bernard L. Reilly was entrusted with the care of souls in St. Mary Parish in 1998.

■ *The old St. Mary church and school*

ST. STANISLAUS KOSTKA

JACKSON

■ *Old Church*

The beginnings of the St. Stanislaus parish are traced to the formation of the St. Stanislaus Club in 1913. The club members purchased a house at the corner of Pringle and Elm Streets in which to hold activities. In 1919 the club sent a delegation to Bishop Michael J. Gallagher of Detroit requesting a second Polish parish in Jackson. The delegation presented a petition with the signatures of 282 Poles who requested a parish in southeastern Jackson. The following year, Rev. Bernard

■ *The Rosary Society, formed in 1919, provides funds for many church needs. Officers, 2003, left to right: Marge Killian, financial secretary; Wanda Marianski, recording secretary; Jenny Augustine, President; Frances Kukulka, Treasurer. Not pictured: Winifred Jeremy, Vice President.*

Ciesielski was appointed the first pastor. The Polish Falcon Hall was the site of the first Eucharist. Later the St. Stanislaus Club house was adapted for use.

In the fall of 1921 the combined church and school building was completed. The Felician Sisters opened the parish school in October with 120 students. The first eighth grade graduation was held in 1923. A further two classrooms were added to the school that year.

During the pastorate of Rev. Joseph P. Nowaczyk (1932–1965) a convent was built in 1936 and Kostka Hall was built in 1937. Building a permanent church was delayed by World War II. The present church was dedicated by the Jackson Dean Monsignor Frank J.

Hardy on May 26, 1957. A new rectory was completed in December 1961.

The parish golden jubilee was celebrated on October 17, 1970. The jubilee Mass was followed by a dinner dance at the Labor Temple. Rev. Hubert J. Rakowski was serving the parish at that time.

The Rev. Canon Darius W. Wyszynski, a distant relative of Stefan Cardinal Wyszynski of Poland came to St. Stanislaus in May 1979. The Cardinal sent an icon of Our Lady of Czestochowa to the parish in 1981. The following year the diocesan observance of the 600th anniversary of Our Lady of Czestochowa was held at St. Stanislaus. Bishop Kenneth J. Povish celebrated the liturgy. Rev. Canon Wyszynski continues to serve as pastor.

■ *A replica of the famous icon "Our Lady of Czestochowa", painted on wood with gold leaf halos and a gold leaf frame, hangs over the altar. It was commissioned by the late Primate of Poland, Stefan Cardinal Wyszynski, and sent to St. Stanislaus Kostka in 1981.*

ST. ISIDORE

LAINGSBURG

The first record of Catholics at Laingsburg is recorded in the St. Mary Lansing annual reports of 1868 and 1869. Rev. Louis Van Driss listed Laingsburg as a station he visited. After that it seems Fr. Van Driss convinced the Laingsburg Catholics to go to St. Patrick church in Woodhull Township, south of Laingsburg.

When Rev. Anton Krams filled out the 1899 report for St. Joseph Parish St. Johns he included Laingsburg as a station visited by him. In February 1900 six lots on Crum Street were purchased for $300. In the summer of 1902 the cornerstone for the brick and stone church was laid. Christmas Mass that year was held in the basement of the church building. Since all the twenty-one families of the parish were farmers, Bishop John S. Foley of Detroit dedicated the church in October 1903 to St. Isidore, the patron saint of farmers.

■ *The old St. Isidore church (1902) and rectory (1910).*

someone younger to oversee the building of a new church. Rev. Paul J. Cummings did that admirably. Bishop Alexander M. Zaleski dedicated the present church in March 1968.

Since August 1977, Rev. Duaine H. Pamment has guided the St. Isidore congregation. In 1979 a parish hall, six religious education classrooms and a parish office were completed. A new parish hall, kitchen, ten additional classrooms and a new parish office were completed in 1997. On September 15, 2002, hundreds of parishioners and four priests joined Fr. Pamment in celebrating the parish centennial.

■ *The interior of the church, c. 1910*

Land was purchased for a cemetery in 1905. The first resident priest was Rev. Edward J. Taylor. He arrived in December 1909 and remained ten years. His arrival necessitated the building of a rectory in 1910. Before his departure, Fr. Taylor saw the $3,000 mortgage discharged.

Tragedy struck on March 9, 1966, when the church was destroyed by fire. The fire was more than Rev. John E. Martin could handle. He had pastored the parish since 1941. He retired in June to allow

(By Dean Peterson/Faith)

CRISTO REY

*L*ANSING

The origins of Cristo Rey parish can be traced to 1954 and to the appointment of Rev. Julius C. Rivera to care for the "Mexican Apostolate" in Lansing. Fr. Rivera lived at St. Mary Cathedral. The following year Rev. Antonio Jose Herrera succeeded Fr. Rivera. In 1957 Bishop Joseph H. Albers established the Mexican Apostolate Office. It was while Rev. William J. McKeon was chaplain of the Mexican Apostolate (1957–1961) that

the Cristo Rey community began to take permanent shape. A former Methodist church was purchased for the use of the Spanish speaking community in early October 1961. On the Feast of Christ the King the converted church was dedicated by Monsignor Herman P. Fedewa, dean of the Lansing region. Bishop Albers created Cristo Rey parish the same day.

Rev. John Walsh, M.M., a Maryknoll priest from New York, was appointed the first administrator of the new parish. Fr. Walsh left in April 1962 due to ill health. After a brief interval, he was succeeded by Rev. Kenneth L. Faiver. In conjunction with being appointed pastor of Cristo Rey, Fr. Faiver was appointed head of the Spanish-speaking Apostolate (formerly called Mexican Apostolate) in the diocese. Fr. Faiver arranged for the first English Cursillo to be held at Cristo Rey in September 1962. Working closely with the Bishop's committee for the Spanish speaking, Fr. Faiver saw the opening of the Cristo Rey Legal Aid Clinic in the fall of 1962. This was the beginning of addressing social needs in the Hispanic Community. The cross-town

expressway claimed the Main Street site and necessitated a move.

North Ballard in North Lansing was the new home of Cristo Rey Community Center in 1968. The center continued to expand services and its chapel became inadequate for worship. It was decided to separate the parish from the social services center. Rev. B. Thomas McCloskey oversaw the transition to South Washington Street. The South Washington church, dedicated in May 1979, also became too small for the growing parish. Rev. Frederick L. Thelen led the parish during its move to West Miller Road. People stood outside because there was not even standing room available for the dedication of the present church by Bishop Carl F. Mengeling on the parish feast day Cristo Rey. During its 40th anniversary in 2001, Cristo Rey continued to celebrate Hispanic culture with its annual fiesta, Cinco de Mayo and El Via Crucis celebrations.

(By Christine Jones/Faith)

HOLY CROSS

ℒANSING

The founding pastor of Holy Cross was Rev. James Hermes, O.F.M. Conv. The Lansing paper of September 15, 1924, had a notice announcing a new parish. The St. Lawrence Hospital Chapel was advertised to be the site of the first Mass. It was later thought that the chapel might be too small. A store building

■ *First church, 1924*

on West Saginaw was procured. Chairs for the first Mass were borrowed from the Lavey Funeral Home. Vestments, sacred vessels, cruets and liturgical books were provided by St. Lawrence Hospital. The first Mass was held September 21, 1924, with 193 people in attendance. The collection was taken up in a sewing basket and a hat by Dr. Fred Drolett and Andrew Risley.

A lot was soon purchased on Clayton Street. A temporary church was erected by the men of the parish, who donated their time and talents. The church was first used in the spring of 1925. A rectory was later built next to the church.

■ *Fr. Pius Poff with the 2002 8th grade graduation class*

Rev. Laurence Martin, O.F.M. Conv., served as pastor from 1929 until 1939. This was a decade of growth for the parish. A basement church, with four classrooms for a school above it, was built on Saginaw Street in 1930. The Sisters of Mercy of the Union from

Farmington staffed the school until the late seventies.

Holy Cross parish grew by leaps and bounds after World War II. Rev. Pascall Murray, O.F.M. Conv., pastor from 1945 until 1951, oversaw the building of the present

■ *Holy Cross from the air, 1956*

church and auditorium. His successor, Rev. Ambrose Finnigan, O.F.M. Conv., built a ten-room addition onto the school, a new convent and a rectory. The church was renovated in 1962. That fall construction began on the present Friary-administration building. The first Auxiliary Bishop of Lansing, M. Joseph Green, dedicated the Friary on August 25, 1963.

The late sixties brought a great change in the Holy Cross-neighborhood that led to the loss of families and financial problems. By the mid eighties things were turning around. In 1984 the eighth grade was re-established in the school and native son Brian Barrons celebrated his first Mass at Holy Cross.

Since 1998 the jovial Rev. Pius Poff, O.F.M. Conv., has served as pastoral leader of Holy Cross parish and brought new life to the parish.

IMMACULATE HEART OF MARY

Lansing

■ *Rev. William Fitzgerald, Bishop Joseph Albers and Rev. Eugene Sears at the school dedication on September 27, 1964*

In preparation for the founding of Immaculate Heart of Mary parish the following July, Bishop Joseph H. Albers purchased fourteen lots known as the Jessop Farm in May 1949. Rev. Joseph E. Wieber was sent as the founding pastor of I.H.M. The Maple Hill Tavern located on the property was converted into a church through the tireless efforts of parishioners. Fr. Wieber celebrated the first Mass in the renovated edifice on Sunday October 23, 1949. The last tiles were laid just a few hours before the Mass began in the "Love and Sacrifice Building". The first Altar Society meeting was held on Halloween.

By 1955 the parish had over 600 families. An assistant, Rev. John M. Steffy, was assigned to help Fr. Wieber in February. Ground was broken for a temporary church in August. Bishop Albers dedicated the building the following year. Ground was broken for a school in 1957. The Sisters of St. Joseph from Nazareth opened the school in September 1958. The new convent was the last thing Fr. Wieber built before he left the parish in June 1961.

During Monsignor Walter E. Mehm's pastorate (1961–1969) the first eighth grade graduation was held in 1962 and a new school cafeteria/social hall was dedicated in September 1964.

In 1971, while Rev. Paul J. Cummings was pastor, St. Casimir and I.H.M. merged their schools at the I.H.M. location. This arrangement continued until the fall of 1985 when the St. Casimir School was reopened as the junior high campus.

The church was renovated and rededicated by Bishop Kenneth J. Povish in June 1991. Monsignor David W. Stotenbur, who had come to I.H.M. in 1990, had laid the plans for the perpetual adoration chapel to be built before his transfer in February 1998. The chapel was dedicated as Holy Spirit Oratory the following October. Rev. John A. Byers has led the I.H.M. congregation since June 1998.

■ *The IHM Mission Rosary Makers spread the Gospel of Christ by providing 15,000-20,000 rosaries free of charge each year to hospitals, schools, jails, etc., around the world, requesting only that those who receive them pray for world peace.*

■ *The Eucharistic Adoration Chapel built in 1998. Adorers are here 24 hours a day. (Faith)*

CHURCH OF THE RESURRECTION

Lansing

In 1922 at the request of Rev. John O'Rafferty, pastor of St. Mary parish, a census of the east side of Lansing had been conducted. The results indicated a new parish should be established. On June 15 of that year, Rev. John A. Gabriels arrived in Lansing with his instructions from Bishop Michael J. Gallagher of Detroit to found a new parish in Lansing to be named Resurrection. The new parish included East Lansing, Okemos, Haslett, Bath and the territories in Lansing east of the Michigan Central and Pere Marquette railroads.

The Resurrection School orchestra, June 11, 1928

For the first six months of the new parish's existence Fr. John, who lived at the St. Mary rectory, celebrated mass for the Resurrection community in St. Mary Parish Hall on Walnut Street. In July 1922 the Haynes property, at the corner of Michigan and Rumsey, was purchased for the new parish site. A temporary church was begun and the first Mass was celebrated in it on December 25 that year.

The Adrian Dominicans came to Resurrection to open the school in the fall of 1926. The school was located in the six rooms built atop the temporary church.

The broadcast on WJIM AM 1240 of the Sunday Eucharist began in September 1934 when Monsignor Gabriels was asked to be on the air once a month. A weekly broadcast began in April 1937.

The school grew rapidly and by 1936 more room was needed. The 1939–40 building project of ten classrooms and an auditorium relieved the congestion. Bishop Joseph H. Albers blessed the new school facilities in May 1940.

The post war era was one of great growth for Resurrection parish. A new thirty-room convent was constructed in 1949. The present church was dedicated by Bishop Joseph H. Albers in October 1952.

Following Monsignor Gabriels' death in 1960, Rev. Francis T. Martin was entrusted with the care of souls at Resurrection. Fr. Martin remained for twenty-six years. The high school, which had opened in 1936, closed in 1963. The sanctuary was renovated in the early eighties and dedicated by Bishop Kenneth J. Povish. The 50th anniversary of the WJIM radio broadcast was celebrated in November 1984. Resurrection received its third pastor, Rev. William J. Koenigsknecht, in 1986. In 1991 a State Historical marker for Monsignor Gabriels and the parish was unveiled by Bishop Povish. The 75th anniversary of the parish was observed in 1997.

(Faith)

ST. ANDREW DUNG-LAC

LANSING

Beginning with Christmas Eve 1984, Bishop Kenneth J. Povish began the tradition of the diocesan bishop celebrating the vigil mass of Christmas with the Vietnamese community. The first such celebration was held at Lansing Catholic Central where there was space for the dinner and program which followed. This tradition has continued with Bishop Carl F. Mengeling.

St. Andrew Dung-Lac was a priest and the protomartyr of Vietnam. He and 116 companions were canonized by Pope John Paul II in June 1988. It was very appropriate that St. Andrew was chosen as the patron of the Vietnamese parish when it was established in 1998, on the Feast of St. Andrew Dung-Lac.

The fall of Saigon in 1975 caused a heavy concentration of immigration to the United States of those who resisted the Communist takeover of Vietnam. Many local Catholic social service agencies helped resettle refugees across the Lansing diocese. Vietnamese priests would come through the diocese to minister to the needs of the Catholics in the Flint and Lansing regions. More regularity for the reception of the sacraments occurred when Rev. Joseph Tran came to Lansing in February 1982. He lived at St. Mary Cathedral and the Vietnamese community began to gather there. Sunday Mass was first held in the Cathedral crypt. When the congregation outgrew the crypt, the Vietnamese Catholic community moved upstairs and held their services at 1:30 on Sunday afternoons.

The Vietnamese Catholic community remained a part of St. Mary Cathedral parish until November 24, 1998, when Fr. Tran was appointed the first pastor of St Andrew Parish. The Vietnamese were given the former Cristo Rey parish site on South Washington Avenue. Fr. Tran was installed as pastor by Bishop Carl F. Mengeling at the last Christmas Eve liturgy held at St. Mary Cathedral in 1998.

■ *Church dedication day, May 30, 1999*

From December 1998 until June 1999 the parishioners worked night and day to renovate their building complex. On May 30, 1999, with traditional Vietnamese instruments and dress, the new St. Andrew Dung-Lac church was dedicated by Bishop Mengeling. Over 700 Vietnamese Catholics and friends joined in the beautiful liturgy.

■ *St. Andrew Dung-Lac carried in dedication procession.*

ST. CASIMIR

LANSING

Even before World War I a number of Polish Catholics had immigrated to Lansing. Monsignor John O'Rafferty, pastor of St. Mary, requested an assistant who could speak Polish. Rev. Leo P. Szybowicz was assigned to St. Mary parish in July 1916. He preached his first Polish sermon to those who gathered for Mass in the St. Mary Parish Hall on Walnut Street. Regular Sunday Masses began in January 1919. Bishop Michael J. Gallagher of Detroit formally established the Polish Catholic Community as a mission in October 1920. Adjacent lots on Barnes and Sparrow Streets had already been purchased. Groundbreaking for a basement church and a rectory was held in October 1921. The St. Casimir community achieved parochial status in September 1921.

The growth of the parish led, in 1926, to the building of a two-story addition to the basement church. The second floor was for a school and the third floor was for a parish hall. A convent was constructed in the summer of 1928. The school opened that fall and was staffed by the Sisters of the Holy Family of Nazareth from Pittsburgh, Pennsylvania. The school closed in 1971 but the Holy Family Sisters continued to minister in the parish until 1983.

■ *Sisters of the Holy Family of Nazareth staffed the parish school 1928-1971*

■ *Bishop Povish receives the gifts at the Polka Mass, March 12, 1982.*

The present church was built during the pastorate (1946–1957) of Rev. Leo J. Kalinowski. The old church was converted into classrooms. The new school and gymnasium were built while Monsignor Michael J. Mleko was pastor from 1957–1971. At the end of his pastorate the parish school was combined with that of Immaculate Heart of Mary. The new rectory and administration building was erected in 1980 when Rev. Albert C. Hornberger was pastor. In 1977, to celebrate the patronal feast, the first polka Mass was held. In the fall of 1985 St. Casimir School was reopened as the middle school under the I.H.M. principal.

During the decade (1987–1997) that Rev. Raymond Rademacher led the parish, a new ambry and baptismal font were installed. Also, the parish celebrated its 75th anniversary with a Mass celebrated by Bishop Carl F. Mengeling on September 27, 1996.

Rev. William R. Lugger has served as pastor of the congregation since June 1997 and enriched the liturgies with his beautiful singing.

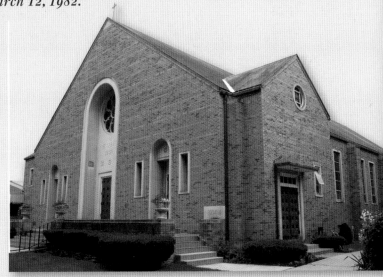

ST. GERARD MAJELLA

*L*ANSING

Rev. John Weber shows off the proposed school addition, November 3, 1961.

In 1953 thirty-nine acres of land were purchased on the west side of Lansing for a future parish. Twenty of those acres were assigned to St. Gerard Majella parish when it was canonically established on June 25, 1958. Rev. John F. Weber was sent as the founding pastor. He resided at St. Vincent's Home until other provisions could be made. The first Sunday Mass was held in Bretton Woods School on July 27, 1958. The Usher Club and Ladies Guild were organized in September.

April 1959 saw the groundbreaking for the 800 seat temporary church and four classrooms. The first Mass in the new building was Christmas Midnight Mass. In September 1960, with 200 children in Holy Cross school, St. Gerard opened a fourth grade classroom as part of Holy Cross but in St. Gerard Hall. The following September the Sisters of Joseph from Nazareth opened the St. Gerard school, grades three to six. In September 1962 Majella Hall and seven classrooms were completed. The first eighth grade graduation was June 1964. The next year a large addition including a library was constructed.

The groundbreaking for the permanent church was held in September 1974. The 870-seat worship space was dedicated by Auxiliary Bishop of Lansing, James S. Sullivan, in June 1975. That fall the old church was converted into a gymnasium. The first "Spring Festival" was held in 1977.

The present administration building was occupied in April 1979. Six years later the offices were enlarged by enclosing the area between the rectory and the church. By the time Fr. Weber retired in 1988 he had completed thirty years as pastor of St. Gerard.

During the decade (1988–1998) that Monsignor Sylvester L. Fedewa led the parish, the school received its fifth addition and the worship space was renovated. In June 1996 the first lay teacher at St. Gerard, Margaret Boucha, retired after thirty-six years. Just before Monsignor Fedewa's retirement the parish held a 40th anniversary celebration in May 1998.

Since his arrival in 1998, Fr. John P. Klein has led the St. Gerard congregation. Because of the continued growth of its population, in 2004 the parish expanded the church to provide more seating. New office space and additional meeting space was also added and the school was expanded to provide more classrooms and support space.

(By Dean Peterson/Faith)

Youth group 2001 (Faith)

ST. MARY CATHEDRAL

LANSING

Thomas and Eleanor Saier moved to Lansing in 1854. That fall, the first Mass in Lansing was celebrated in their log cabin. Rev. Francis Krutil, a Redemptorist from St. Mary's Detroit, was assigned in January 1856 by Bishop Peter Paul Lefevere to minister the sacraments to scattered Catholic groups across the state. In February 1859 Fr. Krutil witnessed the deed by which the Saiers donated two lots to Bishop Lefevere. On the Feast of the Birth of Mary, September 8, Bishop Lefevere paid his first visit to Lansing and laid the cornerstone of the church. The walls rose to a height of four to six feet and funds were depleted. The building was finally dedicated in the fall of 1864.

With the transfer of Rev. Louis Van Driss from Corunna to Lansing on August 4, 1866, St. Mary's future brightened. Fr. Van Driss opened a school in 1872. Two years later the Sisters of Charity from Cincinnati took over the school. They remained ninety-five years until it closed in 1969. A high school was open from 1902 until 1963.

During Rev. Lafayette I. Brancheau's pastorate (1891–1915) the parish totally relocated to a block north of the Capitol. A two-story school was built on Walnut Street in 1902. The next year a temporary church and hall were built. The permanent church was consecrated December 8, 1913, by Auxiliary Bishop Edward D. Kelly of Detroit. Following Fr. Brancheau's death in December 1915, Monsignor John W. O'Rafferty pastored St. Mary until his retirement in 1940. The new high school (now the Diocesan Center) opened in 1939. During Monsignor William J. Flanagan's pastorate (1944– 1954) the parish hall was remodeled and the church redecorated.

Tremendous change marked the pastorate (1955–1967) of

Monsignor Herman P. Fedewa. The high school closed in 1963. The first Mass facing the people was celebrated on November 1, 1964. The stress of the church renovation from 1966 to 1968 and urban blight led to Monsignor Fedewa's retirement. During Msgr. (later Bishop) James A. Murray's pastorate (1973–1998) the parish stabilized, the Cathedral crypt was excavated and the church redecorated in 1986 to prepare for the Diocesan Golden Jubilee. The new parish center was dedicated July 9, 1995, by Bishop Kenneth J. Povish. Since Monsignor Michael D. Murphy became pastor in June 1998 the statues of the Sacred Heart and Blessed Mother were returned to niches in the sanctuary.

The consecration of St. Mary Church, December 8, 1913

The Cathedral is the "seat" of the Bishop, but normal parish events happen here, too. Here Sid and Sandra Dunnebacke exchange their vows with Rev. George C. Michalek presiding. (Photo courtesy of Diane Clark)

ST. THÉRÈSE OF LISIEUX

Lansing

Bishop Joseph H. Albers had the foresight to buy properties for future parish sites. He preferred to acquire them cheap and the parcel he acquired in 1945 as the future site of St. Therése was. Some called the site lowland others called it a swamp. Countless loads of dirt were dumped to make the land usable for a parish. Rev. William J. Koenigsknecht was assigned the task July 1, 1949, of transforming the property and parish into a thriving community.

■ *St. Therese School students, 1951*

The first Mass was held in the Northtown Theater on August 7. The altar was borrowed from Resurrection and the collection was $37.86. In December Bishop Albers blessed the church auditorium built with the help of so many parishioners. Rev. Charles H. Smith, sent as the first assistant pastor in June 1950, focused energy on starting a school. In September 1951 it opened with 306 students. It was staffed by the Sisters of St. Joseph from Nazareth who remained until 1981. The Shower of Roses began in 1954. For many years this card party/

fundraiser was held at the Lansing Civic Center. It attracted people from all over the area.

The tenth anniversary of the parish was marked by the observance of a Novena to St. Therése from September 26 until October 4, 1959. The outdoor closing of the Novena was followed by a pageant at C.W. Otto School Auditorium. The following December the new convent was blessed. An addition to the school and the present church were built in 1962. Just two years before he left St. Therése, in 1967, Fr. Bill celebrated his twenty-fifth anniversary of ordination to the priesthood. Parishioners remember his leading the Our Father, Hail Mary and Glory Be after each Mass for vocations.

In the fall of 1974, Rev. Francis J. Murray presided over a weeklong silver jubilee celebration. Rev. Robert H. McGraw was the celebrant of the 40th anniversary Mass while Fr. Murray was the homilist. Rev. Michael W. Kuchar came to St. Therése in 1994. He oversaw a complete renovation of the church in 2000. The 50th anniversary Mass celebrated by Bishops Carl F. Mengeling and Kenneth J. Povish on August 7, 1999, began a year of special events. The parish school concluded a yearlong celebration of its 50th anniversary with a May 2002 program in the Fr. Koenigsknecht Activity Center. Rev. Michael J. Williams came to St. Therése Parish the following year.

■ *Christmas 2001*

SS. CORNELIUS AND CYPRIAN

LESLIE (BUNKER HILL)

The first Catholics in the Bunker Hill area were the James Markey family who arrived in 1839. Their longing for the Eucharist led to Rev. Patrick O'Kelly coming from Livingston County in February 1845 to celebrate mass in their home. In 1849 Patrick Markey donated land for a Catholic cemetery. When Rev. Cornelius Moutard took up his pastorate at St. John the Evangelist in Jackson in 1857, he was also given the care of the Bunker Hill Catholics. In 1863 a wood frame church was erected in the cemetery. A petition was soon sent to Bishop Peter Paul Lefevere of Detroit for a resident priest. In November 1868 he sent Rev. Theodore Hilary Driessen.

■ *Shepherd and flock outside the first church, begun in 1863.*

Bunker Hill lost its parochial status in 1873 and remained a mission for the next thirty-two years. The mission was under the care of the pastors of St. Mary Pinckney, St. John Jackson or St. Mary Williamston for most of that period. During the pastorate (1898–1905) of Rev. John J. Connolly at Williamston, the Bunker Hill community experienced expansion. A new brick veneer church was built opposite the cemetery and dedicated December 1, 1899. In early 1905, plans were set to build a rectory, convent and school. Fr. Connolly secured the services of the Sisters of St. Joseph from Nazareth to staff the school, which opened in the converted old church.

■ *The interior of the second church prior to the 1906 fire.*

During the pastorate (1923–1942) of Rev. John M. Duffy, Bunker Hill became famous for its picnics. The first one had been held in 1869 but probably the largest was in 1937 when 1,500 attended the dinner. Since 1938 Bunker Hill has also hosted the San Ippolito Festival sponsored by the Italian American Catholic community of Lansing.

Upon Fr. Connolly's transfer in July 1905, Bunker Hill was given its first resident pastor in over thirty years. Rev. James O'Brien's pastorate (1905–1919) combined the best of times with the worst of times. The 1899 church burned down in 1906. The 1905 rectory was destroyed by fire in 1910. A new church (1907), a new rectory (1910), and a school (1912) were built. The school closed in 1964.

The Catholic faith was greatly treasured by the community at Bunker Hill. Thirteen of the parish's daughters and six of her sons entered religious life or the priesthood.

From 1986 until 2003 Rev. Eugene J. Beiter led the Bunker Hill community. Rev. Michael A. Petroski followed.

(By Dean Peterson/ Faith)

ST. MARY

MANCHESTER

The Catholics in Freedom Township were first visited by the Apostle of Washtenaw and Livingston Counties, Rev. Patrick O'Kelly, on April 5, 1835, when the Holy Mass of Passion Sunday was celebrated in the home of John Condon. With the departure of Fr. O'Kelly to Wisconsin in 1839, quarterly or even annual visits by a priest ceased for a time. Fr. O'Kelly's successor at St. Thomas, Ann Arbor – Rev. Thomas Cullen – was preoccupied with building a church in Ann Arbor. After the church was completed in 1845, Fr. Cullen turned his attention to the outlying Catholic communities in Washtenaw County. The help of the German Redemptorists at St. Mary's in Detroit was enlisted by Fr. Cullen to visit the numerous German immigrants in Washtenaw County. In 1848 they visited the Catholics in Freedom and Sylvan Townships.

St. Mary church and rectory, c. 1915

Rev. Raymond Schlinkert, in the church with altar constructed to resemble a chalice, 1971. Fr. Schlinkert's television program "With This Ring" aired for --several years.

A church was built in Freedom Township in 1858 and was dedicated to St. Francis Borgia. When Clinton began a parish in 1863, St. Francis was one of its missions. Rev. Ferdinand Allgayer pastored Clinton from 1867 until 1873. Fr. Allgayer began to visit the Manchester Catholics, which numbered about thirty-five families. In 1871 a frame church was completed and dedicated to the Assumption of the Blessed Virgin. When a lot on South Macomb Street was given to the parish, the church was moved there.

When St. Francis Freedom briefly became a parish from 1874 until 1889, Manchester was a mission of it. The arrangement was reversed in 1889 when Rev. John F. Lovett was made the first resident priest in Manchester. While Rev. Peter J. Ternes was pastor (1890–1895) he celebrated Mass in Manchester on the first and third Sunday of the month, in Freedom on the second Sunday and in Clinton on the fourth Sunday of the month. If there was a fifth Sunday in the month, Fr. Ternes celebrated Mass in Cambridge. The St. Mary

missions had their heyday during Rev. Edwin A. Fisher's pastorate (1909–1917). Fr. Fisher was very fond of fieldstone churches. He oversaw their construction in Tecumseh, Brooklyn, Manchester and Blissfield. The missions were transferred to Clinton in 1944.

During the pastorate of Rev. Raymond R. Schlinkert the parish celebrated its centennial in 1971. Bishop Alexander M. Zaleski celebrated the liturgy. Fr. Schlinkert was well known for his television program "With this Ring".

Since June 2002 Rev. Timothy D. Krzyzaniak has led the St. Mary congregation.

Bishop Povish speaks at the dedication of the State Historical Marker, July 19, 1992. On the steps are members of the 4th degree Knights of Columbus. Next to the marker is pastor Rev. Francis Murray.

ST. MARY ON THE LAKE

MANITOU BEACH

The need for a church at Devils and Round Lakes was first noted by Rev. James B. McCabe who was pastor of Sacred Heart, Hudson, from 1949 to 1953. His successor, Rev. Edward J. Hurley, arranged for Mass to be celebrated for vacationers at the Lakeview Pavilion during the summers of 1956 and 1957. In 1958 eight and one-half acres were purchased for a church at Manitou Beach.

In 1958 a building, one hundred feet by forty-two feet, was begun. The building had an apartment for temporary living quarters for the visiting priest. The first Mass in the new church was held on Easter Sunday 1959. Auxiliary Bishop Henry E. Donnelly of Detroit blessed the church, which was dedicated under the title St. Mary on the Lake.

For about thirty years Rev. Gerald R. Loewen pastored the Manitou Beach community. From 1959 until 1979 he was the pastor of Sacred Heart parish in Hudson. St. Mary on the Lake was a mission of Hudson for that time. When the church was barely six years old, in April 1965, it was destroyed by a tornado. All that remained of the church was the confessional, the sacristy and the outdoor statue of Mary.

The following year the groundbreaking for a new church was held. Once again Easter Sunday was the day Mass was first celebrated in the church. It was not

until 1969 that the church was dedicated by Auxiliary Bishop Walter J. Schoenherr of Detroit.

When Fr. Loewen retired from Hudson he came to live at Manitou Beach. He served as its pastor nine more years until his health failed.

■ *After the tornado of April 11, 1965, everything around Mary was devastated, but she remained - providing a sign of hope.*

The leadership of the parish was then entrusted to a pastoral coordinator. Sr. Helen Walling, I.H.M., was installed as coordinator on August 27, 1988. Rev. Paul Grehl, O.S.F.S., has served as sacramental minister since Sr. Helen's appointment. The parish celebrated Sr. Helen's golden jubilee as a religious in 1992. While Sr. Helen was there, a monument to the unborn and outdoor Stations of the Cross were built. A new rectory was constructed in 1994 and blessed that October.

The second pastoral coordinator, Mrs. Jean Schaub, was installed by Bishop Carl F. Mengeling on the Feast of the Holy Family in 2001.

■ *Breaking ground for the rectory, May 10, 1994*

175

ST. JAMES THE GREAT

MASON

On Christmas Day 1942 the Ball-Dunn Funeral Home in Mason was the site for the first Mass of area Catholics. Rev. (later Monsignor) Charles F. Keating, chancellor of the Diocese of Lansing at the time, was the celebrant of the liturgy. He used the altar kit Bishop Joseph H. Albers had used as an army chaplain in World War I. Fr. Keating continued to celebrate the sacraments for the Mason Catholic community until 1955. Before he left, the Mason Catholics had purchased six acres of land and Bishop Albers had dedicated a church in September 1954. Fr. Keating also secured the services of the Sisters of Charity stationed at St. Mary Cathedral (where he resided) to come to Mason and hold catechism classes in the American Legion Memorial Building.

■ *Rev. William McKeon, Bishop Joseph Albers and the Dominican Sisters visit the school under construction in 1957.*

During the pastorate (1971–1976) of Rev. George B. Zabelka the church and religious education facilities were expanded. Auxiliary Bishop James S. Sullivan was the celebrant of the parish's silver jubilee Mass on September 23, 1979. That same year a new rectory was built. Rev. Raymond J. Goehring was pastor at the time.

■ *A Christmas, 2001*

The parish was transformed during the pastorate (1985–1999) of Rev. Kenneth C. McDonald. Seven charter members turned the first shovels of dirt for a new church and hall on September 3, 1989. Bishop Kenneth J. Povish dedicated the church the following July. Bishop Povish was again at St. James to celebrate the opening Mass of the parish golden jubilee on January 19, 1992. He returned the following January to celebrate the closing liturgy. Many events were held in between, including a homecoming weekend.

The first resident pastor, Rev. Paul J. DeRose, was assigned to St. James parish in July 1955. Fr. DeRose remained for only two years. In this time laid the ground work for the opening of a parish school by buying a building and arranging for sisters. While Rev. James W. Lee was pastor (1957–1963) a rectory was purchased and a parish school opened. When the Adrian Dominican Sisters arrived in September 1957, the four-grade school was held in a renovated former Nazarene Church. The Dominican Sisters remained at the school until it closed in 1970.

Rev. Alan Wakefield came to Mason as pastor in 1999. Bishop Carl F. Mengeling visited his flock in May 2000 to consecrate a new altar and bless the other new sanctuary furniture.

■ *The Memorial Garden*

OUR LADY OF FATIMA

MICHIGAN CENTER

In January 1954 Mr. and Mrs. George Carlson, Jr., and Mr. and Mrs. Chester Bouwens met with Bishop Joseph H. Albers to petition for a new church at Michigan Center. They also donated twelve acres of land for the proposed parish. A potluck was held in February to gauge local interest. Over 200 people attended. On June 30, 1954, the parish, under the patronage of Our Lady of Fatima, was canonically established. The first Mass for the community was held in the basement of the Michigan Center branch of the National Bank of Jackson. Rev. Hugh F. Conklin, the founding pastor, celebrated that first liturgy. Before Fr. Conklin was transferred in 1959, the church and hall were dedicated by Bishop Albers.

The 25th anniversary of the church, July 15, 1979

Rev. (later Bishop) Paul V. Donovan was at Michigan Center from 1959 until 1968. During that time, in September 1960, a school was opened. The Sisters of St. Joseph from Nazareth staffed the school until 1981. The school was dedicated in May 1961. The seventh and eighth grades were added in the fall of 1961 and 1962 respectively.

Since July 1970 the Oblates of St. Francis de Sales have served as pastors of the Michigan Center parish. Rev. Paul G. Gillespie, O.S.F.S., was succeeded by Rev. Andrew Dunne, O.S.F.S., in June 1974. Fr. Dunne oversaw the renovation of the church in 1976 and 1977. The parish celebrated its silver jubilee with ten days of festivities in 1979. Bishops Kenneth J. Povish and Paul V. Donovan concelebrated the jubilee Mass on July 15th.

In June 1982 St. Rita, Clark Lake, which had been a mission of Our Lady of Fatima since 1955, became a separate parish. In 1997 fiberglass statues of Our Lady of Fatima and the three children were placed in the courtyard. The parish looks forward to its golden jubilee in 2004.

IMMACULATE CONCEPTION

MILAN

The Milan Catholic community began in Milan Township in Monroe County in 1854 when an acre of land was given to Bishop Peter Paul Lefevere for a church. A wooden structure was soon built and a cemetery begun.

By 1900 use of the country church had been discontinued and Mass was celebrated in homes in Milan. Soon after Rev. Lawrence H. Soest became pastor of Whittaker in 1909, he met with the lay leaders in Milan to discuss building a church. A new $5,000 structure was dedicated in July 1912.

Rev. John V. Zindler moved to Milan from Whittaker and built a rectory in 1926, not the present. When Rev. Lee J. Laige arrived as pastor in 1927, the parish was heavily in debt and many fundraisers – including chicken dinners – were held. Before Fr. Laige left in 1939 the Ypsilanti State Hospital and the Federal Detention Farm were opened. Fr. Laige was given the responsibility of caring for the Catholics in these institutions.

After Rev. Albert J. Folta became pastor in 1946, he put in place plans to open a school. The Sisters of St. Joseph of the Third Order of St. Francis from Garfield Heights, Ohio, opened the school, which was dedicated by Edward Cardinal Mooney of Detroit in October 1949.

Rev. Roman F. Narkun served Milan as pastor from 1959 to 1965. He set in motion plans to build a new church. Land at the corner of Michigan and North Streets was purchased in 1964. Groundbreaking for the new structure occurred in October. Rev. Joseph S. Strezelewicz succeeded Fr. Narkun and saw the building project to completion. Archbishop John Dearden of Detroit dedicated the new edifice. Fr. Strezelewicz also oversaw the construction of a family center, which contained religious education facilities as well as a banquet hall. The 8,100 square foot center was named for Fr. Strezelewicz and

dedicated by Bishop Kenneth J. Povish on August 20, 1978.

Rev. John M. Bosco succeeded Fr. Strezelewicz as pastor in 1988. While Fr. Bosco was in Milan a grotto and forty-six foot high bell tower were erected at a cost of $113,000. Bishop Povish blessed them on the parish feast day, December 8, 1990. The parish helped Fr. Bosco celebrate the silver jubilee of his ordination in 1996. The following year a new rectory was dedicated on November 9th.

Since June 2001 Rev. Robert J. Pienta has served Immaculate Conception Parish. He oversaw completion of the renovation of the church in 2003. Bishop Mengeling came to consecrate the new altar and bless a new ambo and baptismal pool.

GOOD SHEPHERD

MONTROSE

Rev. John M. Fackler, then the pastor of St. Robert Bellarmine in Flushing, is considered the founding pastor of Good Shepherd parish. He called a meeting of those interested in establishing a new parish on February 1, 1979. About one hundred attended. So, plans proceeded for the first Mass of the Montrose Catholic community. Auxiliary Bishop James S. Sullivan celebrated the first Mass on February 4th. Revs. John M. Fackler, John P. Klein, and Maurice Olk joined Bishop Sullivan and some 385 of the faithful.

Fr. McKeon blesses pets

Within weeks, ushers, lectors, Eucharistic ministers and an altar set-up committee were organized. In May 1979 a parish census was taken and in July voting took place for a parish name. Of the three names submitted, Bishop Kenneth J. Povish chose Good Shepherd. In September a building committee was organized and on November 5, 1979, Bishop Povish canonically established the Good Shepherd mission.

The Montrose Middle School was the site of worship until a church could be built. Ground was broken on July 27, 1980, and the church was dedicated by Bishop Povish the following May.

The Good Shepherd mission became well known for its youth retreats and its charismatic prayer groups. These characteristics are now more associated with the Mt. Zion Pastoral Center, which evolved from the Good Shepherd parish.

The pastoral care of Good Shepherd was transferred from St. Robert Parish to Rev. James B. Bettendorf who also was in charge of the Flint Newman Center. A full time pastoral minister, Connie D. McClanahan, came to the parish in August 1984.

June 1996 -- the mortgage is ended. Thanks be to God!

In 1991 the community experienced another transition. Sr. Josephine McNamara, I.H.M., was assigned to Good Shepherd as pastoral coordinator. She was installed by Bishop Povish in December. She has continued to serve the parish community. The Good Shepherd community celebrated its 20th anniversary in September 1999. Holy Mass was followed by a pig and turkey roast.

ST. MARY

MORRICE

The earliest record of Catholic activity in the area of the Morrice parish is found in the 1868-70 annual reports of St. Mary Cathedral in Lansing. Rev. Louis Van Driss lists Perry, which is just two miles from Morrice, as a station he regularly visited. In Perry Township there were German Catholic immigrants but in neighboring Antrim Township there was an even larger number of Irish Catholic families. In 1871 Rev. Joseph Kraemer began visiting the Irish immigrants. In 1874 land and an old country schoolhouse were purchased in Antrim Township. After renovating the school the following year the first church was dedicated. In the early days Mass was celebrated once a month on a weekday.

■ *The shepherd and his flock gather at the feet of the Good Shepherd at Bethany Cemetery, 1907.*

The Antrim mission began its transition to Morrice when a half-acre lot was acquired in the village for a future church. On September 18, 1892, the cornerstone of the second church was laid. In June 1905 the Wiles, Jordon, Eddington and Flynn families donated two acres for a cemetery, which was dedicated with a statewide Knights of Columbus picnic in the new cemetery on August 15, 1906. The Good Shepherd statue failed to arrive in time for the dedication and was placed there in 1907.

A third ethnic group that formed the parish were the Czechs and Slovaks who arrived before World War I. All three groups rejoiced when Rev. Cecil M. Winters came to Morrice as the first resident pastor in October 1926. The present rectory was built in 1929. Adrian Dominican Sisters from St. Paul's in Owosso taught catechism at Morrice, beginning in 1930, for over thirty years.

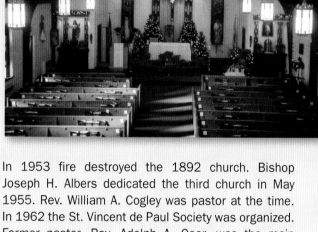

In 1953 fire destroyed the 1892 church. Bishop Joseph H. Albers dedicated the third church in May 1955. Rev. William A. Cogley was pastor at the time. In 1962 the St. Vincent de Paul Society was organized. Former pastor, Rev. Adolph A. Oser, was the main celebrant of the Mass observing the 75th anniversary of the parish in Morrice. A bell tower was dedicated in July 1976. During the pastorate of Rev. James Schmitt (1984–1991) stained glass windows were installed in the church and an activity center was built. While Rev. Matthew J. Fedewa was pastor, the yearlong centennial celebration of the parish in Morrice was held from December 8, 1991, to December 8, 1992.

Since June 2001, Rev. John M. Bosco has served as pastor of the community.

ST. MARY

MOUNT MORRIS

The only Catholic parish in Genesee County, until after the Civil War, was St. Michael in Flint. The visits of St. Michael's pastors Rev. Joseph Kindekins (1850-1854) and Rev. Charles L. DeCeuninck (1854–1869) are among the earliest attempts at organizing the Irish immigrants into a parish in Mt. Morris. In 1865 six acres of land were donated by Christopher Hughes. A church was begun and dedicated to Mary of the Seven Sorrows in September 1868. The Rev. Martin Godfried Canters came to Mt. Morris in September 1870 as the first resident priest.

Rev. Thomas F. Luby began his eighteen-year pastorate at St. Mary in July 1900. By the end of the year, the balcony had been extended to accommodate the faithful. This was not enough so a new church was begun. Its cornerstone was laid October 6, 1903.

■ *The original St. Mary church was built in 1867 at a cost of $1200. It was subsequently used as a school, community building, gymnasium, and social hall before being razed in 1957.*

The parish school was opened during the pastorate (1918–1926) of Rev. Daniel J. Ryan. The Sisters, Servants of the Immaculate Heart of Mary staffed the school until 1993 when Sr. Thomas Mary Kelly ended her twenty-year term as principal.

The school continued to grow while Rev. William M. Gannon pastored St. Mary from 1926 until 1953. In 1927 the cornerstone was laid for a high school. The first graduates were the class of 1930 and the last were that of 1970. Rev. Justin A. Beauvais, pastor from 1953 until 1969, oversaw the church decorated, the convent enlarged, a new grade school built and a new administration building/rectory constructed.

■ *The church interior has recently been painted to conform to the original decor.*

The centennial of St. Mary parish was celebrated in October 1970 during Rev. David A. Bell's pastorate (1969–1985). A centennial Mass, parish festival and homecoming dance marked the event.

Rev. Raymond J. Urbanek has served the St. Mary community as pastor since June 1997.

ST. MARTHA

*O*KEMOS

On Pentecost Sunday 1988, Bishop Kenneth J. Povish canonically established the new parish in Okemos. Rev. Jonathan W. Wehrle was appointed the founding pastor on June twenty-ninth. Fr. Wehrle celebrated the first Mass for the new community on July third in Okemos High School Auditorium. The auditorium remained the site of Sunday liturgies until the church was constructed. Bishop Povish requested that the parish be named after a New Testament saint who was not the patron of an existing parish. A list of names was submitted to the Bishop for his approval before a final vote was taken.

An act of redemption occurred when the Diocese purchased the eighteen-acre site of the former x-rated Crest Drive-In Theater. After some controversy with Meridian Township officials, the go ahead was given to build. The former concession stand was converted into a daily mass chapel and dedicated by Bishop Povish on March 1, 1989. As the parish grew so did the staff. The first pastoral assistant was Jim Thomas who joined the staff in March 1989. Barbara McNicol joined the staff that June. She served the parish until 1997, first as director of religious education and then as pastoral minister. Thomas Quasarano was assigned to the parish as a permanent deacon in September 1998.

Ground was broken in April 1990 for the church and a nine room, two-story religious education wing. Palm Sunday 1991 was when the $2.8 million structure was prepared for the first liturgy. The altar, statues and some of the pews came from St. Vincent Home in Lansing. The chandeliers and some of the stained glass windows came from St. Lawrence Hospital chapel. The three bronze bells came from St. Francis Seminary in Loretta, PA. The first parish mission was preached by Redemptorists that December.

An ardent Catholic school advocate, Fr. Wehrle set out to open a parish school. In January 1993 a preschool was opened. On August nineteenth that year a school opened with kindergarten through fourth grade. The school year was 200 days rather than the normal 180 required by the State. For the first several years the school was staffed primarily by Sisters of Charity from Cincinnati, Ohio.

(Faith)

ST. FRANCIS XAVIER

OTISVILLE

The first visit of a priest to Otisville occurred in 1893. Rev. Francis Clement Kelley came from Lapeer. Bishop Kelley later founded the Catholic Extension Society. Over fifty years later, in 1946, three laymen, Phillip Utley, Gerald Ruddy and Albert Brooks, circulated a petition that was sent to Bishop Joseph H. Albers requesting a permanent mission be established at Otisville. The following year Otisville began to be regularly attended from Davison. Rev. Earl V. Sheridan, pastor of Davison, held masses in the Otisville Community Center.

The Ralph Quaderer family donated land for a church to be built upon in the fall of 1948. The Catholic mission became known as the St. Margaret Mary Mission. Fr. Sheridan in his quest for funds turned to the Catholic Church Extension Society. The Extension Society agreed to give a $5,000 grant toward the $15,000 church provided the church was dedicated to St. Francis Xavier, Bishop Kelley's patron.

The groundbreaking for the church was held Easter Sunday, 1949. By September the church was ready for use. Bishop Albers dedicated the cement block church in December 1949.

Rev. Edward G. Donahoe succeeded Fr. Sheridan as pastor of Davison in 1950. During his ten-year pastorate the mission saw steady growth, reaching one hundred families. In 1953 the church exterior changed by the addition of a brick veneer. A baptistery and bell tower were built at the same time. More land was acquired in 1959. The additional land was used for a rectory, which was erected in 1964. This rectory was built in the hopes that a resident priest would be sent to Otisville soon, but it was not until five years later that Rev. Adolph A. Oser was appointed resident administrator of St. Francis Xavier Mission.

The old church, built in 1949.

A parish hall named in the memory of Rudolf and Genevieve Quaderer, was dedicated in February 1973. The church was remodeled in 1976.

In June 1989 Rev. Frank W. Janson retired after serving a decade as pastor. Sr. Berenice Janszen, C.P.P.S., was entrusted with leading the parish. Sr. Berenice soon began to work to build a new church. Ground was broken in April 1992. Bishop Kenneth J. Povish dedicated the $536,000 edifice on February 21, 1993. In 1997 the parish celebrated its 50th anniversary.

In 1994 Sr. Carol Weber, OP, succeeded Sr. Berenice Janszen, C.P.P.S. as Pastoral coordinator.

Since July 2001 Sr. Elaine LaBell, O.P., has cared for the parish's day to day needs, and was appointed Pastoral coordinator in 2003.

New church dedicated in 1993.

HOLY FAMILY

OVID

The earliest record of a Catholic presence in Ovid is found when Ovid is listed in 1857 as a station of the newly created parish of the Annunciation in Corunna. Almost a century later, in 1956, a petition was sent to Bishop Joseph H. Albers requesting a parish be established in Ovid. Ten years later, in November 1966, Rev. Paul J. Cummings, pastor of St. Isidore Laingsburg, celebrated Mass for the Ovid Catholic community in the home of Larry and Ann Byrnes. There were forty-three people present. The first Sunday Mass for Ovid residents was celebrated November twenty-seventh by Bishop Zaleski's secretary, Rev. (later Bishop) James S. Sullivan, at the Veterans Memorial Building in Ovid. In 1967 twelve acres of land on Mabbitt Road were purchased as a parish site.

■ *Bishop Sullivan dedicated Holy Family Church April 21, 1974.*

For the first decade of its existence (1967–1977), the Holy Family community was a mission of St. Isidore Laingsburg. During that time the Men's Club and the Altar Society were organized. Plans were carried out to build a church. Auxiliary Bishop James S. Sullivan returned to Ovid to dedicate the church in April 1974.

Rev. Howard J. Noeker was sent to Ovid as the first resident pastor in September 1977. He oversaw the building of a rectory and offices. While Rev. Terrence M. Healy was in Ovid (1985–1987) a community room was added to the complex. The room could also be used for religious education classrooms. The parish celebrated its silver jubilee on November 2, 1991. The liturgy was followed by a reception for the charter members and a dance. At the time Ovid was a mission of St. Joseph Parish in St. Johns.

The people of Holy Family were very glad to welcome back Fr. Cummings as their pastor in March 2000.

(By Dean Peterson/Faith)

ST. JOSEPH

OWOSSO

The Czech and Slovak Catholics of the Owosso area gathered in 1920 at the Z.C.B.J. Lodge where the need for an ethnic parish was first discussed. The Catholic lodge members organized a committee to present their plea for a national parish to Bishop Michael J. Gallagher in Detroit. Mr. John Klepko chaired the committee. When Mr. Klepko went to Detroit he had a list of 102 Czech and Slovak households. Among the names were Stasa, Nemecek, Krhovsky, Kuchar, Janik, Gregoricka, Mialik, Czech and Dubovsky. The steering committee first tried to purchase land in Corunna. When that failed six lots and a brick house were purchased in 1922 on East Oliver Street in Owosso.

■ *Rev. John S. Daniel breaks ground for the church March 30, 1954.*

During the pastorate (1934–1939) of Rev. John A. Blasko a two-room school was opened in the basement of the church in 1937. The Dominican Sisters from Oxford staffed the school. The Sisters lived in a house recently purchased for them. Two lots for a playground were also purchased.

The long pastorate (1941–1972) of Rev. John S. Daniel was a period of great growth. A new convent was purchased in 1948. The five-room school was opened in the fall of 1949. Bishop Joseph H. Albers dedicated it on October third. Several lots had to be acquired before ground could be broken for a new church and rectory. The new church was dedicated by Bishop Albers in May 1955. The school was further expanded in 1961.

The 60th anniversary of the parish was celebrated in 1983 while Monsignor Raymond J. Goehring was pastor. A preschool and daycare program were opened in 1989 during the pastorate of Rev. Denis R. Spitzley. Fr. Spitzley oversaw plans to construct a childcare wing to the school. This wing was dedicated by Bishop Kenneth J. Povish in August 1992. Since June 1992 Rev. David E. Fisher has served as pastor of the St. Joseph faith community.

■ *The church is dedicated by Bishop Joseph H. Albers, May 22, 1955.*

The congregation's first liturgy was held in June 1922 in the Corey building above a laundry business. Rev. Joseph E. Nimrichter of St. Cyril's parish in Bannister celebrated the Mass. The costs for the first Eucharist were $3 to rent the hall, $2 to rent the chairs, and $5 for the priest. A church was begun that fall. It was completed about the time the first resident pastor, Rev. John Plavian was appointed to St. Joseph Parish in April 1923.

(By Dean Peterson/ Faith)

ST. PAUL THE APOSTLE

Owosso

In July 1857 the first resident priest, Rev. Edward Van Paemel, was assigned to Shiawassee County. He resided in Corunna where the church was dedicated to the Annunciation to the Blessed Virgin Mary. Fr. Van Paemel had a wide mission territory that included Owosso. When Rev. J. Joseph Kraemer came to Corunna in December 1870 he moved the parochial residence to St. Johns to better supervise the building of the church there. In the fall of 1871 fifty-one Catholics gathered to organize a Catholic community in Owosso. The list of charter members includes the names of Burns,

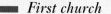 *First church*

(By Dean Peterson/Faith)

Carmody, Cavanaugh, Doyle, Dwyer, Rourke and Sweeney. The founding families were predominantly Irish and very proud of that heritage. Funds were soon being gathered for a church. When Bishop Caspar H. Borgess of Detroit arrived for the cornerstone laying he was greeted by three bands and nearly 150 members of the St. Patrick's Society wearing green ribbon badges. Bishop Borgess directed Fr. Kraemer to move to Owosso and he did so in June 1873. The first Mass in the new church was held Christmas Day 1874.

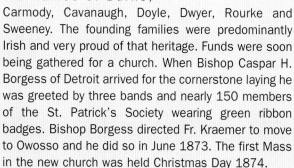

A parish cemetery was begun in 1890 during the pastorate of Rev. Robert F. M. Doman. It was while Rev. Peter J. Slane was pastor (1896–1925) that the school was opened. The Adrian Dominican Sisters staffed the school, which opened in September 1902 with 147 pupils. The first commercial course graduates, four girls, graduated in 1905. The high school closed in 1971. The present school building was erected in 1927 during the pastorate (1925–1944) of Rev. John W. Courtney. While he was pastor (1944–1953), Rev. Herman P. Fedewa oversaw an addition to the church and the building of a new convent. It was the task of Rev. Joseph E. P. Whelan to build the new church. The old church was demolished and the present church erected on the same site. The new church, rectory and administration buildings were dedicated in October 1960.

Since May 1978 Rev. Robert D. Kolenski has been entrusted with the care of souls in St. Paul Parish. The church and school have been remodeled during his pastorate. The parish celebrated the school's centennial with Bishop Carl F. Mengeling in October 2002.

ST. MARY

PINCKNEY

■ *The first church and rectory, c. 1910*

Catholicism was brought to the Pinckney area by Irish immigrants. Henry and Mary Ryan Harris arrived in 1829 and they were later joined by families bearing the names of Brogan, Connor, Dolan, Dunn, Farley, Kelly, Lavey, McCloskey, McDonnels, Monk, Murphy, Quinn, Roche, Ryan, Sheehan and Walsh. The Irish native, Rev. Patrick O'Kelly, first visited these Catholic families. On February 5, 1837, it is recorded that he celebrated Mass and witnessed a marriage in Putnam Township.

In 1854 Pinckney was assigned to the newly created parish of Dexter. In 1867 a brick structure, which could seat 400, was built under the direction of Rev. John F. Van Gennip of Dexter. In 1875 Rev. James Herbert became the first resident pastor. After staying only one year, Fr. Herbert left and Pinckney became a mission of Dexter again.

■ *Fr. Ken Coughlin and crew break ground for the new church in April 2002*

■ *The Seven Sacraments of our Faith in stained glass greet all who enter, the new church.*

When Chelsea became a parish in 1878 Pinckney was assigned to it. A special collection was taken up in 1879 to help pay the $112 debt incurred by the purchase of a buggy for the use of the Pinckney mission. Pinckney became a parish again in 1895.

During Rev. Albert J. Schmitt's pastorate (1948–1958) a parish school was opened. The $125,000 school was dedicated by Bishop Joseph H. Albers on September 9, 1956. The Sisters of St. Dominic from Adrian staffed the school.

In April 1962 a tornado severely damaged the church and rectory. Rev. George P. Horkan was instructed by Bishop Albers to make temporary repairs and begin plans for a new church. Bishop Alexander M. Zaleski dedicated the new church to the Immaculate Conception on January 24, 1965.

The pastorate of Rev. Hugh F. Conklin (1967–1983) brought many changes to the parish. The school closed. A new rectory was built and in 1978 a Senior Citizens Apartment Complex was built by the parish.

During the pastorate (1983–1990) of Rev. John M. Fackler the parish school was reopened with ninety students in September 1983. Bishop Kenneth J. Povish came to Pinckney to celebrate the parish's 125th anniversary in August 1992. Rev. James R. Shaver was pastor at the time.

Since his arrival in June 1995 Rev. Kenneth F. Coughlin has led the parish through the struggles of relocating the entire parish. A thirty-acre site south of Pinckney has been purchased. The new school, offices and temporary church were dedicated in May 2003 by Bishop Carl F. Mengeling.

ST. JOSEPH

ST. JOHNS

The earliest record of Mass taking place in St. Johns is from the mid-1850s. It was celebrated in the Jeremiah and Mary Dooling residence by Rev. George Godez, pastor of what was then St. Peter, Westphalia. In July 1857 the Catholic community in St. Johns was assigned as a mission of the newly established parish in Corunna.

Annunciation in Corunna remained the parochial center from 1857 to 1870. Land for a church in St. Johns was purchased in 1862. Ground was broken in 1866 but progress was very slow. Rev. Joseph Kramer transferred his residence to St. Johns to supervise the completion. Bishop Casper H. Borgess of Detroit dedicated the church in May 1871. Fr. Kraemer later transferred his residence to Owosso. He continued to care for the St. Johns faith community until his reassignment in 1877 when the St. Johns mission became attached to the Ionia parish.

In October 1880 the second resident pastor came to St. Johns. Rev. Thomas D. Flannery also served missions in Portland and Fowler.

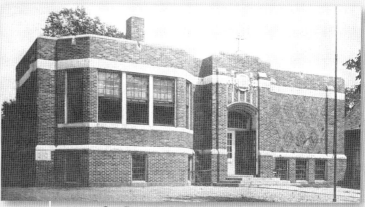

■ *St. Joseph School in 1940*

During Rev. John T. Lynch's pastorate (1906–1919) the long-dreamed-of new church became a reality. Its cornerstone was laid December 8, 1907. Rev. Frederick J. Baumgartner, Chancellor of the Detroit Diocese, presided over the ceremonies. Fr. Baumgartner, as a boy, had come from Lansing with Rev. Louis Van Driss for the groundbreaking of the first church in 1866.

The church was ready for its dedication in October 1908. The first son of the parish to be ordained a priest, Andrew R. Dooling,

■ *Rev. William Hankerd blesses Mt. Rest Cemetery in memory of those who were moved from the old parish cemetery sixty years before.*

celebrated the solemn high Mass.

It was Rev. Thomas R. Carey, pastor from 1919–1923, who initiated plans to open a school. When Monsignor Vincent Hankerd was pastor (1924–1927) the school opened with the Sisters of St. Joseph from Nazareth staffing it until 1989. The school was added on to in 1958 and 1963. Bishop Carl F. Mengeling celebrated the 75th anniversary Mass for the school in February 1999.

Besides the two school expansions while Bishop Green was pastor (1957–1966) the church was also renovated. While Rev. William G. Hankerd was pastor (1966–1987) the church was expanded and parish offices were built beneath the addition. Continued growth led Rev. Timothy D. Krzyzaniak to oversee the purchase of land south of town for future relocation. In July 2001 Rev. Eoin Murphy was entrusted with the care of the souls of the faithful in St. Johns.

(By Dean Peterson/Faith)

ST. ANDREW THE APOSTLE

SALINE

Twenty-two ladies met at the home of Anne and Gordon Prout in September 1950. The purpose of the meeting was to organize Catechism classes in Saline for Catholic children. Out of the meeting grew St. Andrew parish. The ladies worked with Rev. Leon O. Kennedy who was pastor at St. Francis in Ann Arbor. In May 1951 the archbishop in Detroit was petitioned to allow Mass to be celebrated in Saline. The Valentine School on Michigan Avenue was the site of the first Mass in November of that year. The community remained at the Valentine School until a church was built on Monroe Street. Fr. Kennedy celebrated the first Mass there in August 1953.

In June of 1954 Saline was transferred to the care of the pastor at Clinton. The parish remained a mission of Clinton until Rev. Joseph B. Noelke was assigned as the first resident pastor in December 1968. The following year ground was broken for a new church on a 20-acre plot of land on Austin Road. John Cardinal Dearden dedicated this church on October 31, 1970.

■ *Photo of church tower construction*

The parishioners had two reasons for celebration in May 1982. They had paid off the mortgage on the church and Fr. Noelke was celebrating his thirty-fifth anniversary of ordination. When the parish celebrated its 25th anniversary in September 1993, Rev. Roger L. Prokop was pastor. The need for a new church was becoming very obvious. It was during Rev. James G. McDougall's pastorate (1993–1997) that the plans took final shape. Before the first Mass could be celebrated in the new church, Fr. McDougall was

transferred. The honor of celebrating the first Mass went to his successor, Rev. William J. Stevenson. Bishop Carl F. Mengeling dedicated this fourth house of worship for the St. Andrew faith community in November 1997.

■ *"Rejoice in God, all the earth. Clap your hands in gladness!" The bell for the St. Andrew tower calls us to rejoice in the Lord, the building of a new church, and the Great Jubilee Year 2000.*

ST. MARY, QUEEN OF ANGELS

SWARTZ CREEK

The first record of a Catholic presence in Swartz Creek is the 1910 annual report of All Saints in Flint. Swartz Creek is listed as a station attended from All Saints. Over the next two years Catholic families, mostly of Slovak, Moravian, Bohemian and Hungarian descent, formed a faith community. Rev. John B. Hewett of All Saints celebrated the first Mass in the home of Charles and Mary Raubinger. A half-acre of land was donated and on October 16, 1912, the cornerstone of the first church was laid by Auxiliary Bishop Edward D. Kelly of Detroit. The statue of Mary, Queen of Angels, given by the Frank and Antonie Cupal family, determined the title of patronage under which the church was dedicated in September 1913.

■ *The first church and rectory, c. 1940*

When Rev. Raphael J. Shons was sent in 1914 as the first resident pastor, he constructed a rectory and secured land for a parish cemetery. In December 1934 Bishop Michael J. Gallagher needed a Czech-speaking priest to send to Swartz Creek where nearly eighty-five families spoke Czech and another twenty spoke Slovak. He chose the recently ordained Rev. Anthony G. Brakora. Fr. Brakora's temporary assignment became a twenty-three and a half year pastorate. For years, on Sunday the 8:00 Mass sermon was in English and the 10:00 sermon was in Czech.

■ *Teachers and students examine the contents of the new school library, March 1965.*

Fr. Brakora secured the Sister Servants of the Immaculate Heart of Mary, who were missioned at St. Michael in Flint, to teach religious education classes in the church on Saturday, which they did from 1934 until 1952.

Plans for a school began to emerge after World War II. A new parish site on Morrish Road was purchased in 1951. The six-classroom school opened in September 1953. The Franciscan Sisters of St. Joseph from Hamburg, New York opened the four grade school, which was later expanded. The Sisters continued in the school until 1992.

The relocation of the parish to the new site continued after Fr. Brakora's departure. A new church and an addition to the school were constructed during the pastorate of Rev. Joseph R. Robb (1957– 1962). The relocation was completed when the rectory was moved to the new site in 1961.

In 1967 Rev. Amos H. Wischmeyer came to St. Mary as pastor and has remained. In 1984 under Fr. Wischmeyer's direction, the church was completely renovated. Bishop Kenneth J. Povish came for the rededication liturgy on August 19.

(By Dean Peterson/Faith)

ST. ELIZABETH

𝒯ECUMSEH

Rev. Edwin A. Fisher became pastor of Manchester in 1909 and soon began visiting Catholics in outlying areas. Tecumseh became a post of his circuit. Masses were held in private homes and the Old Sage Building in Tecumseh. Fr. Fisher had a love for fieldstone churches. He built four. The cornerstone of the Tecumseh church was laid August 3, 1913. Auxiliary Bishop Edward D. Kelly of Detroit presided. There was a large amount of anti-Catholic sentiment at the time. In a show of support the newly organized Knights of Columbus council in Adrian chartered a special train for 300 Catholics to come from Adrian to celebrate the cornerstone laying.

Tecumseh remained one of the St. Mary missions until July 1944 when it became a mission of the new parish, St. Dominic Clinton. St. Elizabeth became a parish of its own in June 1947. Rev. Michael G. Collins, the first resident priest, didn't reside in Tecumseh until November 1947, when a house was rented for a rectory. Before that, he had stayed at the Clinton and Blissfield rectories.

The old church could only seat 130 people and expansion was desperately needed. In January 1948 the present property was purchased and plans were laid for a new church in 1949. The dean of the Southwestern Deanery of the Detroit Archdiocese, Monsignor G. Warren Peek, presided over the cornerstone laying of the new $74,000 church in July 1950. The edifice was finally ready for the celebration of the Eucharist in November of 1951.

The pastorate of Rev. Thomas J. Collins (1953–1966) was an era of building. In 1953 a school was built. (It remained open until 1971.) A generous parishioner, Mr. C. F. Sage, was benefactor for the entire cost. The parish responded in gratitude and built a convent the next year. Children were bussed in from Clinton and the Irish Hills. Additions to the school and convent and a new rectory followed soon after.

In June 1987 the parish celebrated a double ruby anniversary. The parish celebrated its 40th anniversary and the pastor of St. Elizabeth, Monsignor Vincent J. Howard, observed his 40th anniversary of priestly ordination. Rev. Daniel F. Wheeler succeeded Monsignor Howard in 1988. An extensive renovation program was conducted. On December 13, 1992, Bishop Kenneth J. Povish consecrated the new altar and blessed the new Blessed Sacrament Chapel. New stained glass windows, lighting fixtures and baptismal font were also blessed.

■ *St. Elizabeth School*

ST. MARY

*W*ESTPHALIA

St. Mary's School and Boarding House, Westphalia, Mich

The German Catholic immigrants brought their priest, Fr. Anton Kopp, with them when they came from Europe in 1836. Fr. Kopp was officially appointed pastor of the community on November 19, 1836. A log church was begun in 1837 and completed the following year when the first cemetery was laid out.

■ *St. Mary School and Boarding House, 1915*

Fr. Kopp converted the first church to use as a school where he served as the teacher. The congregation grew rapidly and a second log church was erected in 1843 by Rev. George Godez who arrived that year. This building gave way to a frame building in 1847. This church was dedicated to St. Peter the Apostle. The first recorded parish mission was given by the Redemptorist Father, Rev. George Beranek, in 1853.

The cornerstone for the first brick church was laid in May 1867. The bricks were made in Westphalia. The woodwork and pews were made of black walnut. The edifice cost $70,000. This was the third church Fr. Godez had built during his pastorate (1843–1873) in Westphalia. The former edifice was always refitted to serve as the "new" school.

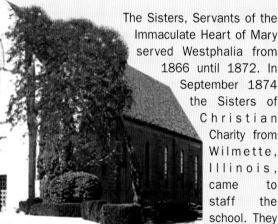

The Sisters, Servants of the Immaculate Heart of Mary served Westphalia from 1866 until 1872. In September 1874 the Sisters of Christian Charity from Wilmette, Illinois, came to staff the school. They

■ *The present church, replacing the one that burned in 1959, was dedicated on May 28, 1962.*

remained at the school for 125 years. In 1906 the Sisters opened a boarding school in the old convent. The boarding school closed in 1920. Because of the close association between the parish and the village, Westphalia High School was renamed St. Mary High School in 1949. It remained open until 1961.

■ *The painting of the Fourteen Holy Helpers: Acacius, Barbara, Blase, Catherine, Christopher, Cyriac, Denis, Erasmus, Eustace, George, Giles, Margaret, Pantaleon, and Vitus (Faith)*

During the decade-long pastorate of Rev. Edward A. Gutha the parish celebrated its centennial. Rev. Aloysius H. Miller was pastor from 1948 until 1971. The church was destroyed by fire in 1959. Groundbreaking for the new church was held September 1, 1960. The present structure, costing three quarters of a million dollars, was dedicated in June 1962.

A new convent was built in 1984. The parish sesquicentennial was held in 1986 and a state historical marker was dedicated. A new parish hall and gym were built in 1988. Since January 2001 Rev. Cecilio C. Reyna has served the Westphalia community as pastor. This cherished memory underscores three things that Westphalia is well known for – its deep Catholic faith, its German ethnic heritage, and its numerous vocations to the priesthood and religious life: twenty priests including one Bishop and 89 sisters.

St. Mary

WILLIAMSTON

Rev. Michael Monaghan was recalled by the pioneers as the first priest to minister the Sacraments in Williamston. Fr. Monaghan was the first resident pastor of St. Michael parish in Flint, from 1847 to 1850. When the parish of Annunciation in Corunna was established in 1857 Williamston was a station assigned to it. In 1866 land was obtained for a parish.

■ *St. Mary School graduates, c. 1960*

Rev. Francis V. McCormick was at St. Mary from 1929 until 1945. The park, which he developed, just north of the church bears his name. A hall was built in 1948 between the church and park while Rev. Joseph Wieber was pastor.

Preparations for a school were begun by Rev. Francis T. Martin. The Thompson house was purchased for a convent in 1956. A school was built in 1959 during Rev. William G. Hankerd's pastorate (1957–1966). The Sisters of St. Joseph from Nazareth staffed the school from 1959 until 1986.

The need for a larger church became more and more pressing. Rev. Steven F. Makranyi was sent to Williamston to see a new church erected. The old church was torn down and an auction of old church articles was held. Bishop Kenneth J. Povish dedicated the new church on May 4, 1986.

■ *The old St. Mary Church, c. 1910*

In 1869 Owen Brannan and Peter Zimmer cut and hauled the first timbers to the construction site. Ten years later, in the fall of 1879, Rev. John Lovett was appointed the first resident pastor. St. Mary remained a parish until 1888 when it became a mission of Howell for ten years. The original frame church was destroyed by fire in 1895 after lightening struck the bell tower.

A brick church was soon built to replace it. In 1898 parochial status was returned to Williamston. Rev. John J. Connolly also oversaw the missions in Fowlerville, Bunker Hill and Woodhull. A rectory was built before Fr. Connolly went to Detroit to organize Blessed Sacrament parish (now the cathedral).

The parish 125th was celebrated during the pastorate (1992–1996) of Rev. Dan J. McKean. As part of the observance, a state historical marker was dedicated in September 1994. In May 1996 ground was broken for an activity and educational center. Since 1999 Rev. Thomas W. Thompson has led the Williamston parish.

HOLY TRINITY STUDENT PARISH

𝒴PSILANTI

The Newman Club's origins at Eastern Michigan University go back to the pastorate (1892–1922) of Rev. Francis Kennedy at St. John Ypsilanti. He fostered the organization of the Catholic Student's Club at the university in 1912. The Catholic Club evolved into the Newman Club and one of the assistants at St. John was appointed chaplain. The students would meet at the Catholic Club house at St. John's.

Of vital importance in the history of Holy Trinity is the arrival of Rev. Leo Broderick at St. John the Baptist parish in June 1961. He was assigned chaplain of the Newman Club. The club was given new life. In the fall of 1962 masses began to be regularly held on the

The students present Godspel

The architect, Charles Hannan, worked with Fr. Broderick to design the triangular church to represent the Trinity. Fr. Broderick's love of pipe organs resulted in the installation of an all-wood tracker-action organ.

Rev. Lawrence P. Delaney served as pastor of Holy Trinity from 1979 until 1989. In May 1982 he received the first Student Affairs Appreciation Award from the university. Since February 2002 Rev. Francis D. Mossholder, PIME, has given pastoral leadership to the Catholic community at Eastern Michigan University.

campus in Strong Auditorium. Property was scouted out and purchased on Perrin Street. Four houses were purchased. Three of them were demolished to build the present church. On September 18, 1965, the chapel/student center was finished. The chapel was dedicated to the Most Holy Trinity and the lower level was dedicated as Pope John XXIII Newman Center. Bishop Henry E. Donnelly of Detroit presided at the dedication. Monsignor John F. Bradley, pastor of St. Mary Student Parish Ann Arbor and National Newman Chaplain, preached at the liturgy.

ST. JOHN THE BAPTIST

Ypsilanti

■ *The old church and rectory, c. 1920*

Needham's pastorate from 1922– 1925. Mass was held in the school and the Wuerth Theater until 1924 when the basement was completed. In 1925 a house was purchased to house the Sisters of St. Dominic from Adrian who opened the eight-grade school in the fall.

Upon the death of Rev. Charles J. Linskey, Rev. G. Warren Peek was appointed pastor in February 1931. He abandoned Fr. Needham's plans and hired a Detroit firm to draw up plans for a new church and adjoining rectory. The new church was dedicated by Bishop Michael J. Gallagher on June 4, 1933.

Local tradition has it that Rev. Patrick O'Kelly was the first to minister to Catholics in the village of Ypsilanti. Fr. O'Kelly's successor, Rev. Thomas Cullen, can be looked upon as the real founder of the parish.

A native of Ireland, Fr. Cullen felt right at home with the Irish immigrants in Ypsilanti. In April 1844 the lot for the first church was purchased for forty dollars. A frame structure was built the following year. In 1856 a larger brick church was begun and was dedicated the following year to St. John the Baptist. Rev. Charles L. Lemagie, a native of Belgium, was sent as the pastor in 1858. He also pastored St. John (now Sacred Heart in Dearborn). The first priest to reside in Ypsilanti may well have been Rev. Edward Van Paemel who came to Ypsilanti in 1862.

In 1880 the Sisters of Providence of Terre Haute, Indiana, were invited by Rev. William DeBever to come to Ypsilanti and teach in the school, which had been opened with lay teachers in 1867. A new school was badly needed, but was not built until 1884. After the Panic of 1893, Rev. Frank Kennedy closed the school in 1895.

The need for a new church and the reopening of the school were the major events of Rev. Dennis G.

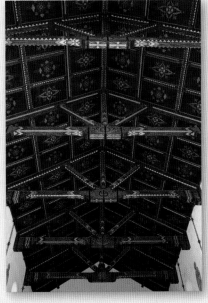

A new school and convent were built in 1955. In 1961 a high school was built but due to financial difficulty the parish voted to close it in June 1969. The grade school, too, has since closed.

Since 1988 Rev. Edmond Ertzbischoff has served as pastor of St. John. He presided over the parish sesqui-centennial celebration in 1995. A major renovation culminated in a rededication liturgy on October 8, 2000.

St. Joseph

Ypsilanti (Whittaker)

For years Catholic families from the Whittaker area traveled the fourteen miles to St. John the Baptist in Ypsilanti. In 1890 a church was built on Whittaker Road in Augusta Township. The Whittaker community was a mission of St. John the Baptist from 1890 until 1904 when the first resident priest, Rev. John F. Needham, was assigned to Whittaker. He lived in a converted store building across from the church.

Rev. Laurence H. Soest became pastor of St. Joseph and its missions shortly after his ordination in 1909. During the pastorate (1921–1927) of Rev. John V. Zindler, Milan became the parochial center and St. Joseph became the mission. The old church was becoming cramped and planning for future expansion began in the pastorate (1959–1965) of Rev. Roman F. Narkun. A fifteen-acre site was purchased two miles north of the old church.

■ *Rev. Klauke at Old St. Joseph Church in Whittaker, Michigan, built in 1904 and closed in 1968.*

In June 1965 the St. Joseph community once again received a resident priest. Rev. Raymond J. Klauke remained until 1971. Members of the parish banded together and built a rectory on the new site. Groundbreaking ceremonies for the present church were held November 6, 1966. Monsignor G. Warren Peek, the area dean, presided. In November 1967 Auxiliary Bishop Joseph H. Breitenbeck of Detroit dedicated the church. The sanctuary was refurbished in 1974 while Rev. Darius W. Wyszynski was pastor.

During the pastorate (1979–1984) of Rev. James W. Lee the parish activity center, now called Fr. Lee Hall, was built. Bishop Kenneth J. Povish dedicated the center in December 1981. Rev. Robert T. Kerr came to St. Joseph parish in 1987 and served until his sudden death in 2001. While he was pastor the parish celebrated its centennial year from June 1989 to June of 1990. The celebration began by blessing the pine grove south of the church and observing the silver jubilee of his priestly ordination. The grand finale was the June 10, 1990, closing liturgy celebrated by Bishop Povish. A tondo depicting Joseph, Full of Grace was also blessed that day. Rev. Nicholas Ritter was entrusted with the pastoral care of the St. Joseph community in June 2001.

TRANSFIGURATION
*Y*PSILANTI

The decree of establishment of Transfiguration parish was signed by Bishop Kenneth J. Povish on January 8, 1994. Transfiguration parish was the result of the merging of St. Alexis and St. Ursula parishes. They were closed the same day Transfiguration parish was born. The first pastor appointed for the new parish was Rev. David M. Franco, O.S.F.S., who still serves.

Rev. Clare A. Murphy had founded St. Alexis parish in 1943 at the Willow Run Housing Project in the recreational hall. The assistants in charge of the mission from 1943 to 1966 all lived at St. John the Baptist parish. In June 1966 St. Alexis was raised to parish status. Rev. Richard V. Bonin was the first resident priest. A new church and school were built during his pastorate. The school, since its opening in

■ *First Communion, St. Alexis, 1992*

The transition of forming the new parish by blending the traditions of two others was made even more difficult by a group of folks who opposed the merger. The loss of good will and revenue resulted in the Transfiguration school (which had opened on June 10, 1994, in the former St. Alexis facility) to close in June 1995. The parish began to band together and in 1996 the church, the former St. Ursula, was air-conditioned and Bednarski Hall was expanded. The Washtenaw Intermediate School District began to lease the former school providing additional revenue for the parish.

1956, had been staffed by Adrian Dominicans. The longest pastorate was that of Rev. Robert J. Burroughs who was there from 1969 until 1981. Fr. Franco was appointed the last pastor in August 1993.

St. Ursula parish had been established in June 1960. Rev. Mitchell J. Bednarski was the founding pastor. He remained at the parish until August 1976. The church was begun in 1966 and dedicated on July 8, 1967, to St. Ursula. Since St. Ursula church was a permanent worship space it was chosen as the worship center for the new Transfiguration parish in 1994 and continues to serve as the present Transfiguration church.

MT. ZION PASTORAL CENTER

Flushing

When anyone hears of the Mt. Zion Pastoral Center they immediately think of Youth to Youth Catholic Evangelization. The youth group is well known throughout the Midwest and Mid-Canada. They were a part of the program at the 2002 World Youth Day in Toronto.

The Mt. Zion community has its roots in the Charismatic renewal, which emerged in the Catholic church following Vatican Council II. A charismatic prayer group began at St. Michael Maple Grove. Members of this group began a group at Good Shepherd Montrose when it was founded early in 1979. That summer the first youth retreat was held in the home of Gordon and Martha Krupp. The forty-seven participants stayed in tents.

YOUTH TO YOUTH CATHOLIC EVANGELIZATION

CHRISTMAS, 2002

The youth held their first Fast–a–thon in 1982. The youth were asked to lead the youth section of the Michigan Charismatic Conference the same year. The first parent/youth conference was held in April 1985. In December 1987, Bishop Povish invited Fr. Donald Sutton, S.J. and Sr. Ellen Rose, S.S.J. to make a visitation to the Community. Among their observations and recommandations were: "its leadership is sound, dedicated and powerful... it would be well to search for a new model in dealing with the Mt. Zion Community...". A chaplain, Rev. Camillus W. Janas, O.F.M., was appointed for the community in April 1986. The group took the name of Mt. Zion Prayer Community. Bishop Kenneth J. Povish approved the status of the community as a pastoral center on July 31, 1988.

The present eighty-acre site was purchased in January 1989. After difficulties in zoning were overcome, the community held a blessing of the land on May 13, 1990. Construction began shortly thereafter. Bishop Povish dedicated the pastoral center complex in June 1991. By 1995 there were two Youth to Youth teams that gave presentations and retreats at thirty-eight locations. Nearly 4,500 youth and parents participated in the four conferences given in Flushing during the 1995–96 season.

Members of the center traveled to Rome for the seventh and eighth International Meeting of the Catholic Fraternity of Charismatic Covenant Communities of the Pontifical Right, in 1997 and 1998 respectively. This fraternity membership has led to exchanges with other communities in Pennsylvania, Virginia, Brazil, Iceland and Mexico.

SACRED HEART OF JESUS PASTORAL CENTER

JACKSON

Jackson area Hispanics first gathered to celebrate the Feast of the Virgin of Guadalupe at St. Mary Star of the Sea. This happened for a number of years before a structured Hispanic pastoral program was begun in 1978. That October, Rev. Manuel Trujillo was assigned to the Jackson area. He celebrated the sacraments at St. Mary parish and began to hold bible study classes there.

In November 1979 a former Seventh Day Adventist church on East Michigan Avenue was purchased by the diocese. Bishop Kenneth J. Povish directed that it be used as a center for Jackson Hispanics. He came to the center in June 1980 to dedicate Sacred Heart Chapel and the Hispanic Cultural Center. A parish council and a religious education program were initiated before Fr. Trujillo's departure in October 1981.

Rev. Timothy Crowley ministered to the group from 1982 to 1984. During this time the first pastoral coordinator/ center director was appointed. Juan Rodriguez served briefly until Sr. Paz de Guadalupe Buccio, C.F.P., arrived in 1985. Since then several of the Passionist sisters, based in Mexico, have helped with study groups at the chapel. Sr. Paz, working with the council, led the community until she returned to Mexico. Sr. Paz was succeeded by Sr. Virginia Alfaro, C.F.P., also a member of the Passionist community. The Sacred Heart of Jesus community continues to grow and nurture the Catholic faith among Hispanics.

SISTERS OF ST. DOMINIC,
CONGREGATION OF THE MOST HOLY ROSARY

*A*DRIAN

The first four Dominican Sisters came to Adrian in August 1879. They came to staff St. Mary Grade School. The following year a second group of four was sent to take over St. Joseph School. Four years later, Rev. P. Casimir Rohowski, C.P.P.S., pastor of St. Joseph parish from 1876 until 1889, once again made a request to the Dominican Motherhouse in New York City. This time it was to open a hospital and home for the aged. Mother Rose Kempton and five other sisters began St. Joseph Hospital on May 20, 1884. This was located on the grounds that were to become the Adrian motherhouse.

In 1892, St. Joseph Hospital became a provincial house. A novitiate had been started the year before with three new novices and three postulants who had been transferred from the provincial house in Traverse City. The first reception took place in May 1892 with Bishop John S. Foley of Detroit presiding. The new provincial house served the Detroit diocese.

Mother Camilla Madden, a native of Ireland, was appointed the first provincial. It was under her leadership that the hospital was closed in 1896 and reopened as St. Joseph Academy for young ladies. The academy was a source for vocations and requests soon began to come from outside Michigan for sisters. The Diocese of Toledo and the Archdiocese of Chicago quickly became familiar with the quality work of these dedicated women and requested their services. In 1923 the St. Joseph Province became a separate order. Mother Camilla was elected founding prioress general.

■ *Holy Rosary Chapel, 1912*

During Mother Mary Augustine Walsh's term as prioress general (1924–1933), the community accepted missions in Florida. The congregation continued to grow and expand under the leadership and direction of Mother Mary Gerald Barry, O.P., from 1933 until her death in 1961. Mother Genevieve Weber, O.P., served as prioress general from 1962 to 1968. Weber Center, which is now a part of the motherhouse complex, was built as a novitiate and completed in the year of Mother Genevieve's retirement. It has served as a retreat and conference center since 1968. Sr. Carol Johannes, Sr. Rosemary Ferguson, Sr. Nadine Foley, and Sr. Patricia Walters have served as prioress general. Today Sr. Janet Capone leads the congregation of just over 1,000 members who serve in thirty states, Canada, the Dominican Republic, Puerto Rico and South Africa.

■ *Golden Jubilarians, June 1985*

SERVANTS OF GOD'S LOVE

ANN ARBOR

The Servants of God's Love evolved out of the charismatic Word of God community in Ann Arbor. In April 1975 six women began residing together in order to pursue a common life as celibate women. Dorcee Clarey was appointed leader of the group. The group developed a Rule of Life based on the rule that the Servants of the Word (a charismatic group for celibate men living in common) had developed. Both groups were ecumenical at the time.

In July 1985 Ann Shields became head of the community. Following philosophical differences of the leadership of the Word of God and the international Sword of the Spirit, the sisterhood became divided in 1990. In the aftermath of the division, all the Protestant women left.

During an annual retreat in August 1992 the decision was made to seek canonical recognition as a Catholic sisterhood. Bishop Kenneth J. Povish was approached and the process of adopting the Rule of Life to Canon Law was begun. Beginning in 1991 members of the community felt called to care for needy children, especially AIDS babies. One of the community's houses was set aside for this purpose in 1992. The constitution of the community was approved in January 1996. The group was constituted a private association of the faithful the following November on the Feast of Christ the King. The community expanded their apostolate by opening a house for the elderly. The community seeks to serve those who have no family or the resources to move into a nursing home. Bishop Carl F. Mengeling blessed Emmanuel House in Ann Arbor on August 5, 1999.

The Servants of God's Love were established by Bishop Mengeling as a public association of the faithful in the Diocese of Lansing with juridic personality on January 24, 2002.

Left to right, standing: Sr. Kelly McDonald, Sherry Kozlouski, Sr. Mary Zielinski, Sr. Fran DePuydt and resident (bedbound) Laura Newell

Sr. Mary Zielinski and Sr. Fran DePuydt (By Christine Jones/Faith)

SISTERS OF MARY, MOTHER OF THE EUCHARIST

ANN ARBOR

The origins of the Sisters of Mary, Mother of the Eucharist, can be traced to Tennessee and the Nashville Dominicans. Mother Assumpta Long was mother general of the order for twelve years. In 1992 John Cardinal O'Connor invited Mother Assumpta to New York to help found the Sisters of Life. In 1996, Mother Assumpta and three

■ *Eucharistic Adoration Chapel*

other sisters, Sr. Joseph Andrea, Sr. Mary Samuel, and Sr. John Dominic, discerned a call to establish a new community. Cardinal O'Connor invited them to come to New York where constitutions for a way of life were composed and sent to Rome for approval. While waiting for approval, Mother Assumpta visited Ann Arbor and met Thomas Monaghan of Domino Farms.

When Mr. Monaghan heard what the sisters were about, he invited them to come to Ann Arbor to help establish the Spiritus Sanctus Academies. After lengthy discussion with Cardinal O'Connor and Bishop Carl F. Mengeling and much prayer seeking discernment, the sisters accepted Mr. Monaghan's invitation. In April 1997 the four founding members of the order moved to Ann Arbor.

Soon after their arrival, young women began inquiring about joining the order, which emphasizes eucharistic adoration and follows Dominican spirituality. In August 1997 the first group of postulants were accepted. On December 11, 1997, groundbreaking for a 28,000 square foot building to house thirty sisters was held. After taking over the academy on Domino Farms, the order opened a second academy on Joy Road in the fall of 1998. The academy on Golfside in Ypsilanti was the third academy to open. The Plymouth Academy on Joy Road opened in the fall of 2000. Mass is held each day in the schools, each of which has its own chapel and chaplain. A school was also opened in Honduras as a mission outreach.

The Sisters of Mary, Mother of the Eucharist, were given official recognition as part of the Dominican Order on May 24, 2002. They are a public association of the faithful in the Diocese of Lansing with juridic personality.

■ *Spiritus Sanctus Academy, Joy Road, Ann Arbor*

ALMA REDEMPTORIS MATER

FENTON

The Alma Redemptoris Mater is currently an Association of the Faithful. Such an association can be a stage in the processes of becoming an institute of consecrated life. The association was founded in 1983 and its inception was fostered by the Sisters of Mercy from Alma, Michigan. The spirituality of the association is based in the writings of St. Alphonsus Maria de Liguori and St. John Mary Vianney. Both of these saints taught extensively on the sacrament of the Holy Eucharist and of Penance. Alma Redemptoris Mater was founded to assist in disseminating the moral teachings of the church. They feel this can be best achieved by catechizing about and encouraging participation in the sacraments, most especially the sacraments of the Holy Eucharist and Penance. Another focus of the apostolate is the care of priests needing medical and psychological services.

Rev. Firestone with German members of Alma Redemptoris Mater who are priests of the Archdiocese of Mainz

The Fenton property of Alma Redemptoris Mater

The association is made up of both brothers and priests. Since its inception Rev. Thomas Firestone, presently pastor of St. Mary Student Parish in Ann Arbor, has served as the moderator of the group. The association's center is located near Fenton. There are at present eight committed members and about fifteen associate members. Members of the association can be found in the Diocese of Lansing, the Archdiocese at Hartford, Connecticut, and in the Archdiocese of Mainz in Germany.

The spiritual fathers of the organization both had Mary as their middle name. The association has been placed under the patronage of the Blessed Virgin Mary under her title "Refuge of Sinners".

Each house of the association is subject to its diocesan bishop in regard to public worship and matters relating to the exercise of the apostolate. Each member makes vows of poverty, chastity and obedience. Those seeking membership are enrolled in a formation program consisting of postulancy, novitiate and temporary vows. Each member pursues excellence in a professional field as well as religious formation.

Paul Augustin Cardinal Mayer, O.S.B., with priests and brothers at the beginning of Alma Redemptoris Mater

ST. LOUIS CENTER

CHELSEA

The apostolate of caring for young people with physical and mental disabilities was begun by Blessed Louis Guanella in Como, Italy, in 1886. That year, Fr. Guanella opened the first resident school for such children. The religious orders, Servants of Charity for men and Daughters of St. Mary of Providence for women, were founded by Fr. Guanella and dedicated to this work. Edward Cardinal Mooney invited the Servants of Charity to come to Michigan.

The St. Louis School for developmentally disabled boys was constructed in 1960 on land located on Old US-12 near Chelsea. The Archdiocese Development Fund provided the funding for construction of the first facility. John Cardinal Deardon dedicated the structure.

Fifteen years later the facility underwent a major expansion. The present chapel was built at that time. The living quarters and administration offices were enlarged in 1982. St. Joseph Hall was built and opened in 1984. This facility cares for young men age eighteen and over

who can benefit from additional training after completing the school's program for six through seventeen year olds. In 1988 the main building was extensively remodeled and Fr. Guanella Hall was built to offer residential services to young men still needing social and personal skill training. Bishop Kenneth J. Povish dedicated Fr. Guanella Hall in September of that year.

Those who help provide support for the school are entitled the "Guardian Angels". These include individuals, corporate sponsors, Knights of Columbus councils, Alhambra Caravans, the Italian American Club of Livonia and the Diocese. Rev. Joseph Rinaldo, S.C., is the present administrator of the St. Louis Center. Besides the school for boys ages six through seventeen the center includes four adult foster care facilities. St. Joseph Hall, K of C Hall and Fr. Guanella Hall are for men. Our Lady of Providence Hall for women was opened in April 2002. The women's facility was opened when the Daughters of St. Mary of Providence closed their facility in Northville.

■ *Fr. Louis Guanella, founder of the Fathers and Brothers of Charity*

HOLY CROSS CHILDRENS SERVICES

(BOYSVILLE)

CLINTON

In 1948 the Archdiocese of Detroit purchased the Ford Vocational School near Clinton. With the assistance of the Bishops of Marquette, Grand Rapids, Lansing and Saginaw, Edward Cardinal Mooney opened Boysville on October 24 that year. From the beginning, two groups have played an integral part in Boysville. The Holy Cross brothers have administered and taught there from its founding. Brother Patrick Cain, C.S.C., was the first Boysville director. He was succeeded the following year by Br. Hilarion Brezik. The other group is the Knights of Columbus, which has consistently been an important source of financial support.

The facility was founded to help troubled boys, usually wards of the court referred to Boysville by juvenile courts or the State social service agencies. Boysville soon became the largest private childcare agency in the state of Michigan. Br. Francis Boylan, C.S.C., became president of Boysville in 1975 and he oversaw the expansion beyond the central campus at Clinton. By 1978 group homes had opened in Detroit, Ecorse, Saginaw and Alpena. In the Detroit metropolitan area a family services program was instituted to work with the families of the boys placed at Boysville.

Dr. Eugene Hausmann is director of pastoral services (By Christine Jones/ Faith)

In 1985 Boysville expanded its services to include girls. The Boysville communities celebrated their 40th anniversary in 1988. That year the St. Thomas Assessment Center Program in Wayne County was chosen as Michigan's most innovative residential treatment program. Boysville of Michigan services included a comprehensive range of treatment services for referring agencies including daycare, latch key daycare, in-home children and family service programs, specialized treatment foster care, short term shelter care, thirty day detention and assessment

■ *The 25th anniversary at Boysville coincided with 75th anniversary at Columbian in Michigan.*

services, residential care including group homes, and a chemical dependency treatment program to over 550 Michigan and Ohio youth on a daily basis.

In 2000 Boysville of Michigan was named the State Child Placing Agency of the Year by the National Foster Parent Association. The following year the name change to Holy Cross Childrens Services was announced.

■ *Brother Francis Boylan, C.S.C., is the Executive Director of Holy Cross Children's Services (By Christine Jones/ Faith)*

ST. JOSEPH HOME RETREAT AND CONFERENCE CENTER

JACKSON

The Felician Sisters came from Detroit in 1911 at the invitation of Rev. Joseph Herr, pastor of St. Joseph parish, to open a girls' academy. The Sisters purchased the William Thompson mansion. During the first year of its existence it became clear that there was a greater need in Jackson for an orphanage for boys. On October 12, 1912, the St. Joseph Home for Boys opened with twenty students. Eventually services were expanded to care for boys ages two to fourteen who came from broken homes, were homeless or were neglected.

The first St. Joseph Home (photo taken in 1955)

In 1976, under the direction of Sr. Mary Noel, the services that St. Joseph Home provided substantially changed. A day care center opened in January and a kindergarten opened in September. The facility became a weekend retreat and conference center for adults.

Sr. Catherine Ryzewicz, C.S.S.F., came in 2002 to direct St. Joseph Home for Children, Inc. During the week, the Sisters are licensed to care for up to 150 children, ages two months through twelve years. On the weekend they host many programs and

The Sisters conducted an elementary school at the home until 1945. After that most of the boys, grades three through ten, were enrolled in neighboring schools. The Sisters continued to provide special education classes for those children unable to be mainstreamed.

The aging facility was in need of much renovation. Sr. Mary Arcadia envisioned a new facility for both boys and girls. The new St. Joseph Home for Children opened in March 1968. It had three units for boys and one unit for girls. Within a decade of opening the residential care program was phased out.

conferences. Sr. Catherine is presently seeking to expand usage to weekdays as well. The Felicians stay connected to St. Joseph parish by renting their gym for the use of the parish school children who have no gym of their own.

ST. VINCENT HOME FOR CHILDREN

Lansing

Three Sisters of St. Joseph from Nazareth moved into the as yet unfinished St. Vincent Home in March 1952. Sister Mary Felix was the first supervisor. The construction had begun in March 1951 and the building was dedicated by Bishop Joseph H. Albers in July 1952. Rev. John D. Slowey, director of Catholic Social Services of Lansing, was appointed the first chaplain and director of the home. The original focus of the home was for dependent and neglected children. In the early 1960s St. Vincent Home became a refuge for a number of Cuban children who were sent to the United States unaccompanied after the overthrow of the Cuban government by Fidel Castro. Beginning in 1962 a six-person board of directors drawn from the membership of the Lansing particular council of the St. Vincent de Paul Society was established. In 1968 the focus of the program was changed to serve children with emotional impairment. This necessitated the development of social work programs. Psychological and psychiatric care began to be provided for residents.

Laying the cornerstone for St. Vincent Home, 1951

On April 2, 1985, the board of directors for St. Vincent Home and that of Catholic Social Services of Lansing merged, creating one unit under the leadership of executive director Donald Ballentine. The merger allowed a full range of counseling services and adoption placement to be coordinated with the residential treatment program.

A tremendous family reunion was held on August 25, 2001, to celebrate the facility's 50th birthday. An all-afternoon picnic was held on the West Willow Campus. The chapel was closed to expand residence space. The facility now has a capacity of thirty-six beds. The average stay is from a few weeks to a few months. Over 200 are served each year.

In February 2002 St. Vincent Home for Children launched the "Building Hope for Children" fund drive. It is the five million dollar campaign to build a new chapel, four additional beds, classrooms and space for family interaction.

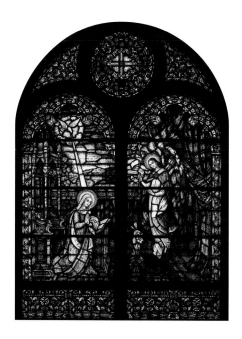

Author
George C. Michalek

Photography
John R. Glover

Design and Layout
Sylvie Reiss

Photoengraving
Editions du Signe - 105760

Publishing Director
Christian Riehl

Published by
Éditions du Signe
1, rue Alfred Kastler
B.P. 94 – 67038 Strasbourg cedex 2
France
Tél. (33) 3 88 78 91 91
Fax (33) 3 88 78 91 99

2003 Éditions du Signe
ISBN : 2-7468-1271-1
Printed in China by Sun Fung Offset Binding Co., Ltd.